PRAISE FOR
MADISON AVENUE MANSLAUGHTER

"Madison Avenue Manslaughter *outlines – in unrelenting, painstaking detail – the decline of the advertising industry and the tone-deaf agency executives who are leading their own businesses to the chopping block. It's about the reality that exists behind the* well ~~ ~~ned *facade of Madison Avenue.*"
Forbes

"*It may take some readers a da*y ~~...~~ge *to open it. But the industry-shaking insights in* Madison Avenue Manslaughter *make it required reading for everyone who works in advertising – marketers and agencies alike.*"
Media Village

"Madison Avenue Manslaughter *is an unforgettable look into the Mad Men's declining world. The book offers key insights into how senior agency executives can restore their agencies to health and deliver improved results over time.*"
Business Publisher's Roundtable

"*It isn't manslaughter, it's industry suicide in slow motion, one FTE at a time.*"
Jon Bond, CEO, Tomorro; former CEO, Big Fuel; co-founder, Kirshenbaum Bond & Partners

"An impressive work. Farmer has convincingly uncovered and documented the strategic problems facing the advertising industry and its refusal to grapple with them. The book provides useful guidance on how to face the problems and deal with them."
Walter Kiechel, author of *The Lords of Strategy*;
former Editorial Director, Harvard Business Publishing Co.;
and former Managing Editor, *Fortune* magazine

"It's more like Madison Avenue Massacre, and the bullets are falling prices, incentives that do not incentivize, mystery benchmarks and scope theft. We need strong and fair economic partnerships to fund creative and strategic brilliance. Michael Farmer's exposé should ignite the debate. Bravo!"
Gary Lee, Global Chief Financial Officer,
McCann Worldgroup

"Michael Farmer is one of the few voices contextualizing the decline of this industry. But not to fear, he also shines a bright light on the path to resurgence. A must read for anyone interested in protecting and preserving creativity as a key business driver."
Lisa Clunie, co-founder and CEO, Joan

This Third Edition is dedicated to the memory of
George "Jay" Hill III, 1932-1999,
co-founder of Hill, Holliday,
Connors, Cosmopulos

MADISON AVENUE
MANSLAUGHTER

AN INSIDE VIEW OF FEE-CUTTING CLIENTS, PROFIT-HUNGRY OWNERS AND DECLINING AD AGENCIES

MICHAEL FARMER

THIRD EDITION

Published by
LID Publishing
An imprint of LID Business Media Ltd.
LABS House, 15-19 Bloomsbury Way,
London, WC1A 2TH, UK

info@lidpublishing.com
www.lidpublishing.com

A member of:

businesspublishersroundtable.com

Printed and bound in Great Britain by Halstan Ltd.
ISBN: 978-1-912555-12-3

Cover and page design: Caroline Li

MADISON AVENUE
MANSLAUGHTER

AN INSIDE VIEW OF FEE-CUTTING CLIENTS, PROFIT-HUNGRY OWNERS AND DECLINING AD AGENCIES

MICHAEL FARMER

THIRD EDITION

MADRID | MEXICO CITY | LONDON
BUENOS AIRES | BOGOTA | SHANGHAI

TABLE OF CONTENTS

"The difficulty lies not so much in developing new ideas as in escaping from old ones."

JOHN MAYNARD KEYNES

FOREWORD

I met Michael Farmer, a former Bain director in the UK, for the first time many years ago, in the 1990s, when he was starting his own consulting firm.

Very early on he identified a major operational deficiency at agencies and agency networks – their inability to carefully define and adhere to scopes of work. At consulting companies, like Bain or McKinsey, the organization would rigidly define their scopes of work, and if the scopes changed, the consultants would stop work, drop their pens and redefine the scopes, which most times would be more expensive to complete. If you didn't, the consultants' bottom line suffered dramatically.

Unfortunately, agencies were not well-disciplined organizations at that time (and they still probably aren't). In fact, they took delight in beating the system, focusing on "keeping clients happy" and failing to stop the work and redefine the scopes of work for fear of angering their clients. Interestingly, Mike Walsh, who was running The Ogilvy Group in the UK at the time, did take Michael's advice, at my suggestion. He did implement some trials and tests of Michael's system, which clearly showed the inefficiencies of agency operations and the fact that a very few projects drove agency profitability and subsidized the projects where there was continuous briefing and rebriefing – as a result, losing considerable sums of money. The pity was that I didn't, or Mike Walsh didn't, insist on deeper penetration of the approach. It was a bad mistake.

At that time, though, it probably didn't matter too much. There was the impact of globalization on corporate growth. Warren Buffett used to say agencies were royalties on the growth of

US companies as they expanded abroad. In fact, there was a mathematical relationship between global corporate growth and agency revenues, as agencies were paid 15% commissions on billings or 17.65% on production costs. In addition, nominal global GDP growth was exacerbated by significant inflation, which gave clients pricing power and more leeway on cost.

The picture is very different today. Basically, since the subprime and Lehman crises of 2008, GDP growth has been subtrend relative to the rate of GDP growth before Lehman. There has been very little inflation, and consequently little pricing power and an increased focus on cost and efficiency, with the current focus instead on ZBB or zero-based budgeting. In addition, the rise of digital has complicated and fragmented the digital landscape, leading to suggestions that the client in-housing might be a better solution or that consulting companies might be able to do the job better or that going direct to Google or Facebook or Amazon is best.

I'm not sure that in-housing works in the longer run. Keeping the best talent in one category or a limited set of categories will be very difficult. Great talent wants to work on many challenges and opportunities. Keeping abreast of technological developments is also difficult for individual clients to do, particularly when they're trying to reduce costs. Although I have to say that at S4 Capital we aid in-sourcing, if that's what clients want to do.

Consultants are not good at implementation or activation and are already running into execution problems. However, they are good at selling digital transformation or disruption projects at the highest management levels to CEOs and CFOs and CMOs and CIOs and CTOs, preying on the digital insecurities that legacy companies have. This is a capability that S4 Capital will try to build through access and partnership.

Finally, Google, Facebook and Amazon are really media companies, although they don't like to admit it, selling their own inventory. You wouldn't entrust your media plan to one traditional media owner, so why do it to a digital media owner?

Partnership with digital media agencies, like S4 Capital, is a better solution, where an agency can demonstrate the independent, transparent case for investment in the platform.

In any event, the clear priority in the current or likely future environment is on increasing cost discipline (not cost cutting). Agencies, both old and new, should take note of Michael's focus on scopes of work and its continuous examination and re-evaluation. It's a critical factor in agency development, or even survival. Listen to what Michael says.

Sir Martin Sorrell
Executive Chairman, S4 Capital plc

EXECUTIVE SUMMARY

The post-World War II growth of advertising agencies is one of the world's great business success stories. Television advertising became a dominant force, and ad agencies were paid via 15% media commissions. The high status and profitability of ad agencies during this period allowed agencies to expand globally, manage themselves loosely and go public in the 60s and 70s.

Ad agencies were subsequently acquired by marketing communications holding companies, and the holding companies themselves grew and showed a track record of increased profits as they continued to acquire agencies and generate bottom-line growth by reducing agency costs. By 1990, their agencies were "at the top of their game," buoyed by inflating media prices that boosted commission income, and their profitable record of success locked in their vision of what they needed to do to stay successful – keep on focusing on creativity and client service.

Today, in 2019, though, the operating and financial health of ad agencies has reversed and is weakening. The holding companies themselves are showing signs of weakness, as both top-line revenue and profit margin growth has slowed down. The commission system disappeared in the 80s and 90s, replaced by fees managed downwards by procurement executives who believed that agencies were high cost suppliers whose value-added was overstated. Clients instituted global marketing practices that put pressure on agency operations and raised their costs. More recently, clients have been adding in-house agencies that divert creative and media activities away from their external agencies. Management consultants displaced senior agency executives as CEO advisors in response to the new corporate "shareholder value" mantra. More alarmingly, management consulting firms like Accenture and Deloitte Digital have been acquiring creative and media shops and aggressively growing as major competitors. Accenture is now the largest advertising agency in the world. Ad agencies came to be seen by their clients as commodity suppliers of creative services, easily replaced through agency searches, and the length of client relationships diminished substantially. Digital and social marketing innovations added specialized agency competitors to the mix of agencies servicing advertisers, and scopes of work expanded significantly at a time when agencies were downsizing in response to fee pressures. Agencies became trapped between low client fees and growing workloads while having to deliver growing margins to their holding company owners. Capabilities were reduced at a time when clients' expectations for increased digital/social know-how and improved results were at a feverish pitch.

The declining fortunes of ad agencies are not visible to those who follow holding company income and profit growth, since ad agencies continue to fuel holding company margins – but they do this the hard way, by squeezing their resources and holding the line on salaries and bonuses. This cost-reduction strategy is in its final stages; agencies have no surplus costs to draw on. They have been "tapped out" over the past 20 years.

Agencies do not document, measure or track their workloads – they focus on being creative, winning awards, delivering service, and generating profit margins. They have little understanding of the growing gap among their workloads, fees and resources. Consequently, senior advertising executives like agency CEOs misdiagnose the strategic problems facing their agencies and fail to mobilize their organizations to respond effectively. Agency senior executives are undermanaging their agencies, and the full consequences of this undermanagement will become very visible in the near-term.

Agencies have not changed their internal cultures in response to these changing circumstances. Loose management practices dominate agency cultures, just as they did during the high-profit past. Client heads are not held accountable for depressed fee levels, unmanaged workloads or insufficient resources for client work. Office heads are not held accountable for the varied performance of their client heads.

Agencies are on a path to self-destruction. Thus far, the level of senior executive response to this problem has been inadequate. Through benign neglect of growing creative workloads, and reluctance to tackle clients over declining client fees, agency CEOs are presiding over the slow decline and overstretching of a diminishing pool of burned-out creative assets. Efforts to develop new clients and grow revenue is their most visible response to client fee pressures, but since every ad agency CEO is going down the same path, this approach leads to further-depressed industry prices that make their situations worse.

Agencies need strong CEO leaders who are prepared to grapple with three clear challenges:

The workload challenge. Agencies must begin to document, track and measure their workloads. This will permit their organizations to do a much more effective job negotiating fees and closing the gap between workloads and fees. This will require new policies, new tools and a new sense of organizational discipline.

The mission challenge. This involves rethinking and then repositioning the *raison d'être* of the agency from "creativity and service" to "results for clients." Only through such a repositioning can agencies begin to set course for higher fees (as measured by billing multiples), begin to close the "value-added gap" between themselves and the management consulting firms, and identify with their clients' need for increased shareholder value. This cannot be done without a wholesale upgrading of the agency culture and skills.

The accountability challenge. The third challenge involves running the agency like a business and creating a strong sense of accountability throughout the organization, especially by office heads and their client heads. The current loose structure, based on the naive principle that *"management needs to get out of the way so that agency people can work creatively on self-defined priorities"* was possible when agencies earned very high levels of commission income, but it is inappropriate today and cannot be justified romantically on the basis of *"this is what is required to run a creative organization."* Increased accountability will require measures, objectives and management reviews to evaluate client-by-client and agency executive performance relative to established goals and targets.

Madison Avenue Manslaughter describes these three challenges and lays out a detailed ten-step transformation programme to be initiated by agency Chief Executive Officers who wish to restore organizational health, financial well-being and renewed strategic relevance for their ad agencies.

ACKNOWLEDGMENTS

This work summarizes my 25 years of experience working as a management consultant and software provider to advertising agencies and advertisers around the world.

I owe a great deal of thanks to the many senior agency executives, procurement executives and marketing executives who called on Farmer & Company to help solve the various workload, fee, resource and relationship problems that they experienced.

Each consulting engagement provided new insights about changing industry and relationship problems. We began in 1990 when agency remuneration was high and scopes of work were relatively simple. Agencies had enough income to staff their work lavishly with talented and well-paid senior and junior people, and this led to the development of high quality brand strategic work and creative ads that improved the competitiveness of advertisers' brands.

As time progressed, though, this comfortable situation frayed at the edges. Remuneration per client declined; marketing became more global; digital innovations disrupted traditional media; brands came under increased competitive pressures and agencies had to struggle to hold on to long-term clients and generate profits for holding company owners. This struggle led to downsizings and salary/bonus constraints that severely limited agency capabilities.

We observed this step by step with our clients, seeing the pieces of an industry puzzle emerge over time.

This book is an attempt to pull the pieces of the puzzle together and to create a picture of the advertising industry that represents the collective experience of those who lived through it and continue to struggle with it today.

I owe a particular debt of gratitude to Sir Martin Sorrell who, in 1990, was the first advertising executive I met. He generously introduced me to many key advertising executives, and we were fortunate enough to begin our agency consulting practice with a WPP agency. Sir Martin has written the Foreword to this third edition, and he provided a retrospective view of his executive career at Saatchi & Saatchi plc, WPP and S4 Capital in Chapter 4. I am deeply in his debt. Later, Jonathan Hirst, John Shannon, Carolyn Carter and Ed Meyer provided leadership and guidance as we worked with Grey Worldwide in various parts of the world.

Tom Rosenwald, a prominent executive search consultant, introduced me to every senior agency and holding company executive in the US after 2001, and eventually through his efforts and the help of others, we expanded our consulting practice in the US.

I am indebted to Kevin Roberts, the former Executive Chairman of Saatchi & Saatchi, who encouraged me to finish the first draft of this book in 2014, and who read various drafts and offered sound words of advice. Bob Seelert, Bill Cochrane, Vaughan Emsley, Brent Smart and Anna Binninger were helpful in many ways; I'm grateful as well to Gary Lee, Laura Turano, Jean-Marie Le Nail, Neil Miller, Andrew Robertson, Dana Perry, Pete Swiecicki, Ian Marlowe, Alain Rhoné, Neal Grossman, Denis Streiff, Rob Schwartz, Chris Sweetland, Rick Brook, John Seifert, Mike Walsh, Steve Goldstein, Ralph Clementson, Toby Drummond, Bob Jeffrey, Lew Trencher, Keith Wilkins, Mike Byrne, Dick Roth, Deborah Wahl, Kristen Simmons, Kevin Everhart, Deborah Hedgecock, Mary Ann Brennan, Jon Bond, Brian Sheehan, Walter Kiechel, Jim Singer, Tom Finneran, Bill Bain, Ralph Willard, Steve Schaubert, Chris Zook, Ken Thuerbach, Kirsten Sandberg, Bob Whittington, Joe Burton and Brian Lipton.

In Mexico, where agencies are taking extraordinary steps to strengthen their operations, I am especially grateful to Sebastián Tonda, Ana María Barquín, Martin Andrés Fernandez, Nora Larios and Sergio A. López.

Many fine individuals made contributions to Farmer & Company's advertising consulting practice during the past 25 years.

I am grateful to Nuri Toker, David Barrett, Nick Ford, Alistair Stranack, Virginia Eastman, James Wolcott, Chris Tidswell (who sadly passed away in 2010), Willow Duttge, Michelle Miller, Jennifer Stingle, Peter Farmer, Julia Schwartz, Marina Bordin, Cameron Jones, Daniel Bellis, Ethan Dennison, Jim Stillman, Brian Suckie, William Wright and Victor Garrido Freyria.

This strategic assessment of the highly stressed advertising industry is not meant, in any way, to criticize or stigmatize individual agencies or executives who provided the various pieces of the industry puzzle described in these pages. My narrative has not given full credit to the senior agency executives who understand their strategic situation and are working very hard to deal with it.

I am solely responsible for the conclusions in this book and for any errors or omissions therein.

INTRODUCTION TO THE THIRD EDITION

"Where is Madison Avenue? You might well ask."

Credit: Victoria Roberts / *The New Yorker* / *The Cartoon Bank*.

This is the third edition of *Madison Avenue Manslaughter*, brought up to date to document the wobbly performance of the holding companies in 2017 and 2018, the departure of Martin Sorrell from WPP, the FBI investigation into media buying practices, the trend for clients to develop in-house agencies, the continued decline of agency fees in the face of nonstop workload growth and other aspects of the continuing saga of the industry's manslaughter.

This book focuses on the "undermanagement" of ad agencies by their senior executives, which tells some of the industry's sad story but by no means all of it. Ken Auletta's *Frenemies*, published in early 2018[1] presents a parallel story through its encyclopedic overview of a media industry in full disarray, as consumers reject the "interruptive" advertising that has supported traditional media channels, like television, and show an appetite for content offered in other, less funded ways. Where will this leave the major media players? Where will this leave society at large? Auletta presents a fascinating picture of the unresolved uncertainties facing the media industry and the 450 executives interviewed for his work.

The global growth and influence of advertising agencies has been one of the world's great business success stories. From modest beginnings, the industry grew and flourished. Today, its prospects are uncertain.

Early advertising involved little more than preparing posters or running display ads in newspapers for patent medicines, soaps, cereals and cigarettes. Today, advertising blankets the world via television, movies, magazines, billboards, radio, newspapers, brochures, electronic displays, computer screens, mobile telephones and online shopper websites – as well as via T-shirts, coffee mugs, pencils, athletic uniforms and anything else that can either catch the eye or be handed out. Digital and social advertising includes Facebook, Instagram, Snapchat, web pages, games, YouTube online videos, and tweets that are designed to create involvement with customers (or trade insults with adversaries, as the case may be).

Advertising reaches out to consumers not only from Madison Avenue, USA, but also from London, Frankfurt, Paris, Moscow, Johannesburg, Tokyo, Ho Chi Minh City, Bangkok, Beijing, Singapore, Melbourne and hundreds of other cities around the world. Advertising is ubiquitous, and so are the agencies that create it.

Historians of advertising mark the end of World War II as the beginning of the global boom in advertising. This was The Golden Age of Advertising, when Bill Bernbach, David Ogilvy, George Lois, Leo Burnett and other well-known giants – typically founders of their firms – made enduring creative marks on the industry. They launched what came to be known as the Creative Revolution, abandoning the hard sell and making advertising entertaining, amusing and palatable. They did this through irony – making fun of advertising and having fun with the products they advertised, treating the consumer as an insider, in on their joke. Not coincidentally, the leading products they advertised grew and established strong competitive market positions, backed by large spends on over-the-air and print media that were promoted by their ad agencies, who were remunerated by commissions on the media and production spends.

Creative Revolution advertising fueled product growth and created memorable ads during the decades after World War II. It remains the template for today's advertising. Agencies, advertisers and consumers expect advertising to surprise, enlighten, and entertain; clients expect it to generate results at the same time.

Creative advertising went global with commercial television, and advertising agencies went global as well, opening up branches around the world. Their success and profitability attracted financiers from New York, London, Paris, and Tokyo, and in a short space of time, nearly every major ad agency was acquired by one of the newly created public holding companies in marketing communications: Interpublic, Omnicom, WPP, Publicis, Dentsu, Havas, MDC – and the holding companies themselves grew and showed a positive track record of profit growth for investors, at least up to 2017/2018.

Despite this historical holding company success, the operating and financial health of the industry's major advertising agencies is weakening. Agency weakness is neither a matter of public knowledge nor the focus of sufficient senior executive action to reverse the trend. Agencies have been squeezed, caught between reduced client fees and growing workloads[2] while having to deliver growing margins to their owners. Agencies have handled this conflict by downsizing or otherwise adjusting their headcounts and costs.[3] This enfeebled the agencies at a time when clients' expectations for more creativity, increased digital and improved results were at a feverish pitch. Client dissatisfaction with their agencies appears to be at a high if we judge this by the rate at which they fire their current agencies, invest in in-house agencies, search for new agencies or employ management consulting firms to carry out marketing communications work.[4]

Client scopes of work are growing substantially, particularly as advertisers experiment with digital and social advertising while maintaining the growth of traditional advertising comprising TV, print, radio and outdoors. With growing workloads and declining fees, agencies have to do more work with fewer, lower-cost creative people. The effort puts a considerable strain on operations and quality. Every year the strain gets worse, and agencies are becoming increasingly stretched and creatively challenged.

A sensible person might assume that agencies are paid by their clients for the work they do. This is not actually the case. Agencies are paid by the head for the number of staff assigned to their client accounts – workload is not technically a part of the headcount equation.

As a practical measure, it's the agencies' clients who determine how many agency staff are assigned and paid for. In the typical process, clients first determine an overall fee, based on their marketing budgets, and agencies in turn assign an affordable number of people based on this figure. For example, if a large client establishes an agency fee of $10 million for the coming fiscal year, a typical agency would assign a number of people that would add up to $4.25 million in salaries and benefits. This might involve 10 creatives and 32 other agency people in client service, strategic planning and production. After covering overheads of $4.25 million, the agency would have $1.5 million left to cover profits, or 15% – thus meeting holding company requirements.

The amount of creative work to be done during the year develops through a separate process. The creative workload "happens" as client marketing plans evolve throughout the year. Creative workloads grow independently, almost as if they were unrelated to agency resources or fees. These creative workloads are not measured or negotiated, although they are discussed in a process called "scope of work (SOW) planning," but because there are no workload metrics – no generally accepted way of quantifying creative workloads so that a required number of agency people can be assigned – the exercise is nearly meaningless from an operational standpoint.

In any case, there are large differences between expected SOWs and the actual amount of creative work that is done. The ten creatives assigned to the $10 million client might or might not be able to handle the workload comfortably. It all depends.

In the end, looking at the past ten years, agency workloads have been growing, but typical agency fees and headcounts have not. My analysis shows that workloads have been growing on the order of 2-3% on a compounded annual basis, while fees (on a constant dollar basis) have been declining by 2-3% on a compounded annual basis. These apparently small numbers have large effects. It only takes 15 years for an agency's compensation to be cut in half for an equivalent amount of work.

This workload-fee problem is not isolated to minor agencies. The big agencies, whose reputations were first made in traditional TV, print and radio, suffer the most: agencies like Ogilvy & Mather, J Walter Thompson, Y&R, Grey, McCann Erickson, FCB, Lowe, BBDO, DDB, TBWA\Chiat\Day, Publicis, Saatchi & Saatchi and Leo Burnett, to name a few. These big-name agencies grew up with the belief that doing any and all client work was simply *part of the service*, as it was originally when they were paid, before 1990, via 15% media commissions. Since then, commissions have been abandoned as the unique form of agency payment. In its place, clients began paying agencies by the head, but this did not change the way agencies thought about servicing their clients. Any and all client work continues to be done for an agreed fee, which remains mostly fixed.

Workloads were not measured during the commission era, just as they are not measured today.

The enduring cultural legacy of the commission days left agencies without the means to measure their workloads. Instead, they were used to making do with the resources they could afford, just as they had been throughout their past, and if the resources were too few or too junior, they would soldier on in any case. They may have complained to their clients from time to time about how inadequate their fees were, but with much less seriousness than the problem actually warranted.

What could have changed their practices was the relentless decline in fees, driven by client procurement departments over the past 20 years, and the growing workloads. Fees divided by workload equals *price*, and price has been in decline for at least two decades. (See below for price graph).

Like the proverbial frog in a pot of cold water, agencies adapt to price declines as frogs adapt to a gradual increase in water temperature – it's fine until it is not, and the frog eventually dies. Agencies are on the same path as their amphibian friends unless something fundamental changes in the way agencies measure their growing workloads and negotiate their relationships and fees.

I have worked as a strategy consultant for advertising agencies and their clients for nearly three decades. This followed a previous 15 years as a consultant, first with The Boston Consulting Group and subsequently as a director of Bain & Company. In 45 years, I've seen a lot of industry changes and nearly as much senior executive action. The advertising industry, though, is an outlier.

PRICE CURVE 1992-2018
(PRICE IN CONSTANT DOLLARS PER SMU)

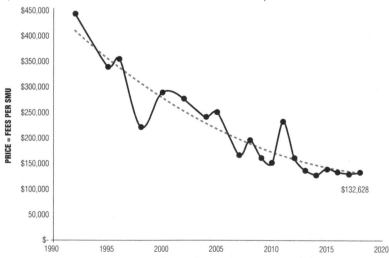

Source: SMU = ScopeMetric° Unit, a uniform measure of scope of work workload developed by Farmer & Company

The industry has undergone more strategic change than any other that I have seen, but the level of senior executive response to these changes has been surprisingly weak. To put it bluntly, senior agency executives have not protected their creative departments or the creative capabilities of their agencies. Through benign neglect of growing creative workloads and reluctance to tackle clients over declining client fees, senior agency executives are presiding over the slow decline and overstretching of a diminishing pool of burned-out creative assets. This is done in the name of meeting holding company profit expectations. Their efforts to develop new clients and grow revenues is their most visible response to client fee pressures, but since every agency CEO and president in the industry is chasing a limited pool of new business, the results are disappointing. Prices are driven even lower by cutthroat competition, and no agency manages to outgrow its competitors.

Jules Verne's protagonist Phileas Fogg burned his ship's furniture for fuel to reach Liverpool on his way around the world in 80 days. There is no Liverpool within reach for today's big ad agencies. The burning of creative assets is a temporary fix for a more permanent problem. At some point, the ship will find itself adrift in the middle of the ocean with no more fuel to propel it.

In this book, I outline the reasons why I believe the industry has reached a critical, even dangerous point in its development. I point out the logical consequences of the failure to act, and I'll offer solutions to avoid inevitable disaster.

Agencies and their clients need to recapture some of the respect, fun and profitability of working in what was once one of the most fulfilling and glamorous of industries but has become a grim sweatshop for the people who do the work.

Agencies complain that clients are demanding and unreasonable, and that agencies are treated as commodity suppliers. They say that it is hard to make money because fee setting is in the hands of procurement and workload is in the hands of marketing. Procurement is rewarded for lowering fees, and marketing wants to experiment, so what can be done? Agencies see a gap in perception between the value they bring and the way they are treated. They accept this as today's business reality – regrettable and unfortunate, but that's simply the way things are. A shrug of the shoulders suggests the futility of their situation.

For their part, procurement executives tend to see agencies as disorganized, chaotic and overpaid for their services. They note the annual holding company announcements of record profit levels and conclude that agencies must be much more profitable than they let on. Ad agencies have long-standing reputations for excess, fuelled especially by the annual June Festival of Creativity in Cannes. High agency fees might be acceptable if agency work were creating reliable brand growth and profitability, but brands are not exactly flourishing. Award-winning creativity is not enough; clients want improved brand performance that hits their bottom line. Agencies are not willing to be on the hook for guaranteed results. Advertisers feel entirely justified, cutting what they perceive as the fat out of agency fees.

Growing workloads and declining fees; it's a recipe for disaster. Agencies are already compromising their holding company owners by failing to grow or deliver the necessary profit margins. WPP stumbled badly in 2017, seeing its share price decline by 30%. The new leadership of WPP is struggling to restore share price growth. MDC Partners saw its share price decline by 60%, and its CEO, Scott Kauffman, was forced to step down.

Wall Street and The City should be asking better questions – what is actually going on that is compromising share price performance?

This book was written in advance of the inevitable holding company disasters – to outline the industry problems and encourage agencies and their clients to take management actions to keep disaster at bay. These actions form the basis of the required strategic response by agency CEOs and their clients' chief marketing and procurement officers.

SECTION I –
HISTORY: THE WHEEL OF FORTUNE

"Yes, rise up on my wheel if you like, but don't count it an injury when by the same token you begin to fall, as the rules of the game will require."

Boethius

Credit: Ted Goff / The New Yorker Collection / The Cartoon Bank.

A senior ad executive sat behind his desk, smiling and waving at me to sit down as he hung up the phone. He was excited: "Our third invitation to pitch this month! Things are really heating up – we're on everyone's list!"

The agency world is under constant financial pressure, and people under pressure understandably look for solutions. New business wins are seen as a big solution. The hope is that won business will add incremental revenue, offsetting lost clients and absorbing overheads, making it easier to generate profit margins for the holding companies. Holding companies, too, are very much in the game, competing with one another for "holding company relationships" that lock in clients to use the exclusive services of the holding company agencies.

Of course, every agency and holding company in the industry has the same thought, so new business pitches are highly contested. There are many new business opportunities, but only because clients are changing their agencies at more frequent rates. It's a strange kind of opportunity, because it adds more economic downside than economic upside. There is excess capacity in the industry. Competition for new business drives fees downwards, and no particular agency wins more than its fair share of new business. In short, the new business game is just an expensive game of musical chairs, and the constant shifting of accounts from one agency and holding company to another depresses agency economics by raising costs and pushing fees down. New business wins are necessary, but the new business outcome for the industry is an economic disappointment.

The agency world has experienced many dramatic changes during the past several decades: a shift in remuneration from commission to fee; the rise of holding companies; the involvement of procurement in fee-setting; client and holding company obsession with quarterly profits; globalization of relationships; and global growth of new media, especially in digital and social media, where the exploitation of "big data" is supposed to lead to new insights and increased marketing effectiveness. The addition of in-house agencies and competition from management consulting firms have increased industry complexity to an exceptional degree.

All of these changes have inevitably led to declining fees, rising workloads and stretched resources. Workload growth and fee declines are strategically and economically incompatible. Tragedy is a current outcome for strategically weakened agencies. This is not an industry that has unlimited potential for economies of scale or productivity increases, like the computer industry. There is no Moore's Law for the advertising industry.

In the chapters that follow, I will outline the key historical events that have shaped the industry. and then propose what can and needs to be done.

CHAPTER 1 –
REMUNERATION

"Money is life's report card."

Credit: William Hamilton / *The New Yorker* / *The Cartoon Bank*.

For more than 100 years, up to the 1980s, advertisers created budgets for advertising, of which most of the costs were for media space (print) and air time (radio and television). Their agencies kept a percentage of this spend to plan and develop the associated advertising. This percentage was called a "media commission," and it was meant to cover all of the agencies' in-house costs and profits. It did not matter how many agency people were involved or how much work the agency carried out. The commission was simply a percentage of media spend, and the basis of the calculation was very straightforward. Additionally, agencies charged a mark-up on bought-in production expenses – identified, in many cases, as a "service charge" for handling production logistics (Barton, 1955, p. 9).

Most business historians attribute the commission system to agency N.W. Ayer & Sons. In 1874, N.W. Ayer implemented its "open contract," a contract with a standard media commission rate of 15% (N.W. Ayer & Son, 1909). The rest of the industry noticed. In 1893, the American Newspapers Association, representing the sellers of advertising space, formally recognized agency commissions and the prevailing rate. Importantly, the association stated that these commissions *would only be available to advertising agents, not to advertisers*. This meant that advertisers could not get an equivalent discount by buying direct from the publisher. As N.W. Ayer & Sons wrote in its self-promotional book *Forty Years of Advertising*: "The [commission system] pulled the advertising business out of the muck and mire of bidding and faking, and made the advertising agent an agent of the customer rather than an agent of any publication or group of publications" (N.W. Ayer & Son, 1909). By extension, the advertiser was now positioned as the agent's client. Advertiser-agent interests were more closely aligned than ever before.

In 1901, magazines followed the newspapers and agreed to adhere to the fixed commission system. Decades later, when radio and television came along, the 15% commission was so well established that it was accepted as a matter of course (Barton, 1955, p. 7).

In 1917, the commission system got one of its strongest lobbyists, the American Association of Advertising Agencies (4As). In a statement later attributed to the 4As, the association argued that the 15% commission standard was the *lifeblood of the advertising agency*. Without it, 4As argued, agencies would die a slow and painful death. A fee system would only encourage competition on price, and price-cutting would see agencies give less and less service to advertisers. If agencies did not have to compete on price, the only question advertisers would have to decide was "which agency will give the best and most service" (Haase, 1934, p. 128).

Advertisers, on the other hand, were disenchanted with commissions. In 1934, Albert E. Haase wrote a paper for the Association of National Advertisers (ANA) bashing the practice of fixed commissions and calling the practice out of date. Fixed commissions were simply the "easiest way for agencies to keep getting paid," he argued. Furthermore, there was no relation between the agency's task and the remuneration it received, and commissions encouraged agencies to prioritize one medium over another based on potential income. Finally, it was unfair for agencies to buy space in publications at a discount when advertisers could not (Haase, 1934, p. 60).

It would take a few decades for the balance to tip in the direction of ANA, away from commissions in the direction of labour-based fees. In the meantime, remuneration during the commission era was very high relative to the amount of work to be done and costs of the agency people required for the work. Clients were aware of this, of course, since they could see that agencies were both exceptionally well-paid and ostentatious about it. Anyone working as an account person could buy an expensive lunch any time for anyone, reported Martin Mayer in *Madison Avenue USA* (Mayer, 1959, p. 9). There were in-agency bars, private chefs, first-class travel, town cars, and pricey décor:

- J Walter Thompson in 1958 had more than 100 private offices decorated to the tastes of the individual – one vice chairman, for example, had a round gaming table with cups for chips in his office. The agency maintained an executive dining suite composed of an 18th century farmhouse from Ipswich, Massachusetts, which the agency purchased in 1920 and reconstructed in its headquarters building.
- In the mid-1960s, the Interpublic Group of Companies, parent of McCann Erickson, owned a fleet of five airplanes known as the Harper Air Force (after Marian Harper, the Interpublic CEO). The fleet, which included a DC-7 for the boss, was furnished in French provincial. Harper's flying suite boasted a king-size bed, a private library, and a sunken bath. Harper was unrepentant about this luxury. "We can't support people with little thoughts or little dreams," he said (Fox, 1984, p. 266).

During the commission era, agencies used the high remuneration from commissions to "staff up" their work rather than earn super-high profits. They assigned multiple creative teams[1] to creative briefs[2], which permitted agencies to develop a generous number of creative ideas for client consideration. This required highly staffed creative departments with a mix of senior and junior people. Additionally, agencies maintained high headcounts in the client service (or account management) department, keeping on the payroll at least 1.5 to 2.0 client service people for every creative person in the agency. The client service people were charged with the responsibility to sell the creative ideas to the client and to manage the relationship to assure continuity and provide high levels of service. Furthermore, client service people were "media salesmen" on behalf of the agency, encouraging clients to spend more aggressively on media. This made great sense, because the more the client spent on media, the more the agency earned through its 15% media commission. A large investment in client service people kept the financial gears of the agency well-oiled.

Writing in 1948 on the financial management of the advertising agency, accountant Ira W. Rubel advised agencies to seek a 20% margin, with "direct expenses" (client serving people costs) at 55% of income and "indirect expenses" (overhead costs) at 25% (Rubel, 1948, p. 121). This would suggest a high ratio of direct-to-indirect costs of 2.2x – a much higher proportion of direct costs than exists today, where the ratio of direct-to-indirect is closer to 1:1x.

The commission edifice began to tumble in 1960, when Shell decided to change both its agency and its form of compensation. Shell announced that it was replacing J Walter Thompson with Ogilvy, Benson & Mather, but the real drama was the new way Shell was going to pay Ogilvy. At Shell's insistence, Ogilvy would work for a fee instead of the usual 15% commission. The fee amounted to the actual cost of operating the account, based on salaries and other cost-accounting variables, plus 25%. This formula would give the agency a 20% profit margin.

Many years later, David Ogilvy took credit for this new fee system, outlining its four advantages, as he saw them:

1. The advertiser pays for the services he wants – no more, no less.
2. Every fee account pays its own way. Unprofitable accounts do not ride on the coat-tails of profitable accounts, which is the case with the commission system.
3. Temporary cuts in clients' [media] budgets do not oblige you to cut staff.
4. When you advise a client to increase his advertising, he does not suspect your motive *(Ogilvy, 1983, p. 55).*

During subsequent years, other Ogilvy clients, including Sears, KLM, American Express and IBM adopted fee arrangements. To the advocates of fees, the method put the agency-client relationship on a more professional basis, like that of attorney or physician, instead of depending on agency salesmanship to persuade the client to spend more on media. *"The commission system is an anachronism,"* Ogilvy proudly declared (Fox, 1984, p. 260).

There were compelling economic reasons for changing to fees from commissions. Advertising was a "hot" industry in the 1960s, and media space and time were in short supply. The insatiable demand for advertising drove up media prices at double the rate of GDP inflation – a phenomenon that lasted until the late 1980s, when cable television began to add significant advertising capacity in media. Until then, though, agencies rode the price curve up, earning more and more as their commission income rose proportionately with the rise in media prices. Jay McNamara, a former president of agencies Young & Rubicam and McCann-Erickson Worldwide, looked back on the industry from the vantage point of 1990 and characterized media price inflation as one of the *three key drivers of agency revenue growth* (McNamara, 1990, p. 99).

Advertisers, in contrast to agencies, suffered, having to dig deeper into their pockets every year to pay for increased media costs.

Consequently, beginning in 1960 and continuing thereafter through the 1990s, clients began to experiment with fee-based systems, whereby agencies were paid essentially *by the head* for the people who worked on the clients' accounts. This system paid for the relevant proportion of agencies' client service, strategic planning, creative and production people. Clients paid a proportionate share of the salaries and benefits of these people, in proportion to the time they were expected to allocate to the client, plus an additional markup for overhead and profit. Agencies and their clients negotiated the number and seniority of these people, since the agency staff plan was the principal driver of agency fees.

Fee-based remuneration was seen as the solution to the media price-inflation problem. The desire to shift to fee-based systems developed a head of steam during the period of media price inflation, and by the next decade, after 2000, the commission system was essentially dead, as nearly all advertisers had converted agency remuneration from commissions to fees.

The commission system had been a rigid, industry-wide 15% fact of life. The shift to fees broke the commission-based price monopoly, and although the shift took decades to accomplish, once it was done it gave advertisers flexibility to exercise new fee-setting powers – they were now in a position to dictate fees on an individual agency-by-agency basis. Remuneration became a private and individual affair between client and agency rather than a broad industry convention.

Astonishingly, though, the shift from commissions to "by the head" remuneration did not lead either advertisers or agencies to think through scope of work issues.

"If we're paying 'by the head,' how do we figure out how many heads are required?" could have been a key question. Scope of work workloads could have provided the answer, but that's not the direction the industry took.

CHAPTER 2 –
THE GOLDEN AGE

"Promise me you'll keep the buzz alive."

Credit: Donald Reilly / The New Yorker / The Cartoon Bank.

The charmed period of advertising was 1945-1975. Let's call it The Golden Age. It was golden in the sense that headline agencies during this period participated in its growth and profitability, creatives saw their creative reputations enhanced, and commercial activities turned over vast sums of money. This period established the ad agencies' template for success, defining what advertising was (or could be), how relationships ought to be conducted, and what the internal culture of the agency needed to be to assure commercial and creative success.

It may be conventional wisdom that we learn from our failures, but history shows that companies continue to emulate and reinforce what made them successful in the past, even if their marketplaces change beneath them in fundamental and life-threatening ways. (For an in-depth analysis of this, see Clayton M Christensen's classic *The Innovator's Dilemma* (Christensen, 1997))

Pay close attention to the legacy of The Golden Age, 1945 to 1975, because today's agency cultures are built on the factors that were perceived to have created success during that wonderful era.

Television was a fresh technology after World War II, and the television media owners – the television networks and the local station owners – had plenty of advertising time to sell to potential advertisers. Over time, the demand for television advertising proved to be insatiable, adding to but not replacing radio advertising. TV media owners sold their available advertising time, and excess demand drove up media prices. TV media owners got very, very rich. So did the advertising agencies that created the advertising content, filling the advertising pipeline with innovative and creative work, earning commissions from the growing stream of income that flowed to media owners.

The post-war period created a perfect alignment of factors for the creation of wealth:

1. the population was growing, fueled by the post-war baby boom
2. there was an insatiable post-war demand for products and services, well above the growth of the population, plus
3. banks and tax policies made credit available and desirable, permitting the demand to be financed.

The US growth statistics for this period are extraordinary:

"Between 1950 and 1973 the US population increased by 38%, while disposable personal income increased by 327%. New housing starts went up by 47%, energy consumption by 121%, college enrollments by 136%, automobile registrations by 151%, telephones in use by 221%, number of outboard motors sold

by 242%, retail sales by 250%, families owning two or more cars by 300%, frozen food production by 655%, number of airline passengers by 963%, homes with dishwashers by 1,043%, while homes with room air conditioners rose by 3,662%" (Kleppner, 1979).

During this time, television ruled the marketplace. Households with televisions increased from 9% of all households in 1950 to 87% in 1960 and 97% by 1975, and television drove product sales with print and radio playing supporting roles (Mierau, 2000). The media choice for advertisers was a simple one – TV, print and radio, in that order – and advertisers were ready and willing to pay high prices for the media, in that order. Advertising expenditures rose from $5,780 million in 1950 to $28,320 million in 1975 – a growth of 490%.

Historian Stephen Fox observed the growing influence of TV:

"Though TV still accounted for only about one fourth of gross advertising expenditures, that flickering screen in a box now controlled the ad industry, commanding the best and priciest talent in the business and dominating discussions of the most inventive, effective commercials" (Fox, 1984).

Television was the most expensive medium for advertisers, so the agencies loved it because it made the most money for them – the 15% media commission saw to that. Furthermore, TV ads required the same kind of creativity as Hollywood, so it brought out the closet Hollywood fantasies of the Madison Avenue crowd. Furthermore, TV ads were perceived to be more effective than other types of advertising. TV worked! And because it worked, advertisers fell over themselves buying more and more TV time, encouraged by their advertising agencies. Writing in 1959, author Martin Mayer gushed about the power of television:

"Television is undoubtedly the greatest-selling medium ever devised, for those relatively few advertisers whose market is so large that they do not waste most of television's enormous audience and whose advertising budget is big enough to carry television's enormous costs. The combination of the moving picture and the speaking voice, both in the consumer's own living room, gives the television advertiser something that is almost the equivalent of a door-to-door sales staff – which makes its visits at a cost considerably less than one cent per call. When the personality presenting the sales pitch is himself a great salesman – an [Arthur] Godfrey, a Steve Allen, a Tennessee Ernie Ford – the advertiser's cup runneth over" (Mayer, 1959).

The agency's client service people assured that their clients understood the message about television's effectiveness. Client service people were, in reality, salesmen for the concept of TV advertising, convincing their clients to spend big on television and to buy ever-growing amounts of national advertising time. The message rarely failed. As long as their clients bought TV advertising, the agency's 15% commissions guaranteed a positive inflow of cash, enough to cover all the work and all the costs of the agency, with plenty left over for profits.

This was one of the beauties of the commission system. The agency sold the client on the effectiveness of TV rather than on the special capabilities of the agency. It could be shown that advertisers who outspent their competitors on a consistent basis gained market share, and the advertisers who dominated category spend – companies like Procter & Gamble in detergents, for example – protected their leading market share positions. *"If you want to be as dominant as P&G,* agencies would say, *you have to spend like P&G – outspend your competitors, year after year, in good times and in bad times."* It was hard to argue with the logic. The television research data, established by AC Nielsen in 1950, proved the case.

Client service people didn't just talk about agency capabilities – they *showed* agency capabilities on a daily basis. They provided unlimited service and brought a steady stream of clever creative ideas for approval. This was easy and fun, even if it was deadline-intensive. It required very little in the way of genuine management expertise. As long as there was 15% commission income, an agency could afford great creative talent and give the client as much service as it needed: sales meeting materials, management presentations (to make client executives look good), competitive reviews, restaurant bookings, sports tickets – anything was possible. Unlimited service bought good will up and down the client's organization, and this made the ground fertile for the hard sell on increased TV advertising.

Fee negotiations, too, were relatively simple during The Golden Age. The agency did not have to put forward a proposal for agency compensation, justifying how many people worked on the account or what they did. Compensation was worked out by how much money the client was prepared to spend on media.

A senior ad agency executive would get the client's CEO and chief marketing officer (CMO) excited about a high level of next year's media spend – and the market share increases that might be expected – and once this was done the client service organization could be turned loose on the rest of the client's marketing organization, lining them up to expect and desire a big year with big advertising budgets. Once the media budgets were agreed and approved, the agency had to deliver the goods: provide unlimited service, create and deliver great ideas and produce terrific ads. It was hoped that the clients' products would sell well in the marketplace. This was easier said than done. If a client's sales fell short of expectations, then media budgets would be cut, usually in the fourth quarter, to make up for any product sales or profit shortfalls. This would certainly affect agency income for the year. It was important, then, for agencies to convince their clients that media expenditures be viewed as sacred and untouchable, whatever the circumstances, in good sales years as well as bad, rather than as spigots to be turned down or off in a reactionary manner.

This is why agencies' client service teams worked so hard to influence the thinking about media spend at every level in the clients' organization. Agencies staffed their accounts to provide "cover" at every hierarchical level, from lowly assistant brand managers at the bottom to the chairman and chief executive at the top. This took a large number of client service people – from 1.5 to 2 client service people for every creative who worked on the account.

Service was not exclusively a client service responsibility during The Golden Age. Creatives had a role to play, as well. The head of the creative department would assign multiple creative teams to work on client briefs – in effect, assigning extra creatives to the work – so that the agency could generate a *surplus* of creative ideas. The idea behind this was simple. *Take ten ideas to the client rather than three. Give the client a choice. Show the client how creative the agency can be. Exceed their expectations. Some ideas will be rejected, to be sure. Others will "stick." Rework the positive material until you get it right and get the client to give approval for production. Help the client feel good about spending so much on media. Over-deliver!*

Global advertising network BBDO highlighted this work ethic with their well-known motto: "*The work, the work, the work,*" featuring its creative work prominently in its communications to clients and potential clients.

"Work" really meant "work it until you've generated the slam-bang big idea" for the brand – the kind of idea that generates brand successes and makes the client want to spend even more on media.

WE'RE IN THE BIG IDEAS BUSINESS

In the vocabulary of 2019, these "big ideas" are "taglines," and they're meant to sum up a brand's meaning in an enduring way. Past and present taglines include McDonalds': *I'm Lovin' It.* Budweiser: *The King of Beers.* Nike: *Just Do It.* Kentucky Fried Chicken: *Finger Lickin' Good.* De Beers: *A Diamond is Forever.* You get the idea – you've been bombarded with taglines your entire life.

David Ogilvy, founder of Ogilvy & Mather, described the "big idea" concept in 1983:

*"**What's the big idea?** You can do homework from now until domesday, but you will never win fame and fortune unless you also invent big ideas. It takes a big idea to attract the attention of consumers and get them to buy your product. Unless your advertising contains a big idea, it will pass like a ship in the night. I doubt if more than one campaign in a hundred contains a big idea. I am supposed to be one of the more fertile inventors of big ideas, but in my long career as a copywriter I have not had more than 20, if that. Big ideas come from the unconscious ...But your unconscious has to be well informed, or your idea will be irrelevant. Stuff your conscious mind with information, then unhook your rational thought process. You can help this process by going for a long walk, or taking a hot bath, or drinking half a pint of claret"* (Ogilvy, 1983, p. 16).

If big ideas are the Holy Grail, it's easy to see how agencies persist in seeing themselves as being in the big ideas business rather than in the advertising deliverables business. "You can't measure the effort to develop big ideas," I was told by an ad agency office head. "It could take five seconds or five weeks. Your interest in measuring agency outputs is noble but misguided." Big ideas are generated by creative teams. Creative teams consist of an art director and a copywriter – an images/sounds person and a words person – who work closely together, often for years, bouncing concepts back and forth to one another, feeding on each other's capabilities, functioning as a self-contained ideas machine within the creative heart of the agency.

The industry had been in the creative doldrums in the years immediately after World War II. Leo Burnett, founder of the agency that bore his name, long held the opinion that his industry had had "too much dull advertising, pages and pages of dull, stupid, uninteresting copy that does not offer the reader anything in return for his time taken in reading it" (Fox, 1984, p. 221).

He celebrated *creativity* and encouraged his agency and others, as well, to celebrate "the creative men who are the men of the hour.

It is high time that they were given the respect that they deserve," he wrote in 1955. He pushed his creatives to find "the inherent drama in the product itself and present it believably, like a news story, using non-verbal archetypes and symbols, often drawn from American history and folklore." Under his leadership, Leo Burnett created the Jolly Green Giant, the Pillsbury Doughboy, Tony the Tiger and the Marlboro Man (Fox, 1984, pp. 221-223).

Separately, Bill Bernbach, the creative founder of Dane Doyle Bernbach, developed innovative 1950s ads for Volkswagen (*Think Small*) and Avis (*We're No. 2; We Try Harder*), while David Ogilvy invented *The Hathaway Man* in 1951 for Hathaway Shirts.

The industry coined the phrase "The Creative Revolution" for the change from dull advertising to the whimsical big ideas of the 1950s and 1960s.

Jerry Della Femina, head of Della Femina & Partners and well-known creative figure in his own right[1] celebrated these accomplishments in 1970: *"In the beginning, there was Volkswagen. That's the first campaign which everyone can trace back and say, 'This is where the changeover began'. That was the day when the new advertising agency was really born, and it all started with Doyle, Dane, Bernbach. They began as an agency around 1949 and they were known in the business as a good agency, but no one really got to see what they were doing until Volkswagen came around"* (Femina, 1970).

The Volkswagen campaigns turned the industry on its head – this was *creativity writ large*. Every advertiser wanted and sought comparable *Creative Revolution Big Ideas* for their campaigns. *Creativity* sold products! The Creative Revolution kicked off a burst of sustained demand for advertising that increased industry growth, created excess demand that drove up the price of media and lined agency pockets with 15% commissions.

Mary Wells established Wells, Rich, and Greene in 1963 with one $6 million client, and she grew the agency spectacularly to more than $100 million in billings in five years by focusing on Creative Revolution work, including *"I can't believe I ate the whole thing"* for Alka-Seltzer and *the 100-millimeter cigarette* for Benson & Hedges (Fox, 1984, pp. 268-269).

Fifty years later, in his 2011 memoir, John Hegarty, the creative founding partner of Bartle Beatty Hegarty, reiterated the Creative Revolution refrain:

> *"Ideas are what advertising is built upon. We worship them, we seek them, fight over them, applaud them and value them above everything else. Walk round the floors of any agency and the phrase you'll most hear is: 'What's the idea?'" (Hegarty, 2011).*

"Big ideas" and "creativity" combined with "unlimited service" defined the formula for agency success. These factors came together during the 15% commission era, during The Golden Age, and they have served as guideposts for agency executives ever since.

GOING PUBLIC

The advertising business was financially attractive for agency owners. The 1960s would be remembered not only for the Creative Revolution but also as the decade when advertising agencies went public, rewarding themselves for their successes to date and setting themselves up with strengthened finances for global growth and other initiatives. Papert, Koenig, Lois (PKL) took the plunge in 1962, setting a trend which was initially frowned upon by the industry (Fox, 1984). PKL was followed by Foote, Cone & Belding and DDB in 1964, Grey in 1965, Ogilvy & Mather in 1966 and J Walter Thompson in 1969.

During the first seven months of 1969, attracted by high industry growth and the prospect of wealth, nearly 100 new agencies were launched. *Newsweek* put the Creative Revolution on its cover in August 1969. Advertising was the place to be for would-be entrepreneurs.

The 30 years of The Golden Age, 1946-1975, was a period of growth and wealth creation. Agencies focused on creativity and service. The commission system provided high levels of income, making the large cost investments affordable. The Golden Age was successful for advertised brands, and what was good for clients created success for agencies. Agency executives hammered home the simple themes of creativity and service, and in doing so they created an enduring theme for agency culture for the decades to come.

Agencies also continued the practice of over-staffing their offices and clients in order to "over-deliver" creative ideas. The 15% media commissions generated such high levels of income relative to agency workloads that 50% or 60% margins would have been possible if staffing was leaner and more reasonable. However, no publicly quoted agency wanted to show such high levels of profitability. It would have looked like highway robbery to their clients.

Instead, it made more sense to "staff up" to the highest levels possible and show "reasonable" profits on financial statements. The surplus resources could be used to over-service client accounts.

With surplus resources, everything and anything became possible, and the need to "manage the agency" was minimal, indeed.

CHAPTER 3 –
THE HOLDING COMPANIES

"Who is our most creative accountant?"

Credit: William Hamilton / The New Yorker / The Cartoon Bank.

The success of ad agencies during the Creative Revolution attracted financial acquirers and, eventually, as author Mark Tungate observed in his highly readable history of global advertising, *Ad Land* (Tungate, 2007), "almost everyone in advertising works for one of five different companies." Those five companies are, of course, the behemoth holding companies WPP (British), Omnicom Group (American), The Interpublic Group of Companies (American), Publicis Groupe (French), and Dentsu Inc. (Japanese), which together bought up during the past 30 years a significant portion of the world's global advertising agencies, direct marketing agencies, digital and social agencies, market research companies, media agencies and public relations firms.

These five major holding companies are joined by five other diversified and acquisitive competitors who have made recent inroads in the marketing communications industry: Accenture Interactive, PwC Digital Services, Deloitte Digital, Cognizant Interactive and IBM iX – all of whom come from management consulting and digital transformation heritages (see Table 3-1).

TABLE 3-1: TOP TEN HOLDING COMPANIES 2018 – GLOBAL GROUP RANKING

Ranking	Agency Group	Revenue (Millions of U.S. Dollars)
1	**WPP**	**$19,703**
2	**Omnicom Group**	**$15,274**
3	**Publicis Groupe**	**$10,921**
4	**Interpublic Group of Companies**	**$7,882**
5	**Dentsu Inc.**	**$7,822**
6	**Accenture Interactive**	**$6,512**
7	**PwC Digital Services**	**$5,060**
8	**Deloitte Digital**	**$4,065**
9	**Cognizant Interactive**	**$3,942**
10	**IBM iX***	**$3,490**

Source: Ad Age Datacenter (Agency Report 2018)
Asterisk indicates Ad Age Datacenter estimate

The holding companies developed a dominant ownership position in the industry and changed the equilibrium between ad agencies, who focused on creativity and service, and their clients, who wanted from the agencies whatever "worked." The new imperative brought by the holding companies required agencies to generate higher and growing profit margins, year after year. Early in the holding company/agency relationships, when agencies were well paid and "fat" with resources, this new imperative did not pose problems – agencies could easily cut costs to improve their profits. This caused no damage to their operations or their ability to service clients. Later, when industry conditions deteriorated with lower fees and greater workloads, the profit generation imperative would begin to stretch if not cripple agency capabilities.

After 2005, without diminishing its emphasis on agency margin improvement, the holding companies began to negotiate for "holding company relationships" to secure increased revenues for their extensive portfolios of agencies. They recognized that clients had broader needs for diversified agency services – from TV to digital and (later) social – and they offered "one-stop" shopping for major clients.

Each holding company came into existence for different reasons, as discussed below. In chronological order, here is a brief sketch of early holding company histories:

Interpublic. The Interpublic Group of Companies was the grandfather of them all, born in 1960 as the handiwork of McCann-Erickson's merger-obsessed president, Marion Harper Jr, who rose from the mailroom at age 23 to become president of the agency by age 32. Harper had grand ambitions, and he was bent on leaping to dominance in the industry through account wins and acquisitions of other agencies. Marschalk & Pratt, an acquired agency, was maintained as a separate entity with its own office and identity. Further agencies were acquired, and in 1960, Harper announced a rescrambling of the ensemble into a new conglomerate, Interpublic, with four initial divisions: McCann-Erickson, to handle domestic accounts; McCann-Marschalk, a second "traditional" agency, to handle competing accounts; McCann-Erickson Corp. (International), to handle nearly 50 overseas offices; and Communications Affiliates, offering various research, public relations, and sales promotion services (Fox, 1984, pp. 198-199).

On 1 May 2008, The Securities and Exchange Commission (SEC) filed enforcement actions against IPG, McCann-Erickson Worldwide, and two former executives for their roles in an accounting fraud involving intercompany transactions that had the effect of purposely and falsely inflating McCann-Erickson's and IPG's earnings between 1997 and 2005.

IPG and McCann agreed to settle the SEC's charges, and McCann agreed to pay a $12 million penalty.[1]

The SEC's legal action led a change of leadership at IPG, where Michael Roth was brought in from the outside to run the holding company. John Dooner, the previous IPG head, was "demoted" to become CEO of McCann-Erickson Worldwide, a post he retained until his retirement in 2010, when he began to collect pension benefits of $37.7 million.[2]

The SEC's complaint provided a detailed picture of the holding company's annual quest for profits:

"IPG and McCann had a deep-rooted culture that emphasized profits as the company's prime objective. The drive to deliver profits was very aggressive. Every year from 1997 through 2001, Price Waterhouse Company UK listed 'pressure from parent company to produce results in line with budget' as one of several risk assessments in PwC's internal audit strategy memorandum. Every fall, McCann conducted 'Forward Planning Meetings.' At these meetings, McCann's management met with regional management and local heads of agencies and proposed budgets and profit targets for the following year. McCann management then either accepted or rejected the budget. If rejected, the agencies had to return with a higher number to attain. After McCann management accepted the budget for all of its agencies, McCann management then submitted the budget on a consolidated basis to IPG management, who then either accepted or rejected it.

"This planning process was updated twice throughout the year – in the Spring and Summer – based on actual profits achieved by the agencies and any other developments. During the updating process, new profit targets were set, often above the original target set in the Forward Planning Meeting. Consequently, these targets were called 'stretch targets.'"[3]

Interpublic's marquee advertising agencies today include Deutsch, FCB, The Martin Agency, McCann and RG/A;

media is bundled under the banner IPG Mediabrands, of which Universal McCann is the best-known entity. In 2018, IPG forked out $2.3 billion to add Acxiom Marketing Services to its portfolio, reflecting the recent interest by holding companies in adding data service providers to their creative and media capabilities.

WPP. Next in line some 25 years later was a pure holding company start-up, WPP, begun by Martin Sorrell (Sir Martin from 2000 onward) and stockbroker Preston Rabl, who raised a loan to acquire Wire & Plastic Products, a manufacturer of shopping baskets, to serve as a shell company for a straightforward programme of ad agency acquisitions. Sorrell, a Harvard Business School graduate with an MBA, had worked at Saatchi & Saatchi since 1975, and after 1977 he had been their group finance director. He learned the acquisitions and ad agency business thoroughly. During his stewardship, Saatchi & Saatchi completed more than 15 agency acquisitions in the UK, US and elsewhere in the world, using Saatchi & Saatchi stock, debt and "earn-out" structures that motivated agency owners/managers to improve their financial performance as a way of earning a higher final price for their companies.

In June 1987, Sorrell borrowed heavily and WPP completed the industry's first hostile takeover, acquiring JWT for US $566 million. Subsequently, in 1989, Sorrell pursued and won Ogilvy & Mather for US $860 million, using debt and preferred stock rather than equity. By 2000, he secured Young & Rubicam for US $4.7 billion, and in 2005, Grey Global Group for US $1.75 billion (Tungate, 2007, pp. 164-165). Along the way, WPP completed many other acquisitions in various media, and Sorrell consolidated the media departments of his various holdings into GroupM, a media powerhouse. Later, WPP pursued an aggressive programme of digital agency acquisitions and by 2013 had 150 major holdings in advertising, media, research, public relations, branding, healthcare, direct marketing, digital, promotion, and specialist communications (Annual Report, 2013).

WPP fell on difficult times in 2017 and 2018, when its share price declined by 30% in the face of disappointing growth and profitability. Concurrently, the WPP board instructed the US law firm WilmerHale to investigate an anonymous allegation that Sir Martin had used petty cash to pay for expenses incurred other than in connection with his duties as CEO of WPP. Sir Martin strenuously denied the allegation. No written report was prepared by WilmerHale, and the investigation concluded. No findings were made against Sir Martin in relation to the allegation. However, when news of the investigation leaked to the press, Sir Martin concluded that it was no longer in the best interests of WPP for him to remain on its board of directors, as he considered that the leak was indicative of a relationship breakdown between Sir Martin and certain other members of the WPP board. Sir Martin then resigned.

Sorrell was an industry innovator, having created a diversified financial conglomerate that bought well-paid, cost-rich companies, like JWT and O&M, and diversified by marketing discipline to balance the risk. WPP's real goal was to deliver growing income and improved margins to WPP shareholders, who would benefit from rising share prices. Improved performance would be achieved through tough budget negotiations with acquired companies., with a focus on reducing their excess costs. WPP became expert in buying companies and squeezing better performance out of them through annual budget negotiations.

There was some financial manipulation at O&M during the same years that McCann was artificially inflating its earnings. In 2005, two senior New York Ogilvy & Mather executives were jailed by the federal government for 14 months and 18 months, respectively, for their part in a scheme to overbill the government on Ogilvy's Office of National Drug Policy account. The fraud involved timesheet manipulation rather than financial accounting. At the trial, prosecutors accused the executives of leading a plot to falsify timesheets in order to make up for a projected revenue shortfall on the account in 1999. The invisible hand of holding company profit pressures certainly played a role in this, although at no time did WPP ever encourage any operating company to falsify its accounts.

WPP's individual companies were specialized and encouraged to stay that way. "People of specialist skills work best and contribute more when recruited, trained and inspired by specialist companies," stated WPP's 2003 Annual Report.

Client needs for "best in class" agency expertise across marketing disciplines drove WPP into becoming an operating company as well as a financial holding company. Sorrell saw this need and put a lot of personal energy into developing new WPP client relationships under his "horizontality" banner. He became an indefatigable salesman for the bundling of WPP agencies to serve clients like Ford and others. (In October, 2018, WPP agencies lost most of their creative responsibilities on the Ford account to BBDO – breaking the near-monopolistic grip that WPP had on the Ford account).

He never lost his zest for micromanaging agency costs, though, and year after year, especially in the face of fee cuts by procurement, Sorrell continued to impose "stretch" budgets on WPP's portfolio agencies.

Sorrell's energy and focus on acquisitions, cost reductions, "horizontality" and industry conferences was legendary. So was his desire to be well paid for his successes.

This, of course, made him vulnerable when WPP's share price declined. Although Sorrell blamed clients for "short-sighted" cuts in marketing spend, he missed an important fact: WPP agencies, like all holding company agencies, had been cost-reduced into weakness, and they had less to give the holding company in 2017.

The other holding companies were subject to the same pressures.

WPP includes the Grey Group, Ogilvy & Mather, Young & Rubicam (merged into VML in September 2018 as VMLY&R),

Landor Associates, and JWT. Digital holdings include Wunderman, AKQA, Geometry. Public relations includes Hill+Knowlton Strategies, Ogilvy PR, Burson Cohn & Wolfe. Media agencies include GroupM, Mindshare, MediaCom, Wavemaker, Essence, m/SIX and Xaxis.

Martin Sorrell has provided his reflections on his executive career in Chapter 4.

Omnicom. Concurrently in 1986, but along very different lines, Keith Reinhard of Needham Harper sought to pair his agency with the highly regarded BBDO and DDB agencies, seeking scale in an industry that was then highly fragmented. The three agencies eventually came together as Omnicom, a mega-agency that segued into a three-legged structure involving two surviving (and competing) agencies, BBDO and DDB Needham (a merger of DDB and Needham Harper), and a third entity called Diversified Agency Group, which gathered together the assorted direct marketing, public relations and sales promotion activities of the member agencies.

The press nicknamed the deal "The Big Bang" (Tungate, 2007, p. 166). Allen G Rosenshine, Chairman and CEO of BBDO, called the new agency entity "nothing less than advertising's global creative superpower," capable of providing extra creative resources for clients, providing a structure that could hold on to restless creative talent, and introducing a higher-level organization to handle new business pitches.

Of all the holding companies, Omnicom remains the most wedded to the creative legacy of its major agencies, BBDO, DDB and TBWA. Each agency aggressively touts its creative excellence; creative awards remain particularly important to BBDO and TBWA. Omnicom, as a holding company brand, maintains a low public profile. This is not to say that Omnicom does not aggressively pursue holding company relationships – it has recently sought and won a number of highly contested relationships, like McDonald's – but Omnicom's Chairman, CEO and President, John Wren, stays out of the press and avoids industry conferences, working instead behind the scenes to maintain Omnicom's performance.

Media companies operating in the Omnicom portfolio include media networks OMD Worldwide, PHD Worldwide and Hearts & Science. In addition, data and analytics are covered by Annalect and the digital marketing agency, Resolution Media. The DAS Group of Companies is made up of more than 200 companies in public relations, CRM, healthcare, events, promotional marketing, vehicle testing, branding and research. Omnicom's major ad agencies today include BBDO, DDB and TBWA.

Publicis Groupe. Publicis, the French advertising agency founded by the innovative Marcel Bleustein-Blanchet in 1926, went public in 1970 and expanded along European lines until 1988, when under its Chairman and CEO Maurice Lévy it entered into an alliance with FCB. Publicis-FCB became the largest European network with one worldwide footprint via Publicis' 40 agencies in Europe and the US and FCB's 176 agencies located in 40 countries. However, when FCB's Chief Executive Norman Brown retired and was replaced by Bruce Mason, Mason was not favourable to the alliance, and in 1996 it was dissolved. To make up for lost time, Lévy set off on an acquisition trail, buying Hal Riney & Partners, Fallon McElligott and, in 2000, the fabled Saatchi & Saatchi. Subsequently, in 2002, Lévy negotiated a merger with Bcom3, the temporary holding company for Leo Burnett and the MacManus Group (D'Arcy Masius Benton & Bowles, along with N.W. Ayer and Partners) (Tungate, 2007, pp. 176-179).

Subsequent acquisitions were designed to turn the holding company into a digital giant: Digitas (USA), Business Interactif (France), CCG (China), Tribal (Brazil), Phonevalley, Performics and Razorfish, purchased from Microsoft Corporation.

In 2013, Publicis and Omnicom announced that they would merge "as equals" and become the number one holding company in size, but much to the embarrassment of both parties, they were unable to pull off the deal in 2014 as a result of tax complications and disagreements over who would be the finance director, a Frenchman or an American. After the failure of this deal, Publicis bought Sapient, a digital technology provider with digital advertising interests, for $3.7 billion.

Management of Publicis Groupe changed at the top with the 2017 retirement of the charismatic Chairman and CEO Maurice Lévy, who first joined Publicis Groupe in 1971. Lévy was succeeded as CEO by 46-year-old Arthur Sadoun, a 1997 MBA graduate of INSEAD who pursued a career in advertising.

Sadoun has made it clear that Publicis Groupe must become a "superagency" under the Publicis Communications brand name, and he has aggressively promoted the Groupe's services accordingly. The major communications brands – BBH, Fallon, Leo Burnett, Publicis Worldwide, Saatchi & Saatchi are expected to work in a fully-integrated fashion with Publicis Media (Starcom, Zenith, Spark Foundry, Digitas, Blue 449 and Performics) and Publicis Sapient.

More than any other holding company, Publicis Groupe seems committed to becoming a fully integrated operating company rather than a collection of individual brands.

Dentsu. Dentsu had long been the world's largest advertising and media *agency*, operating from a dominant position in Japan and having strategic Dentsu outposts throughout South East Asia and elsewhere. In recent years, particularly since 2007, Dentsu made a number of focused acquisitions of limited scale – the US creative hotshops Attik (2007) and mcgarrybowen (2008); the US digital firms 360i (2010), Ignition One (2010)[4], Netmining (2010), Firstborn (2011) and Steak (2011); the PR group Mitchell Communications (2013), and in India Taproot (2012) and Webchutney (2013). Then, in 2013, Dentsu upped the ante through a $5 billion acquisition of London-based media company Aegis, owner of Carat, iProspect, Isobar, Posterscope, Vizeum and Aztec, putting Dentsu in the number five position in the industry with income of $6.4 billion

(Adage Data Centre, 2013). Consistent with its increased globalization and geographical reach, Dentsu announced that it would launch Dentsu Aegis Network, which would manage all Aegis Media work and non-Japanese Dentsu operations worldwide, and it upgraded its management structure, anointing Jerry Buhlmann, CEO of the Aegis Network, as a Dentsu executive officer in June 2013 – joining his boss, Tim Andree (director and executive VP of Dentsu Inc.) as the second of only two non-Japanese to be named executive officers (Dentsu Taps Aegis Executive, 2013). In November 2018, Jerry Buhlmann resigned as CEO, having served for nine years in the job, and Tim Andree was promoted to fill the vacancy.

Unusually among the holding companies, Dentsu (or more accurately, Dentsu Aegis Network – DAN) decided to keep its books "by region" rather than by individual profit centre. DAN Mexico, for example, can make financial trade-offs among its various operating units, and only the country has to deliver the required profit margin to the centre. This, it is argued, makes it easier to instill a culture of cooperation among business units in a defined geographical area – avoiding the cutthroat competition among operating units in other holding companies, each of whom have to meet financial targets along with cooperating with one another on holding company initiatives.

Despite the differences in formation history and articulated strategies, each holding company has certain goals and concerns that are common to each of them.

1. **Improve the financial performance of portfolio companies**. Each holding company demanded improved profit performance out of each of its owned agencies. This was not a one-time request to be accomplished after an agency was acquired; instead, it was a major ongoing activity that dominated the relationship between the holding company and its owned agencies, from budget setting time (typically during October-December

for the following fiscal year) through quarterly reviews and end-of-year closings.

Like any owner of a diversified portfolio, the holding company established profit margin goals for each agency, and these goals were documented in the agreed agency budget with specific revenue and cost targets by client, region and office. It goes without saying that these holding company profit goals were "stretch" goals, and that the "stretch" became harder to achieve in the face of ongoing client fee reductions. The typical holding company came to expect a 15-20% operating margin from its operating companies.

One common metric used by holding companies to evaluate agency operations was "staff-cost ratio," or the cost of all agency personnel divided by agency income. Staff-cost ratio took the total of staff costs and divided them by income, yielding a "ratio" or "percentage." The holding company would set a "benchmark," like 50%, for the staff-cost ratio, on the assumption that this would optimize agency operations and deliver an appropriate profit margin. If an agency had a higher ratio of (say) 55%, meaning that staff costs were 55% of agency income, then the agency was deemed to be "high cost," and agency management was expected to cut agency staff costs accordingly. The alternative interpretation, that the agency was "low income" rather than "high cost" was not considered. This metric was effective during the decade of the 1990s and shortly thereafter, when agency remuneration was high and agencies were staffing their clients heavily with multiple creative teams and a full complement of client service people. However, as agency income eroded, and declining income mathematically drove up staff-cost ratios (the denominator was declining, so the ratio rose), agencies were still expected to reduce costs and get the ratio in line. It did not matter if workloads were growing and more staff was required; the staff-cost ratio dictated a lower agency headcount and cost structure. Agencies did their very best to meet holding company staff-cost ratio targets.

2. **Use purchasing leverage to negotiate lower costs with key suppliers**. The holding company's purchasing scale was an obvious source of lower-cost value-added for individual agencies. Prices of hotels, airline travel, telecommunications costs, IT costs, stationery/paper supplies and like items were negotiated effectively by procurement executives at the holding company to give their agencies lower costs in key parts of their cost structures.

3. **Seek to grow organic top-line revenue by acting as an integrated operating company**. Apart from encouraging revenue growth from the individual agencies, holding companies acted independently, selling the concept of "holding company relationships" to large global advertisers. In this type of scheme, clients agreed to use principally, or wholly, the agencies owned by the holding company. In return for this exclusivity, and on the assumption that there were genuine economies of scale from holding company relationships (a debatable claim), the holding companies offered a fee discount of some type. Needless to say, many of their agencies saw the promotion of holding company relationships as directly competitive with agencies' new business marketing activities, with the holding company "brand" eclipsing ad agency brands. As one senior agency executive explained to me, "It's one thing for us to go out there and win a new client. It's another thing to be a cog in the wheel of a low-priced holding company relationship. I've appreciated the revenue that it brings us, but I'm concerned about damage to our agency's brand name."

4. **Grow holding company size through further acquisitions**. All the holding companies developed considerable acquisitions experience, not only in negotiating terms of acquisitions but in integrating acquired agencies into the holding company's portfolio. New or upgraded budgeting, financial and reporting systems had to be put in place, and the holding company's budgetary and cost controls implemented immediately.

Holding companies were aggressive acquirers of marketing services companies around the world, not only in digital and social technologies, but also in strong-growth markets, like Brazil, Russia, India and China (the BRIC countries). Hardly a week could go by without the announcement of new holding company acquisitions in one part of the world or another.

The consolidation of holding company power and position in the industry is one of the fascinating aspects of advertising industry change since the 1980s. Industry spokesmen evolved from agency CEOs (i.e., David Ogilvy, Leo Burnett, etc.) and famous creatives (Bill Bernbach, Jay Chiat, Lee Clow, Hal Riney, and so on) to holding company CEOs. Freewheeling and undisciplined agency spending on people, parties and creative pitches were replaced by sober agency consideration of salary levels, head-counts, overhead rates and profit margins. Holding companies brought discipline and profit consciousness to the creative free-for-all that had been the trademark of ad agencies during The Golden Age. Holding companies did not kill all the fun, to be sure, but their involvement was like that of a sober spouse at a cocktail party, reminding you of tomorrow's hangover if you indulge too much.

Today (2019), though, the holding companies themselves are under threat, struggling to maintain their growth rates and profit margins in the face of new competitors (consulting firms), in-house agencies and their own understaffed and underpaid agencies.

The holding companies have taken much of the value-added out of their agencies over the past one or two decades, so there are new challenges to address. It will be interesting to see how Mark Read, the new CEO of WPP, and Arthur Sadoun, the new CEO of Publicis Groupe, deal with their own performance challenges.

Accenture Interactive, PwC Digital Services, Deloitte Digital, Cognizant Interactive and IBM iX are technically marketing services holding companies along with the Top 5 discussed above, but they act and compete more like management consulting firms than holding companies.

We will deal with these disruptors in Chapter 7, The Rise of the Management Consultants.

CHAPTER 4 –
SIR MARTIN SORRELL: REFLECTIONS

"*Grab some lederhosen, Sutfin. We're about to climb aboard the globalization bandwagon.*"

Credit: Robert Weber / The New Yorker / The Cartoon Bank.

Sir Martin Sorrell sat for a taped interview in September 2018, after his departure from WPP and the acquisition of MediaMonks by S4 Capital, his newly-formed company. He reflected on his many years as an executive in the global marketing communications industry.

I was at Harvard Business School in the late 60s as a relatively young man, having gone to HBS directly from Cambridge. Most of my classmates worked in industry or finance for two or three years before getting their MBAs – no matter; for me it was fun and instructive. At Harvard we talked about globalization, which was then a new concept, and the growth prospects for companies if they looked more broadly at the world. I remember hearing Howard Morgens, CEO of Procter & Gamble and the father of one of my classmates, talk about Procter as a global company, and at the time I think international was only 10% of its operations.[1] Even for Procter, globalization was in its infancy before the 70s.

Later, I was finance director at Saatchi & Saatchi plc in London from 1975 to 1985, and we were involved in acquisitions, with globalization a big part of our strategy, acquiring US agencies and increasing the number of global clients. China was opening under Deng Xiaoping, and P&G and British Airways were expanding internationally. Saatchi was responsible for the launch of Pampers in the UK. P&G had a Pampers manufacturing plant somewhere in the middle of America. P&G was testing the product in the UK, and for a long time it was spending nothing on UK media, so we had no income on the brand – we were paid on media commission. That's the way it worked. Procter finally finished its UK product development and set a market share objective, and once they started marketing, they blasted away with media until they hit their target, and they spent whatever it took. The media commission was a bonanza. We benefited enormously from P&G's globalization, as did its other agencies and all agencies that worked on global accounts for global clients.

Saatchi was committed to globalization, pure and simple. I remember in 1983, Maurice Saatchi rushed into my office, waving a *Harvard Business Review* article by HBS Professor Ted Levitt[2], which said something like "everyone will consume everything in the same way everywhere," and he said, "this is it. This is what we are. This is what we have to be."[3] Levitt was eventually appointed to the board of Saatchi.

I left Saatchi in 1985 with my own ideas about globalization, and I put together WPP, a holding company, from Wire and Plastics Products plc. At first, we focused on acquiring below-the-line agencies, which we thought were both underappreciated and affordable. The industry had a snooty attitude in those days to "shelf wobblers" and "sales promotion," much as some agencies today have snooty attitudes towards digital and data. We were not then looking to acquire creative agencies, but because of circumstances, JWT hit hard times in 1987, having gone into loss in Q4 of 1986, and it was vulnerable. JWT was 13 times our size, but all we had to do was to pay twice our value, and once we did this we found that JWT had undervalued property in Japan. We sold the property, and it helped to pay for the deal.

JWT was global, and we were committed to global expansion with the clear realization that Asia and Latin America and Africa and the Middle East and Central Eastern Europe would become more important in the future. Later, these parts of the world would be called the BRICs[4] and the Next Eleven[5] by Goldman Sachs, but for WPP they were then "global opportunities." We were going to expand in the world with a global portfolio of marketing communications companies. We continued to acquire agencies in a variety of media, and to add Ogilvy & Mather and later Y&R and Grey as our creative agencies, with their other capabilities, too.

Our organizational situation was more complicated than Saatchi's. Saatchi & Saatchi was a storied creative agency expanding globally through the acquisition of other storied advertising agencies, like Ted Bates, all of them with growing, globalizing clients. By contrast, we were WPP, a somewhat strange and small manufacturing company buying famous creative agencies (JWT, O&M, Y&R and Grey) and below-the-line agencies. Little old WPP, the wire basket manufacturer, didn't mean anything to anybody.

I knew that we needed to expand globally, and to utilize our diverse technologies in useful ways, and to co-ordinate clients increasingly on a worldwide basis, and to handle country management in an effective way. All of this meant better integration of the resources we owned. What I faced as CEO, though, was "how do we manage integration" from the centre? How could the WPP centre bring about effective change within our diverse portfolio? In some ways, it was amusing that a wireworks manufacturer controlled all these brands. The brands were much more important than WPP, and they were much more famous and involved with famous clients, and funnily enough, each of them was a mini-WPP in a way – they had all been publicly listed, and each had a diverse portfolio. The agency brands were important, and the CEOs were proud and independent, and they had fixed ideas about who they were and what they should do, and this made it difficult for us at the centre to bring about change.

The people running the agencies were more aligned to their brands than to the holding company. I had to bring about a change in this alignment if we were to achieve something important. The brand CEOs were dead set against co-operating with one another. This is understandable – many of them had spent 20 years of their life at their agency brands, and they viewed the other agencies as deadly competitors and the WPP centre as an interfering presence. My history was entirely different from theirs – it was easier for me to see what we could achieve through co-operation.

We couldn't have a holding company that had a number of businesses that operated independently in 115 or 205 countries, whatever the number was – my thinking was *"it has to be WPP, one united company,"* so we can operate efficiently and competitively on behalf of our clients. We had to become one company, like a McKinsey or Goldman Sachs. The uncertainty about "what do we do to create one company," and "what is an appropriate pace of change" consumed much of my thinking. If you try to change too fast, you'll kill the businesses. If you go too slow, you never get anywhere, and the centre will be rendered impotent.

That led me to creating our first WPP-wide incentive programme in 1992, what we called our first five-year Leap Plan. The first year, I put up a million pounds of my own money, and there was the opportunity for this to generate five million pounds of incentives if we hit four share price targets in the coming five years. We had to hit the target for 30 trade days each year for the plan to kick in. You know, we hit our targets, and this helped to create a WPP identity and incentives for the 18-20 people who ended up in the pool.

To my annoyance, though, I found that incentives didn't really change people's behaviour. They re-enforced existing behaviours. Individuals are motivated in certain ways and you can stimulate that motivation by providing incentives and targets. But you can't get around the fact that you have to have the right people in the right jobs, and you need to change the people when it's clear that change is moving too slowly. In one of our creative agencies, we've had three changes of CEOs over the years, and with each change we've seen improvements in the degree of intercompany co-operation and integration. Change takes time and sometimes it requires new people.

Media posed another challenge for us. Each of the storied creative brands had its own media operation, and the media people within the agencies did not have corner offices or Ferraris. They weren't the feted heroes of their agencies. They were like Harry Crane, the media guy in *Mad Men* who hopes for a partnership but will never get one. Media was considered lower status and lower priority than creative, but it was media that was making the money, and over time, with the fragmentation of media due to direct marketing, CRM, digital and social, media would be ascendant. I used to upset creatives by saying that *the medium is more important than the message*. It's a bastardized version of McLuhan, but it's fundamental. Media could not blossom inside the creative agencies. For them, it was always "*creative first*," and "*media take the hindmost.*"

That's why I had to form Mindshare in 1997, pulling out media and merging the media operations of JWT and Ogilvy & Mather – to allow media to flourish on its own within WPP. Later, we upped the ante and created GroupM in 2003 to serve as a parent media company for our many media properties – Mindshare, MediaCom, Wavemaker, Essence, m/SIX and Xaxis. This was a necessary WPP initiative.

There were further issues that we had to influence. Country management was a key one. For each of our 30 or 45 or 50 global clients, we had global client coordinators across the world. At the same time, we had country managers who were consolidating people into one building and running country operations. There were always matrix problems between global coordinators and country managers. For most of my time at WPP, the global coordinators were primary. But at some point, you had to flip the switch. At some point, the country managers, who were running WPP operations in growing and big countries, had to become the primary movers, the primary focal point. When you start appointing country managers for China and India, for example, the global coordinators lose influence and power. It's the right direction to go, but it's an uncomfortable change for many, and when there are uncomfortable changes, you can expect resistance.

In fact, there have been many uncomfortable changes in the past 30 years, and they've all had to be managed one way or another, with leadership coming from the WPP centre. Although globalization has been a constant source of growth, it's changed since 2008 with the collapse of Lehman Brothers and the financial crisis. Before 2008, you had modest levels of inflation, and this gave our clients the ability to influence the pricing of their products and to grow appropriately. There used to be a linkage between GDP growth and advertising, but more recently the link has been broken, particularly in the mature countries. We're now in a low-growth situation, with no inflation, no pricing power, lower growth of advertising – and this has reduced the effectiveness of marketing and the power of the CMO. Brands have stopped growing. The emphasis has shifted to cost management and the rise of procurement. Clients have become finance-driven rather than marketing-driven. Agency fee budgets have been slashed. Clients have been investing in in-house agencies in a quest to reduce costs. Marketing has really taken a back seat.

Looked at broadly, marketing was in the ascendancy in the 80s and 90s, but it is now finance and procurement that are getting more and more ascendant. This is unfortunate.

Additionally, the change in marketing technology, from TV, radio, print to direct marketing and digital and social has had a major influence at the same time, and while the CMO was declining in importance to procurement, you had the rise of the Chief Information Officers (CIOs) and Chief Technology Officers (CTOs). You could not draw a sharp line between CIOs/CTOs and marketing; CIO/CTO technological decisions were affecting the way marketing was conducted, and the CMOs had very little influence over this.

Unfortunately for agencies, this situation favoured Accenture Interactive, Deloitte Digital, PwC and other consultants, and agencies did not really have the technological skills to compete in the same way. Instead, WPP and other holding companies were getting pushed around by finance and procurement while the consultants were pitching the C-Suite about digital transformations and zero-based budget (ZBB) programmes that would slash media and agency costs.

It would have helped if clients had worked with agencies and holding companies to bring about necessary relationship changes, but if you're a client, when there are problems you think that your suppliers must be the ones who need to change. So, clients put pressure on payment terms, on structure, on fees, and on relationships in the hope of getting better results. It was mostly cost-driven.

What clients didn't do was change the way their organizations and their middle managers behaved. Middle management resists change because it's pressurized to produce results. Middle managers must deliver the goods, so even if top management tells them that "they need to transform and disrupt," middle managers will nod their heads and go on behaving as they have always behaved. They see transformation as a threat to achieving results. So, middle managers become part of the problem, and they impose transformations on their suppliers, not on themselves.

A further problem with clients is the separation of marketing and sales. Most packaged goods companies have separate media, marketing and sales functions, and the lack of coordination in these areas leads to enormous inefficiencies. One executive looks after creative agencies, another looks after media relationships, and sales is in a different part of the organization. By contrast, the tobacco companies, like BAT and Philip Morris, who have faced limitations on advertising, unified the marketing and sales functions, and their experience has been very positive, allowing for more effective deployment and coordination of marketing funds and programmes.

With all the performance challenges that clients face, what they want from their marketing partners are "the best people" – not "Agency A" or "Agency B." Clients don't care where the best agency people come from. The only reason to have separate agency brands is to navigate "client conflict" problems. You can't have a single agency work for two competing clients. That's understandable. Apart from this, the agency brands are much less important today, but this message has (understandably) been a hard one for agency CEOs to embrace. Even the concept of the big idea has changed. Years ago, the big idea was 80% of the process ... because there was mainly one channel of distribution, television. Today, by definition the big idea is still central, but its distribution is not 80% TV anymore, it's something less than 80% due to the fragmentation of media. Execution throughout the media landscape is critical. *The medium is more important than the message.*

My theory has always been that everybody has a contribution to make, every employee knows something, and every organization has untapped skills. The job of the CEO is to help to mobilize these skills for the benefit of clients. That's what we tried to do at WPP, and progress was made over many, many years.

Most observers of WPP were unable to see the complexity of its operations and of its need to evolve as it globalized, exploiting technology, reorganizing country management, and integrating its capabilities. WPP was always an organization "in process," and that remains the case today.

At $20 billion in income, though, it's like a battleship or an aircraft carrier that needs to be turned around. It's not a motor torpedo boat. It's harder to grow when you're this large, but growth is still the strategic imperative. If a holding company cannot restore and maintain its growth rate, its future is not at all assured, and its CEO is dead mcat.

Of course, after I left WPP or was pushed out or assassinated or whatever, the job of manoeuvring WPP fell into the hands of professional management – and Mark Read was appointed CEO. This was a big change. I loved WPP because I started it. I never regarded it as being a nine-to-five job. Starting a business is the nearest thing a man can do to giving birth to a baby. Not physically, but mentally. It's like that old Bill Shankly quote about Liverpool: "*Some people think football is a matter of life and death. I assure you, it's much more serious than that.*"

For the people who are now at WPP, however good they may be, it's a job. There is no way that anybody at WPP can apply themselves in the same way. No way. That may be a good thing, by the way: work/life balance; macromanagement as opposed to micromanagement…Who knows?

WPP was and is manageable, and if I had stayed, I would have done what was necessary to continue the necessary changes. There are some ill-informed people who think that the job involved micromanaging 400 profit centres, but that's rubbish. You have JWT, Ogilvy, Y&R and Grey as four verticals. Then Kantar; Hill & Knowlton and Burson Cohn & Wolfe in PR; WPP Branding and Design; the Media companies; WPP Health & Wellness; and digital verticals like AKQA and Wunderman. – no more than 15 or 16 organizational units, and today that's a manageable number of direct reports for the CEO. There are opportunities to consolidate some of the operations within the large organizational units, and especially within GroupM, for example.

Still, WPP is a very big battleship, and so are the other holding companies. Publicis Groupe has moved very fast and has a great strategy, moving to one brand, but the speed of change may kill them, and in integrating their agency brands so rapidly they may have killed what was good within. The pace of change, as I mentioned before, is critical. Omnicom, by contrast, has no apparent strategy, but they have great businesses. They have no obvious strategic logic or direction – just a street fight among the businesses. IPG is somewhere in between.

As far as the future is concerned, there are a lot of uncertainties. It may be that there's an inevitability, with the speed of technological and geographical advances, that the life cycle of companies like holding companies is compressed, leading to more rapid cycles of creative growth and then destruction. Change may be continuous, with companies coming and going. The holding companies are going to go through some major structural shifts. Between now and 2020 there's certain to be a market crack, and as the tide goes out, all boats are exposed. MDC and Havas appear to be going through this now, with their futures uncertain.

I'm in a different place, putting together an agile motor torpedo boat rather than a battleship. Maybe I'll be in a position to take advantage of those structural shifts and to pick up some of the pieces on the beach at a future date.

One thing is sure – China remains very, very important. The West might not like to hear this, but China is so technologically advanced … so far ahead of the West … that it's likely to win in any battle. The fight between the US and China is a fight for who will be top dog. China has a longer view and apparently more political stability. Xi Jinping is in place for a long time. China's long-range planning, their socialist form of capitalism, or more accurately their state-directed capitalism, will allow China to do a very effective job. And they have 1.3 billion or more people. For us, China is essential.

At S4 Capital, we're just getting started. We're about digital content and digital media, planning and buying in all forms, globally. We're about using data where we can, first party data. Our data will help inform content decisions. One of the things that really excited me at WPP was Hogarth, where we were getting massive traction, which is the area S4 Capital is now in.

We've got massive traction on the data side. Content, production, data and digital. We'll add media, and we'll expand globally to get to scale. Scale for us will be achieved when we can work with clients and be assured of delivering results. We will achieve scale at a lower level of income and significantly lower costs than the current holding companies today.

Looking back, I can't say that I had a crystal ball about WPP's development or could anticipate all the opportunities and challenges and problems that we encountered. No one is this good. You live from day to day while working to a vision and strategy. Then you find out what happens, and you adjust accordingly, and it's a constant effort.

The same is true with S4 Capital. We're just beginning our journey. The marketplace is fluid. Competitors face uncertain prospects. I feel liberated from the responsibility of managing the battleship, but I miss it and its scale at the same time. WPP will always be a part of my heritage – more accurately, my parentage. S4 Capital is my present and future, and I relish the coming weeks and months and years as we move ahead.

CHAPTER 5 –
MIXED OUTCOMES:
1973-1990

"These are our golden oldies."

Credit: Joseph Farris / The New Yorker / The Cartoon Bank.

Global events beginning in 1973 led to major hurdles in the post-World War II economic boom, and they were followed by a number of changes in the advertising business that had long-lasting consequences. However, from 1973 through to 1990, ad agencies continued their successful and astonishing financial performance, riding a wave of inflated media prices and earning media commissions along the way. Agency revenues and profits continued to rise even though the major economies of the world were having difficulties and advertisers, themselves, were struggling:

"... billings at the top agencies and total advertising expenditures increased faster than the GNP, even faster than inflation or any other economic indicator. In a time of generally stuttering economic growth, advertising enjoyed remarkable, almost giddy leaps forward. Total spending on advertising grew from $19.6 billion in 1970 to $54.6 billion in 1980; TV as usual led the way, from $3.6 billion to $11.4 billion. In 1970 world billings [were] $773 million for J Walter Thompson, the leading agency. Ten years later, 13 agencies [were] billion-dollar operations" (Fox, 1984, p. 327).

OAPEC and the first oil shock. In October 1973, the Organization of Arab Petroleum Exporting Countries (OAPEC) announced an embargo against countries that supported Israel in the Yom Kippur War against Syria and Egypt. The embargo was lifted in 1974, but it was followed by an upsurge in oil prices as OAPEC began to use its leverage by raising world oil prices.

This first oil shock raised energy costs for corporations. Prices rose for all products, particularly those with high-energy content (steel, aluminum, and so on) or made from materials based on petrochemicals, such as plastics. Prices could not be raised enough to cover cost increases, so all-important corporate earnings were threatened. Executives responded in a number of ways, particularly by creating energy task forces to identify energy usage in their manufacturing and distribution operations and by developing conservation measures to cut costs.

The 1974 energy task forces, out on the hunt for energy cost savings, established an early precedent for what would later become, for different reasons, procurement-led hunts for cost savings within marketing departments and from marketing suppliers like ad agencies.

High prices, driven by higher energy costs, and high unemployment from the associated recession took the growth out of consumer markets. In addition, traditional industries like steel-making and automobile manufacturing suffered as newly industrialized countries stepped up the competition through low-cost exports. The stock market crashed in 1973-1974 and the associated pain was felt until the spring of 1975. In the UK, the oil crisis was compounded by the imposition of a three-day week amid fears of power shortages following the announcement of a coal miners' strike. There were widespread power blackouts across the country. UK inflation peaked at 20%.

Recovery, then 1980-1982 recessions. Economies began to grow in late 1975, along with inflation, but in 1980, followed by 1981-1982, a severe double-dip recession resulted from a variety of factors. One of these factors was another energy crisis, this time created by the Iranian Revolution of 1979 and the subsequent interruption in the smooth flow of oil from the producing countries to the oil-consuming world. This second oil shock initiated a second round of energy cost investigations in the corporate world and helped to institutionalize what later became permanent cost reduction initiatives in major corporations.

Media inflation cushion, 1975-1990. Advertising agencies were relatively insulated from these adverse economic factors, since media price inflation provided a revenue and profit cushion during the 1970s and 1980s. Media airtime remained in short supply, and the excess of media demand over media supply drove up media prices and the agency commission income that was tied to them. As welcome as this was for agency executives, it was probably not in their best long-term interests, since their hard-pressed clients were footing the bill during the difficult times of the 1970s and 1980s, and resentments were building up. Agencies looked fat and arrogant at a time when their clients were making sacrifices.

Visible agency wealth. Strong financial performance encouraged ad agencies to go public, and public ownership took certain agencies on the acquisition trail, providing a degree of visibility about agency richness that was both embarrassing and irritating. "At the centre of it all was Saatchi & Saatchi," remarked journalist and author Mark Tungate (Tungate, 2007). Saatchi & Saatchi went public in 1976. By 1987 Saatchi & Saatchi plc had acquired more than 35 marketing services businesses, including four significant ad agency networks (Goldman, 1997). Tungate put the total price tag of these acquisitions at over US $1 billion, and with a minimum of organic growth Saatchi & Saatchi plc expanded to 18,000 employees in 500 offices across 65 countries (Tungate, 2007, p. 101).

Saatchi & Saatchi's 1986 acquisition of the privately held Ted Bates Worldwide agency had industry-wide reverberations. The price, more than $500 million, was five times larger than any previously paid for an advertising firm. The deal gained Bob Jacoby, the Ted Bates CEO, a personal fortune of $111 million and turned 100 other Bates employees into instant millionaires. The transaction also turned Jacoby into the industry's most prominent outcast. "A living symbol of greed," Tom Delaney, [then] a senior editor for the trade journal *Adweek*, put it (Kleiner, 1987).

Nearly 30 years later, advertising people still remember the Jacoby affair. Writing in Forbes.com in 2012, Avi Dan, who was an account director at Benton & Bowles in the 1980s, recalled the shock:

> "Marketers were flabbergasted. They did not realize that their agency partners were able to monetize their relationships for so much money. Clearly, they concluded, agency profits were much higher than the agencies were letting on.
>
> "They quickly decided that it was now time for reassessing how agencies are compensated. Heretofore, agencies were collecting a commission of 15% on the media they placed for marketers. With media inflation rising on average 10% every year as far back as the eye can see, the agencies doubled their profits every seven years.
>
> "Once marketers realized that the commission system favoured the agencies disproportionately and unfairly, they started switching to a more equitable compensation system" (Dan, June 21, 2012).

Internal cultural shifts. Public ownership (and later, holding company ownership) brought about internal cultural shifts that many executives later regretted. Increased public or holding company ownership was marked by "a shift from the creative departments to management, from little boutiques to bigness and mergers, from vivid personalities to corporate anonymity," according to historian Stephen Fox (Fox, 1984, p. 314). "In retrospect," George Lois said of his experience both pre- and post-public ownership at Papert, Koenig, Lois (which went public in 1962 and shut down after client and management losses in 1969), "public ownership was the catalyst for destroying our partnership. People became rich quick and choked up. They started to think, 'We now have obligations to our stockholders'" (Fox, 1984, p. 317).

J Walter Thompson, Foote, Cone & Belding, DDB, Grey and Ogilvy & Mather were all public companies by 1969, and the need to focus on profits was top of mind. This focus would intensify in later years when each was merged into or was acquired by one of the holding companies.

Globalization. Global growth added an additional complexity for large agencies, as their global clients reorganized to produce and sell homogeneous, high-quality, low-priced products throughout the world. "Success in world competition," wrote Theodore Levitt of Harvard Business School in a landmark *Harvard Business Review* article in 1983, "turns on efficiency in production, distribution, marketing, and management, and inevitably becomes focused on price. The world's needs and desires have been irrevocably homogenized" (Levitt, 1983). Levitt's emphasis on globalization made him one of Maurice Saatchi's favourite mentors, and Levitt was eventually appointed to Saatchi & Saatchi's board of directors.

Globalization turned traditional marketing on its head. No longer could companies treat the local consumer as king, serving them with locally produced advertising for customized products and services that met local preferences. Instead, according to Levitt, "The global competitor [must] seek constantly to standardize its offering everywhere ... customers will prefer its world-standardized products."

Globalization struck at the heart of local agency office operations and began a process of agency reorganization. Previously, local agency offices around the world created local ads for their local advertiser clients – like Grey Germany working for P&G Germany, for example. Grey Germany addressed the needs of German P&G customers, using the full capabilities of agency people in Grey's German office – and earned local media commissions from the airing and printing of ads in German markets. The New York, London, Paris, Dusseldorf, Madrid and Milan offices of a global agency like Grey might have the same name on the door and serve the same global client – but they operated as six independent entities, dealing with their US, UK, French, German, Spanish and Italian clients in independent ways.

Globalization changed this structure. Instead of producing six different ads for a consumer product, globalization encouraged *the homogenization of ads*, much in the same way that the client's products were homogenized for sale in global markets. In fact, globalization required the homogenization of ads, so that the brand message could be uniform and consistent, completely aligned with the product, around the globe.

Globalization led to the *centralization of ad creation*, typically in New York or London, with Paris, Dusseldorf, Madrid and Milan (and many other offices) *adapting* centrally produced ads for local consumption. A genuine adaptation would require very little new creative time from the local market and very few client service resources to get the ad through the local client's approval process. Consequently, a global policy of centralized ad creation with local ad adaptation was a lower-cost strategy in total, and it certainly involved lower costs in the local office.

Clients figured this out quickly, and as globalization practices were put in place around the world, clients considered changes in agency remuneration plans. Instead of paying agencies on a 15% commission basis, global clients reasoned that since globalization was reducing agency headcounts, agency remuneration should be reduced as well. By 1990, clients began cutting the standard 15% commission to as low as 11%, and a majority of agencies went along (Goldman, 1997, p. 107). Later, commissions would give way to labour based fees. This shift in remuneration took years to work its way through the list of big-spending advertisers, but the logic was established early in the globalization game, adding another source of downward pressure on agency remuneration.

Agencies found themselves ill-equipped to deal with globalization. Local offices, fighting to maintain their size and income, resisted globalization efforts and conspired with their local clients to thwart the takeover of marketing by the global guys. Their local clients, too, learned that they had much at stake. If globalization was a success, then local marketing organizations had only a limited marketing role to play. Local agencies and local clients dug in their heels and resisted global efforts. They complained that centrally created ads missed the mark in their unique local markets. Globalization surfaced new conflicts between local operations and headquarters operations. In the meantime, the executives at the centre of the storm – at advertiser or agency headquarters – scratched their heads and fumed over the organizational resistance. They were relatively powerless to dictate terms to their regions, but they could not stand back and watch globalization fail.

The requirements of globalization forced agencies to confront the management and operational independence of their local offices. Up to this point, each office operated under an office head as a standalone entity with its own responsibility for income and costs. Office heads were perceived as the real centres of power in the agency network, and they were capable of telling senior executives in the agency centre to "stick it" if they felt like it. After all, office heads had their own clients and revenues, and they developed new clients. No one at the agency headquarters really knew what any office head was doing. Traditionally, office heads were left alone to run their shops, and headquarters stayed out.

Globalization, though, cut out the local offices in ways that undermined the stature and power of office heads. In the worst cases, at least in the eyes of an office head, global client fees came to an office as an *allocation*, a piece of a global pie. The pie was negotiated by a centrally-based finance director, a CEO, a holding company executive or a global client head. The size of *the local piece of pie* was determined in an arbitrary way. Inevitably, local offices felt left out and short-changed by this, and they resented globalization initiatives – they diluted the power and position of local offices and created a confusing network of ambiguous relationships within the agency. Who was more important – an office head or a global client head? Vocally, office heads complained that globalization hurt their profits. If office profits fell short at the end of a year, office heads pointed the finger at low global client fees as the culprit. Too little money for too much work, they said. And there was nothing they could do about it except grouse and fight territorial battles with global client heads, who were elsewhere in the world, flitting about between their global clients and the network of agency offices, responsible for big visible bucks, leaving the painful aspects of globalization for the local office heads to sort out. It did not matter if global income was high or low; local office heads still had to deliver required profit margins. Globalization made this harder, they said.

Supply chain efficiency. Globalization had other effects, and one of these was to motivate corporations to develop programmes that would lower global costs while improving global quality. This went beyond finding the energy cost savings that they sought as a result of the oil shocks. Competitors were global competitors; global companies had to achieve cost positions at least as low as their major global competitors. Economist William Shepherd estimated that industry deregulation, together with anti-trust actions by the government, had served to increase the portion of the US economy "subject to effective competition from 56% in 1958 to 77% by 1980" (Kiechel, 2010, p. 174), so there was some urgency for US corporations to get it right. Remember what Ted Levitt wrote in 1983? *"Success in world competition turns on efficiency in production, distribution, marketing, and management, and inevitably becomes focused on price."* Increasingly, companies who sought these efficiencies went down a predictable path, building on the experience of the energy-reduction efforts, organizing internal task forces and hiring management consultants to carry out wide-ranging studies that examined not only the efficiency of the corporation's own operations *but those of their suppliers as well.*

1. **Global supply chain management**. Global companies shuttered their inefficient internal manufacturing operations and expanded their use of outside lower-cost strategic suppliers, who were expected to design, produce and deliver products and services at low cost with high quality. This required a revolution in the way companies worked with suppliers. A new science of supply chain management sprang into being, along with quality management programmes and certification programmes like ISO 9001 to guide the transformations. Outside suppliers obtained quality certifications and opened up their operations to make their costs and processes transparent; they worked hard to achieve the rigorous quality and cost standards established by their customers. Significantly, they were given a larger role to play in their customers' operations. The list of qualified suppliers was significantly pruned, so that only a handful of suppliers remained on the list of strategic suppliers, and each of them became responsible for significantly larger volumes of design and production. Additionally, strategic suppliers were given design-and-produce responsibilities rather than produce at the lowest cost. Strategic suppliers became an integral part of their customers' operations, engaging in proprietary R&D as well as production design. This tied the fortunes of suppliers with the fortunes of their customers, and vice versa.
2. **Procurement departments**. Global companies empowered their procurement departments (sometimes called strategic sourcing or purchasing) to lead supply chain improvements.

Often, procurement brought in outside management consultants to help provide analysis and direction for the supply chain and process review programmes. As procurement departments uncovered and eliminated inefficiencies, they grew in corporate power – here was a department that could deliver increased efficiencies and profits on a reliable basis. Incremental dollars invested in procurement activities provided a reliable return – a better return on investment than the speculative dollars invested in marketing, some thought.

3. **Process reviews.** Procurement departments examined and overhauled the processes that generated costs, inefficiencies and waste – and sought to eliminate all non-value-added activities, which were believed to add up to more than 30% of value-added costs. In the 1990s, this concept was popularized as business process reengineering (BPR) by Michael Hammer and James Champy in their *Reengineering the Corporation: A Manifesto for Business Revolution* (Hammer & Champy, 1993). The process to uncover process inefficiencies cut across all departments and all organizational structures in a corporation. The process became a horizontal cost hunt across vertically organized corporations, facilitating an inspection of previously protected domains, and it empowered procurement departments with their operational specialists and analysts at the expense of previously untouchable silos, like manufacturing and marketing. Indeed, BPR activities threw the organizational chart out the window. Although the traditional organizational chart continued to show vertical management structures, the actual power structure was as much horizontal as vertical. As Hammer and Champy described it, *"Once it is restructured, process teams – groups of people working together to perform an entire process – turn out to be the logical way to organize the people who perform the work. Process teams don't contain representatives from all the functional departments involved. Rather, process teams replace the old departmental structure."* (Hammer & Champy, 1993, p. 70).

When BPR investigations later migrated to analyse media and advertising costs, agencies and their fees became more broadly exposed to procurement's analyses, and chief marketing officers were no longer in a position to protect their favoured agencies. Marketing began to lose control over what happened to its ad agencies. Procurement entered the picture in a big way and soon would be the driving force for the determination of ad agency fees. Marketing was reluctant to intervene; they had their own problems justifying their own cost structures. Agencies would have to sort out procurement on their own.

CHAPTER 6 –
SHAREHOLDER VALUE:
1990 AND ONWARDS

"It was at this point, gentlemen, that reality intruded."

Credit: Jack Ziegler / The New Yorker / The Cartoon Bank.

Ad agencies had their hands full after 1990. There was another belt-tightening recession, this time in 1990-91, and the recession added to an already existing slow-down in advertising expenditures, particularly in the US (Goldman, 1997, p. 107). An expansion of cable television capacity was putting an end to the media shortage that led to media price inflation. Commission rates were on the decline and fee-based compensation was replacing commission-based income in any case.

One accelerating factor for the shift to fee-based remuneration was the strategic spin-off of media buying and selling operations from full-service ad agencies, leading to the formation of stand-alone media agencies that left behind the creative service parts of their previous agencies.[1] Full-service agencies had been spinning off their media planning and buying capabilities so their media operations could compete more successfully against stand-alone media agencies like Carat and CIA, which were picking up the media needs of advertisers through aggressive selling and pricing. Stand-alone media agencies operated on commissions in the range of 4-5%. This left a 10-11% commission from the original 15% commission for the residual creative services agencies, but the justification for a media commission of any magnitude for creative agencies was a weak one. Advertisers used this argument as a basis for shifting creative agency remuneration from commission-based to fee-based arrangements.

Procurement departments were flexing their muscles, and media costs and agency fees were starting to come under their scrutiny. The early fee and commission cuts that resulted from this process were modest, and they were small cuts relative to the high levels of remuneration that were being paid, so the pain was negligible. Nevertheless, the agency remuneration pattern was set – the direction was clearly downwards.

Separately, clients were globalizing, and agencies were doing their best to respond, but the fragmented agency organizational structure was a difficult one to tame, and resistance to global initiatives was very real and highly frustrating. Agencies were new at this globalization game, and it would take time and sophistication to figure out how to manage the decentralized agency network structure.

JWT and Ogilvy & Mather began the 1990s under new ownership after Martin Sorrell's WPP acquired their shares in two transactions that came close to being called "hostile take-overs" by industry insiders. Subsequently, both agencies would be required to improve their profit margins at the behest of WPP.

Saatchi & Saatchi plc went through a management upheaval, with Maurice and Charles Saatchi leaving the company in 1995. Public ownership, delightful as it had been when everything was heading up, had its perils when profits and share prices went the other way. Saatchi & Saatchi's free-spending acquisition binge caught up to it, and the company's bottom line was hurt by over $1 billion in client defections associated with its programme of agency acquisitions, which created client conflicts (Goldman, 1997, pp. 189-193). Shareholder dissatisfaction led to board of director actions, and the Saatchi & Saatchi management drama was played out in full by the British press.

Recession, advertising slow-downs, media spin-offs, procurement department investigations, client globalization initiatives, fee-based remuneration schemes and holding company ownership added significant complexity to ad agency operations by 1990. The simplicity of The Golden Age and the Creative Revolution was long gone, whether recognized or not.

There was more difficulty to come after 1990. It sneaked up on agencies in the form of a newly adopted corporate concept, "*shareholder value*," defined as "*the value delivered to shareholders because of management's ability to grow earnings, dividends and share price – the sum of all strategic decisions that affect the firm's ability to efficiently increase the amount of free cash flow over time*" (www.investopedia.com).

Shareholder value became the mantra that boiled down corporate purpose to matters involving money, wealth and a performance obligation to owners – period. Boards of directors and executive compensation consultants used the concept to justify explosive increases in senior executive remuneration tied to improvements in corporate profitability and share price. CEOs used the concept to hire investment banks and strategy consultants to recommend and integrate mergers and acquisitions that added growth and incremental profits to their current companies. Procurement departments and their hired-in management consultants used the concept to initiate company-wide cost-reduction programmes and to outsource entire departments to reduce corporate costs. Corporate raiders used the concept to criticize existing corporate leaders and to justify the acquisition and breakup of underperforming companies.

It was never mentioned at the time, but the widespread pursuit of shareholder value initiatives put marketing in the back seat among other strategic priorities. There were easier ways of growing the top- and bottom-lines than by gambling on marketing. Marketing was uncertain and difficult in the recession-prone, post-Golden-Age decades. The cozy relationship between chief executives and advertising agencies had unravelled, as other strategic advisers like investment bankers and strategic management consultants jumped to the head of the queue.

The shareholder value concept was originally attributed to economist Milton Friedman, who wrote, "The Social Responsibility of Business is to Increase its Profits" in the *New York Times Magazine* (Friedman, 1970). The concept finally developed traction in the 1990s, when executive pay went through the roof, as various compensation consultants and corporate advisors recommended higher performance-related pay to tie CEO actions to company marketplace performance. Companies quickly responded by handing out options and restricted shares to CEOs and other senior corporate executives.

In 1989, Michael Eisner of Disney performed as hoped for, and he earned $57 million based on a bonus formula that was applied to the pro forma financial results of the company. He delivered the promised financial results, and he had a generous bonus package in his contract that rewarded him for doing just that.

By 1990, there were seven "$10 million men" in corporate America (Crystal, 1991). A few years later, in 1994, Michael Eisner made $203 million. Sandy Weill got a pay package worth some $151 million for running Citigroup in 2000. Jack Welch's pay for managing GE in 2000 totaled about $125 million. Larry Ellison's 2000 pay as Oracle's chief was $92 million (Colvin, 2001).

The number one earners in each of the years 1995 to 2000 received packages valued cumulatively at nearly $1.4 billion, or $274 million on average (Colvin, 2001). By 2011, the average numbers were stratospheric – median pay of the US's 200 top-paid CEOs was $14.5 million (Popper, 2012). In 2017, the median pay for the 200 highest-paid chief executives was $17.5 million, and they received an average raise of 14%, compared with 9% in 2016 and 5% the year before that.[2]

Stock options were the vehicle that fueled senior executive growth. Writing in *Fortune* magazine in 2001, Geoffrey Colvin reflected on the "highway robbery" of CEO pay: "*Although stock options had been available since 1950, the options culture began in the bull market of the 1980s. This made perfect sense since stocks essentially went nowhere from 1964 to 1982, and options during that past era didn't exactly make a CEO's heart beat faster. But once stocks took off, options suddenly became an excellent vehicle for getting rich, and companies began delivering them in truckloads. Besides, corporate raiders like Boone Pickens were arguing, rightly, that most CEOs didn't have enough skin in the game – they didn't own enough company stock to care about increasing the share price. Institutional investors and shareholder activists were pressing the same case*" (Colvin, 2001).

There were quicker ways to increase shareholder value than by investing in marketing and hoping that the investment paid off, particularly as consumer markets were becoming saturated and domestic growth was slowing down. Additional corporate profit growth could be achieved through financial engineering, cost reduction and mergers and acquisition (M&A) activities, and Wall Street advisers could provide the roadmap and the financing, particularly through junk bonds and other financial instruments. The payoff from financial initiatives was a big one, and it was significantly more certain than the payoff from marketing.

Writing in 2002, Robert Korajcyk of the Kellogg School of Management at Northwestern University identified 131 published papers from 1991-2000 on the subject of value-based management. The list included the highly influential 1991 book by G Bennett Stewart III, *The Quest for Value* (Stewart III, 1991), updated in 2013 as *Best-Practice EVA: The Definitive Guide to Measuring and Maximizing Shareholder Value*, that preached the gospel of "economic value added (EVA)," defined as the profit earned by the firm less the cost of financing the firm's capital. According to the EVA theory, CEOs should maximize EVA on behalf of shareholders, and CEO compensation should be structured to encourage them to do so. In practice, CEOs who were paid on EVA principles had very elevated levels of compensation. EVA principles and publications provided the intellectual underpinnings used by board compensation committees to set and manage CEO compensation levels.

The obsession with quarterly earnings came about because personal compensation was increasingly tied to what happened to the share price. Improving market capitalization became the number one job for senior executives. Success would lead to personal wealth.

Sadly, as often happens with business ideas that make some people a lot of money, shareholder value caught on and became the conventional wisdom. Executives were only too happy to accept the generous stock compensation being offered. In due course, they even came to view it as an entitlement, independent of performance.

Moreover, an apparent exemplar of the shareholder value theory emerged: Jack Welch. During his tenure as CEO of General Electric from 1981 to 2001, Jack Welch came to be seen – rightly or wrongly – as the outstanding implementer of the theory, as a result of his capacity to grow shareholder value and hit his numbers almost exactly. When Jack Welch retired, GE had gone from having a market value of $14 billion to $484 billion, making it, according to the stock market, the most valuable and largest company in the world. In 1999 he was named "Manager of the Century" by *Fortune* magazine (Denning, 2013). (Whatever goes up, though, must come down. GE was worth about $600 billion in 2000 and only $100 billion in 2018. Jack Welch's successors managed to destroy $500 billion of shareholder value, although during the process they each became fabulously wealthy through generous annual remuneration schemes.)

It was hard for ad agencies to influence CEOs, touting the latest "big creative idea" for television ads as the secret for corporate success. In addition, there was growing suspicion about the cost and effectiveness of television advertising, given the advances made in direct marketing and the exploitation of customer data through various CRM (customer relations management) database systems. There were direct and lower-cost, more effective ways of reaching the consumer, the direct markers said. Direct marketing and loyalty programmes could provide more targeted messaging, but it required investing in a database of existing customers, tracking their purchase preferences and having retail data capture systems in distribution to monitor purchases. CRM systems lacked the glamour of big ideas, but they provided better measurability.

Direct marketing agencies, which previously were involved in direct mailing campaigns, began transforming themselves into customer data processing businesses, and they competed with their brethren traditional advertising agencies for marketing dollars. Increasingly, marketing total spend was less important than the *mix* of spend – some traditional, some direct – and later, some digital and social as well. The media alternatives grew and grew, and traditional advertising agencies no longer had the field to themselves. The choice between traditional advertising and direct marketing became known as the "above the line" versus "below the line" choice, based on an outdated accounting treatment of previously commissionable costs (above the line) and non-commissionable costs (below the line). Below-the-line advertising was growing faster than above-the-line advertising, and this was a cause for concern by the above-the-line traditional agencies, who were having their own problems breaking through "clutter" on the airwaves.

These debates took place far from client CEOs. Agency senior executives were still useful and needed in large relationships, coordinating the agency's creative work, but they were no longer striding the corridors just outside the CEO's office. There was nothing dramatic about the change in their status. There were no uncomfortable discussions. It was more like a marriage whose passion had faded.

The compensation consultants, investment bankers and management consultants were hotter and younger, and they were driven to please in new and exciting ways. Their work generated increased share prices and increased profits – and helped to make senior client executives very rich.

The concept of shareholder value encouraged companies to cut costs wherever they could, and this responsibility was passed on to procurement departments. They had had their hands full in the 1980s with manufacturing and distribution suppliers and costs, and as a result, media costs and agency remuneration were then left alone. Later, though, during the 1990s and after 2000, procurement was increasingly directed to look at marketing and media costs.

Procurement did more than accelerate the shift from commission to fees. Once the fee system was in place, procurement could manage the fees for year-on-year declines.

The fee system divided agency remuneration into three "packages," and each of the three was subject to tough negotiations by procurement: 1) **Direct costs**. Direct costs were the salary costs of the agency people working on the account, plus statutory benefits, calculated by multiplying the headcount by the average salary and benefits rates. Procurement negotiated fewer heads and challenged average salaries, using "industry salary benchmarked data"[3] as their source of authority. 2) **Overheads**. An agency's total overhead costs divided by the agency's direct costs determined the "overhead rate." Typically, overhead rates were on the order of 100% or so, since overhead costs were approximately equal to direct costs. Procurement challenged the composition of the agency's pool of overhead costs and disallowed certain items, like new business prospecting costs and holding company management fees. Procurement also used "industry overhead rate benchmarks," which were always lower than actual agency costs, to beat down agency overhead rates. 3) **Profit margin**. Finally, in the fee calculation, agencies submitted their profit margin expectations, usually in the range of 15% to 20%. Procurement often negotiated this downwards to 10%.

Thus, in the fee arrangement, agencies were paid on a cost-plus basis, with procurement seeing this as an opportunity to negotiate costs ever-downwards, as they had with other types of suppliers. (More accurately, agencies were actually paid on a "costs-as-procurement-defined-them" basis, which was certainly less than actual costs.) Unlike other suppliers with whom procurement had previously worked, ad agencies were generally uncooperative in providing data, and when they were pressed, they showed what was perceived to be an astonishing ignorance about the economics of their "ad factories," as some procurement people called them. Procurement assumed that the lack of cooperation was real but the ignorance was not; they assumed that agencies had something to hide, which was "extreme profitability" and "high degrees of inefficiency." Consequently, procurement felt safe in negotiating fees ever-downwards, even if the basis for this was arbitrary. As one automotive procurement executive told me "we whack their salaries or overheads by 10% or so if we feel that their numbers are soft. They protest, but they always accept it, so we must have figured them right – they've got plenty of fat."

The arbitrariness was widespread. Agency workload was not a factor used to justify agency headcounts. "Benchmarked data" were of questionable origin. Profit margins were arbitrarily selected. Year after year, post-1990, agency fees were chipped away, and the unbroken complaints from agency finance people about the "unfairness of it all" fell on deaf ears.

Looked at from an agency perspective, there was something unfair about the way agencies were being treated by their clients, and the unfairness was baffling. Weren't agencies still working hard to generate big ideas and create memorable ads? Weren't they safeguarding and building brand equity, helping to assure consumer loyalty well into the future? Weren't they expanding their capabilities from traditional advertising into direct marketing and providing "integrated services" for these two previously separate disciplines?

Yes, they were doing all these things, and yet their remuneration was eroding under the relentless questioning and assaults of procurement. It was easy to conclude that the deterioration in agency relationships was caused by these newcomers – these procurement people – who knew nothing about the subtleties of marketing, like consumers' emotional connections to brands, and who spread stories about agency inefficiency and phony accounting numbers among their peers at ANA meetings.

Was there nothing that could be done to neutralize these barbarians?

Procurement, though, was on a mission to support shareholder value. "Nothing personal," they could have said. "It's just business." Cutting fees was one of the new ways the game had to be played.

Agencies missed the significance of "shareholder value" and the change in priorities that it represented to their clients. They assumed, perhaps, that creativity and big ideas were eternal verities – that they were what clients needed under any circumstances. Shareholder value was just another management trend, buzzword of the month – nothing to worry about.

The management consultants did not see it this way. Early in the decade of the 1980s, as one example, Bain & Company adopted a mission statement that made "improved client results" as its single-minded mission. "Bain's mission," it said, "is to help our clients create such high levels of economic value that together we set new standards of excellence in our respective industries." That was a mission worth a CEO's attention and protection from procurement fee-cutting.

Shareholder value became, from the 1990s onwards, a driver of management consulting success and, somewhat sadly, of advertising agency marginalization.

CHAPTER 7 –
THE RISE OF THE
MANAGEMENT
CONSULTANTS

*"Somewhere out there, Patrick, is the key to increased sales. I want
you to find that key, Patrick, and bring it to me."*

Credit: Robert Weber / The New Yorker / The Cartoon Bank.

W hen "shareholder value" began to seriously influence CEO thinking from 1990 onward, there was an army of skilled management consultants ready to jump on board. For 20 years or so, from 1990 to 2010, the consultants only had an indirect impact on advertising agency operations. Management consultants did not then directly compete with advertising agencies, of course, but they did muscle in and dominate CEO time and attention while trying to improve shareholder value by working with CEOs and procurement departments on inefficient corporate processes and high costs. From 2010 onwards, though, Accenture Interactive, Deloitte Digital, PwC Digital Services, Cognizant Interactive, IBM iX and even McKinsey began to acquire agency operations and now compete directly with advertising and media agencies. This direct competition represents a sea-change in the role and threat from management consulting firms.

After 1990, the management consulting firms grew and flourished, and as they expanded their mandates within their clients' organizations, they developed ideas about marketing strategies, channels of distribution, product pricing, media mix (traditional, social and digital) and other areas that might have been deemed to belong, in happier times, to the advertising agencies. This is evident today through any perusal of the consultant's websites[1], which are filled with insights and ideas about how marketing can be conducted in a more efficient and results-oriented manner.

I was a strategy consultant with The Boston Consulting Group in the 1970s and a partner and director of Bain & Company in the 80s, so I participated in the growth and expansion of each of these firms during their relatively early years. Later, after founding Farmer & Company in 1990, I worked with advertising agencies as their strategy consultant, seeing first-hand the kinds of pressures they were under from their marketing clients and related procurement departments. My consulting practice with advertising agencies and their clients has allowed me to observe and measure, first-hand, the ever-changing dynamics of their relationships with one another. This experience has provided the basis for this book – and given me the desire to document what I have seen and learned.

My experience with The Boston Consulting Group and with Bain & Company was enriching, to say the least. I joined BCG in early 1973, just ten years after Bruce Henderson founded it. The firm then had about 100 consultants. In early 1979, I joined Bain & Company, six years after Bill Bain left BCG and founded this competing and very successful firm. Bain, too, had about 100 consultants when I joined, all of them in the company's single Boston office (by 2015, Bain had 51 offices in 33 countries). I was only somewhat aware at the time that BCG and Bain were leading *revolutions* in the way their clients thought about growth, profitability and investments among their portfolios of businesses. Instead, I was satisfied, as were most of my colleagues, to be working happily alongside one another in a stimulating environment that surfaced difficult corporate problems to analyse and solve. Only later, through the prism of 20/20 hindsight, was it obvious that the two decades of the 1970s and 1980s were a very special time to have worked in strategy consulting.

Author, editor and journalist Walter Kiechel documented the special character of the strategy consulting firms in his outstanding work, *The Lords of Strategy* (Kiechel, 2010). Kiechel focused on the ideas behind the growth and development of three firms (BCG, Bain, and McKinsey), and in the works of the famous business school thought-leader, Professor Michael E. Porter of Harvard Business School, author of *Competitive Strategy* (Porter, 1980), *Competitive Advantage* (Porter, 1985), and *The Competitive Advantage of Nations* (Porter, 1990).

Kiechel recounts the birth and evolution of *strategy as a paradigm* – a set of 1970s and 1980s ideas that refocused chief executives on the need to seek competitive advantage in the industries within which they competed. The focus on competition was new. In the search for competitive advantage, companies and their strategy consultants analysed *costs* (relative to competitors), *customers* (pricing, segmentation and relative satisfaction), and *competitors* (relative market shares, corporate portfolios and ambitions) to determine a starting point; they then formulated and implemented action plans to achieve improved growth, profitability and competitiveness. BCG first developed and articulated the "price and cost experience curve" and the "growth-share matrix" in the 1970s[2] as diagnostic and conceptual tools; Bain developed and popularized "best demonstrated practices" in the 1980s to serve as performance benchmarks

(Kiechel, 2010, p. 90); McKinsey developed in 1980 the "elements of a business cost system" as a guide to understanding all the cost elements that made up a product (Kiechel, 2010, p. 193); and Porter developed the "five forces" (1980) and the "value chain" (1985) to add to the list of intellectual frameworks that underpinned the strategic paradigm (Kiechel, 2010, pp. 127, 196).

The conduct of strategic assessment and the development of strategic action plans was a highly analytical exercise. It required more than a bag of strategic tools and concepts – it required highly trained, data-hungry young consultants with first-class MBAs and (after 1990) personal computers with Excel and other analytical tools. The young consultants could operate successfully within their clients if they had sufficient "air cover" from the CEO, whose job it was to make sure everyone (*yes, everyone*) in the client organization cooperated with them.

Gaining this kind of CEO support was a critical part of success in strategy consulting, and no one understood this better than Bill Bain, who articulated a confidential set of binding "client principles" to the Bain partners. Only those potential clients who met Bill Bain's highly selective criteria would be taken on.[3] Appropriately structured relationships rather than mere consulting studies would prove to be the key to Bain's long-term success.

CEOs during this period were overseeing highly diversified and global operations, relying on the executives who ran each "profit center" to develop strategic plans and deliver improved results during each budget cycle. For many corporations, though, the results were disappointing. One of my frustrated CEO clients in 1988 complained about his organization. "I don't know if I have the right strategies and right budgets but the wrong people, or the right people and the wrong strategies and budgets. All I know is that we never achieve our budgets or our strategic targets."

What Bain & Company could promise, as did the other consulting firms, were detailed analyses that would get at "two truths": 1) why the various businesses were then performing below par, and 2) what the "full performance potential" of the businesses would be if different strategies were implemented. Each business would be analysed separately, and the "truth of the situation" would be uncovered.

Strategy reshaped the concept of consulting and the kinds of people who practiced it, moving consulting from the realm of sage advice-giving by grey-haired industry experts to a world where business insights were *discovered in the data* by bright-faced hyperactive MBAs, whose only industry experience may have been in the consulting industry. Full credit for this reshaping must go to Bruce Henderson of BCG, who broke the mold and set the example through his early recruiting and marketing activities at business schools. Henderson valued high IQs and people who were intensely interested in data, concepts and ideas. In a famous recruiting ad for BCG in the Harvard Business School newspaper *Harbus* around 1969-1970, Henderson taunted the Harvard MBA student body: *"Are You Good Enough?"* The ad went on to describe the current consultants at BCG – their age profile (young), the percentage of consultants with PhD degrees (high), the percentage who had already published papers or books (also high), the percentage of valedictorians and honors graduates (nearly 100%), and so forth. The message was clear: BCG would hire only the best, the cream of the crop, and age didn't matter. Strategy consultants could be 23 years old if they were brilliant enough. Most of the HBS students scoffed at this display of BCG's arrogance, and the firm was then much hated (or much envied) on campus, but Henderson did not care about *most* of the students. He only wanted those who were attracted by the message, and in this he succeeded.

While the strategy paradigm was developing a head of steam in the 70s and 80s, advertising agencies were suffering a slight hangover after the growth and success of the Creative Revolution. The 1971 recession, followed by the energy shocks and recessions, caused most large agencies to suffer losses in total domestic billings (Fox, 1984, p. 314). However, media inflation was on the rise, and media commissions held steady in perhaps three fourths of all agency-client dealings (Fox, 1984, p. 317).

Importantly, this meant that agencies could operate as they had always operated, focusing on creativity and service, and agency account managers could continue to service their clients and sell-in the idea that their clients ought to spend even more on TV media – the kind of spend that generated agency income through media commissions. Nothing in the loss of domestic billings suggested that the fundamental business approach needed to be changed.

If there was any change going on at any of the agencies, it was in response to being acquired by a holding company and, separately, dealing with the shift from commissions to fees. In both cases, the attention of top management turned to internal operations and the shedding of excess costs – to meet aggressive holding company targets for operating margins on the one hand, and to respond to the beginnings of the fee declines triggered by the shift from commissions on the other hand.

There was a new trend for agencies to hire and parade before their clients "strategic planners," an idea originally imported from the UK; but these were not strategists in the same way that management consultants were strategists. Instead, agency strategic planners were experts in customer segmentation and behaviour, excellent at designing market research and reading the results of market research reports. The planners were called, in some quarters, "the conscience of the consumer" – they upheld long-term brand values on behalf of consumers and helped to resist any attempts by the creative department to go "off brand" in the pursuit of cute ideas that would dilute "brand values." In short, the strategic planners were consumer experts, brand developers and brand policemen. They were an important innovation, but they hardly signaled new strategic directions for ad agencies, and their efforts did not have the slightest impact on their clients' concerns about achieving improved shareholder value.

Ironically, the increase in numbers of the strategic planners had the effect of releasing the client service people from any previous responsibilities they had for brand strategic thinking

– leaving them free simply to coordinate with their clients and give them all the service they needed.

One agency executive told me "the arrival of strategic planners signaled the final dumbing down of the client service department."

We should recall that during the commission era, client service people were relationship managers, brand guardians, strategists and salesmen – selling in the idea that clients should spend, spend, spend on TV media to steal a march on their competitors. In support of this, they were armed with research studies and Nielsen data that showed that big TV spenders tended to gain market share and succeed in their marketplaces. This was pure strategy – success was proportional to the degree to which clients outspent their competitors in a product category. What better justification could there be?

When commissions gave way to fees, though, client service executives lost their salesman role. Sure, they could continue to tout high TV media expenditures, but this time it made no difference to agency income or profits. Agencies were now paid on the basis of headcounts, and it was not so easy to sell the client on the idea that what they really needed were more agency people working on the account. Since workloads were neither documented nor tracked, the basic data to support this conclusion were missing in any case.

So client service executives became client servicers, and the arrival of strategic planners to shore up brand planning took substantive intellectual responsibilities away from them, further reducing their status in the eyes of their clients.

The contrast between the bright-eyed management consultants, who were working for the CEO, spreadsheets in hand, and the ad agency client service people, who were working for the marketers, could not have been more dramatic. Agencies were dismissive of the consultants, in any case. They looked askance at the MBA credential, finding that young men and women with MBAs, smart and analytical as they were, were also very expensive, and that kind of expense could not be easily borne in an environment where clients were cutting fees while holding companies were squeezing for more profits. Besides, there was nothing obvious in the skill set of client service people that required an MBA. The MBA made no sense at all to ad agencies.

It's fair to say that the management consultants tightened their grip on their clients as the strategy paradigm and the related shareholder value concept became corporate foundations. At the same time, advertising agencies began to slide down the slippery slope of their clients' organizations. Increasingly, procurement developed a louder voice in matters involving agency fees, CEOs disappeared as direct clients, marketing experimented with greater quantities of marketing deliverables across all media types and agencies responded, unsuccessfully, by overinvesting in client service in an attempt to regain control of their relationships.

Whatever opportunities there were for agencies to become key players in corporate strategy and shareholder value by focusing on "improved results" was lost during this critical period. Agencies retained their primary cultural and commercial focus on "creativity and service," even though their market was shifting out from underneath them.

This lost opportunity has afflicted advertising agencies for more than 20 years. Even the advent of the more measurable digital and social advertising innovations was not enough to bring agencies squarely into the camp of those whose mission is solely to "deliver results."

Ironically, it was the management consulting firms who seized on the confusions wrought by the digital and social revolutions to create a large and growing new business for themselves. Accenture and Deloitte, in particular, positioned themselves to "help clients transition successfully to the new digital/social world," asserting that any advertiser who was slow in this transition would soon become uncompetitive – they could forget about increased shareholder value and huge pay packages for top executives. The consultants exploited the insecurities of CEOs, who watched brand growth disappear during the 2008 financial crisis and did not have confidence that either their CMOs or IT professionals were on top of the momentous technological changes occurring in the market-place. Marketing required a complete overhaul, and the consulting firms seemed to know more about this than anyone else. Accenture and Deloitte had all the necessary credentials; they were already working on large scale projects in most companies, so why not hire them to accelerate the transition to digital and social marketing?

For Accenture and Deloitte (and others like PwC and IBM), digital marketing initiatives allowed them to expand and extend their existing relationships. Further expansion and extension could be achieved if creative and media agencies were acquired. They could then say, "We've helped you build a digital and social capability; we can now help you implement it through our newly acquired expertise in creative and media operations."

By 2017, Accenture Interactive, the most acquisitive and aggressive competitor, was managing $6.5 billion in digital revenue from its clients, having made 23 agency acquisitions since 2012, including London-based Fjord and Karmarama (creative shop), Media Hive (e-commerce solutions provider), Clearhead (digital optimizer), SinnerSchrader (German digital agency) and HO Communication (Chinese digital agency). Still, says Accenture Interactive's CEO, Brian Whipple, "We are not principally an ad agency. We do advertising, but we do it in the context of reinventing clients."[4]

Competition from management consultants has created a new identity crisis for ad agencies. At one end of the spectrum, there are those agency folks who dismiss consultants as "linear-thinking spreadsheet analysts who look at the past," while agencies are "lateral-thinking creative thinkers who create visions for the future." At the other end of the spectrum are the ad agencies that are rushing to reposition themselves by developing consulting operations, like Ogilvy & Mather, which established Ogilvy Consulting (formerly OgilvyRed) in 2012, and Omnicom, which established Omnicom Consulting Group in 2015.

Martin Sorrell, late of WPP and now Executive Chairman of the newly formed S4 Capital, sees three trends that principally affect his new operation:

1. Advertising spend is shifting towards an increasing number of digital channels. The shift to digital has also added importance to the ability to capture data to derive meaningful customer insights and has contributed to the emergence of digital brands;
2. A drive to disintermediate advertising has increased the strength of the relationship between brands and content producers; and
3. Consulting companies with strong IT experience are developing or acquiring creative content capabilities (e.g. IBM iX, Accenture Interactive and Deloitte Digital).[5]

As a result, S4 Capital will take on management consultancies and others by creating a "new era, new media solution, embracing data, content and technology, in an always-on environment for multinational, regional and local clients and for millennial-driven digital brands."

As long as clients have performance problems and are led by ambitious and/or anxious senior executives, the consulting firms, who have a 30-40 year culture of "results-improvements for clients" are likely to succeed. Agencies, whose equally long "we're creative and we give great service" culture are less well-equipped, and they currently lack the talent and the pay levels that permit them to recruit and retain the right kind of people.

Between these two extremes are new entry consulting aspirants, like Martin Sorrell, who has committed to put together a single company through acquisition.

It's a new era in the industry, but I suspect it will only accelerate Madison Avenue's manslaughter.

CHAPTER 8 –
MEDIA EXPANSION, MEDIA FRAGMENTATION AND THE BALKANIZATION OF THE INDUSTRY

"This 'digital revolution'—can we muscle in on that?"

Credit: Robert Mankoff / The New Yorker / The Cartoon Bank.

Much is made today of big data in advertising, a new 'big' to worry about – The Big Bang, Big Foot, The Big Idea and now, Big Data.

Big data comprises the computer-analysis of consumer purchasing data and online behaviours to guide advertisers in their ad-creation and ad-buying decisions. One branch of big data leads to the development of new tools to permit more focused and programmatic (automated) ad buying, in which online and offline ads are bought through automated exchanges, often in real time. This is a relatively new development in recent years.

There are other uses and purposes of big data, most of them designed to improve the odds that John Wanamaker worried about – *"Half the money I spend on advertising is wasted; the trouble is I don't know which half."* Big data is supposed to help decision makers identify and spend on advertising that really works and to increase the percentage of effective spending to levels well above Wanamaker's 50%.

Big data in its current incarnation has existed without a name for the past 50 years, for at least as long as accessible data processing and customer databases have been around. Computer power has always made it possible for clever people to find and crunch consumer data and draw conclusions accordingly[1]. What's new about big data is the quantity of consumer data available from online purchases, customer reviews, Twitter, Facebook, LinkedIn, Google, Pinterest, Instagram, Yelp and other such sources. The internet, computing power and vast quantities of mineable information have come together in a "perfect storm" that has, for the moment, dominated discussions about marketing needs and marketing capabilities. Everyone is getting in on the act – IBM, in a recent ad in the advertising trade press, asked "How do leading organizations use big data and analytics to increase revenue, operational efficiency and more?" All you had to do was sign up for an IBM webinar to find out. There are many interested companies in the big data game, and they all are frighteningly competent when it comes to data crunching and analysis. During the summer of 2014, the UK affiliate of US political consulting firm Cambridge Analytica hired a Soviet-born American researcher, Aleksandr Kogan, to gather basic profile information of Facebook users along with what they chose to "Like." About 300,000 Facebook users, most or all of whom were paid a small amount, downloaded Kogan's app, called This Is Your Digital Life, which presented them with a series of surveys. Kogan collected data not just on those users but on their Facebook friends, if their privacy settings allowed it – a universe of people initially estimated to be 50 million strong, then upped to 87 million. It used such data to target voters with hyper-specific appeals, including on Facebook and other online services, that go well beyond traditional messaging based on party affiliation alone. This is known as "psychographic" targeting or modeling, and it could, of course, be used to create audiences for real and fake political messaging.[2]

In many ways, new players have been the challenge in advertising for a long time, but we did not have to worry about the use of data by unscrupulous players to undermine democratic processes. We must now add this to the list of things to worry about. New capabilities and innovations appear to be specialized and distant from one another in the beginning, giving those with existing strengths a false sense of security, but over time advertising capabilities converge. Traditional advertising now competes with the formerly specialized direct marketing agencies, CRM agencies, and digital/social agencies. Computer programmers become highly desired agency resources. Is big data an area where data and analytical nerds will invade and dominate?

Well, in some ways it already has by 2018. The 2016 election was a case in point. The raging debate about "fake" versus "real" is another. The inroads by the consulting firms is another straw in the wind. So is the ongoing concern by the holding companies about the need to become "analytical" for the benefit of clients. This is no longer a debate on the fringes of the industry.

The advertising landscape was once a homogeneous one, dominated by the traditional advertising agencies and the traditional advertising media in which they worked: print, radio and television. The traditional Mad Men and their creatives were the aristocrats of the industry, operating with big media commissions to carry out very visible and important work. Toiling at a lower level in the industry were the unwashed: the "below-the-line" practitioners of direct marketing and sales promotion, working in low-prestige below-the-line agencies, pencils behind their ears, estimating and bidding on local direct mail or promotional point-of-display projects that always went to the lowest bidder.

Apart from competing with one another for client dollars – *How much budget for above the line? Below the line?* – the two worlds co-existed and largely ignored one another. The traditional agencies certainly ignored the direct agencies, which were beneath them. The direct agencies ignored the snubs.

The below-the-line agencies had a number of things going for them, though. First, compared to the above-the-line agencies, they were able to measure the results from their work. If a mail shot of 100,000 letters went out at a known cost, and there was a positive response rate of (say) 2,000 letters (2%), then the benefits and costs were known, and the marketing ROI could be calculated.

Second, the below-the-line agencies were paid on a per-project basis, so they had to develop sound estimating, bidding and project-management skills. They were paid for all the work they did. Because margins were paper-thin in this highly competitive business, volume was key, and sales practices were sharp and aggressive. This package of skills never developed at the above-the-line agencies, even after commissions gave way to fees. Indeed, above-the-line agencies are just awakening to the need for better project management capabilities, and they would consider being paid for all the work they do a small miracle.

Third, the below-the-line agencies were inevitably wedded to consumer and customer data, and technological and social developments were going to assure that data became more plentiful and powerful. History would prove to be on their side. Practitioners of heavy-duty data analysis, like Bain & Company's Fred Reichheld, were discovering and proclaiming the economic benefits of such things as increased customer loyalty, for example (Reichheld, 1996), and these efforts put an increased economic value on the development and exploitation of sophisticated customer databases.

Below-the-line agencies began to grow faster during the 1990s as advertisers lined up to experiment with improved CRM and loyalty programmes. This phenomenon might have been overlooked by the traditional advertising agencies, but it did not go unnoticed by Martin Sorrell and WPP, who aggressively acquired specialized below-the-line agencies, reasoning in a practical way that advertising might take several different paths in the future, so it was wise to have all the alternatives under one roof. By 2003, WPP owned well-known below-the-line agencies Wunderman and OgilvyOne, but it also owned A Elcoff & Co, Brierley & Partners, Dialogue Marketing, Einson Freeman, EWA, Good Technology, The Grass Roots Group, Headcount Field Marketing Group, High Co, Imaginet, FullSix, KnowledgeBase Marketing, Mando Brand Assurance, Maxx Marketing, rmg:connect, RTC, Savatar, sygyzy, ThompsonConnect Worldwide, VML and 141 Worldwide.

WPP identified a central feature of these specialized companies – they each loved working independently in their specialized fields, even though their clients had broader needs. Read here from the 2003 WPP Annual Report:

- Our clients all live in competitive worlds. Whether Fortune 500 multinationals or single-nation charities, their first requirement, always, is an intrinsically appealing product.
- But for many years now, to compete successfully, they have needed more. They need access to high quality information, strategic advice and specialist communications skills. And it is in the nature of specialist talent that it is unlikely to flourish within the confines of a single marketing company. People of specialist skills work best and contribute more when recruited, trained and inspired by specialist companies.
- Within the WPP Group, our clients have access to companies of all the necessary marketing and communications skills; companies with strong and distinctive cultures of their own; famous names, many of them.
- WPP, the parent company, encourages and enables operating companies of different disciplines to work together for the benefit of clients and our people.
- There can be no doubt that discrete and sharply honed specialist talents working together with single-minded unity towards a common end is becoming a rapidly growing contributor to client success and therefore to group revenues (WPP, 2003).

In effect, WPP (like the other holding companies and the rest of the industry) accepted the Balkanization of the ad agency world as an accepted industry fact of life. Actually, "accepted" is less than accurate; the holding companies then had a strong interest in maintaining the fragmented structure of the industry, if only for management convenience. Let's remember that the holding companies did not really manage their portfolio companies. They owned them and established annual profit targets for them. Once an agency or company was bought, and an earn-out arrangement struck with the current executives, the subsequent ongoing dialogue between the parties was about profit margin – are the current targets going to be met? Over time, the targets are raised, so there is always plenty to talk about, especially in view of declining industry prices – profit targets are always a stretch, and they always risk not being achieved.

With a fragmented portfolio on the one hand, but a strong client need for integration on the other hand, the holding company became the "integrator." The WPP argument in 2003 anticipated the "holding company relationship," whereby holding companies cut exclusive deals with major advertisers and provide all of the specialized agencies required for the highly varied SOWs.

Balkanization has been a feature of the ad agency industry, but it is not a universal phenomenon across all service industries. Somehow, management consulting firms (again!) expanded their technical capabilities and specialties under one brand name. They added specialist consultants, to be sure, but at the same time, they expect their senior partners to become adept at understanding a growing number of disciplines. Senior consulting partners who manage large relationships with clients need to be multifaceted – capable of working in mergers and acquisitions, cost reduction, organizational design, management information systems, corporate strategy and the like – and able to shift in and shift out of their assignments any required specialized resources. Indeed, one of the selection requirements for partnership in a consulting firm is an individual's intellectual capacity to learn and master a number of disciplines.

The cultural divides within the advertising industry became wider when web pages became part of the marketing mix, beginning in 1995. Early web pages were like printed catalogs, and traditional advertising agencies knew how to design catalogs – they were just pictures and words in a different medium, right? The rub was that web pages seemed to clients and agencies more like the domain of software folk, like computer programmers, rather than the domain of traditional copywriters and art directors. An automotive company that wanted to put up web pages to help consumers choose car models and features was more likely to go to a group of programmers than to a traditional agency. The web production costs were exceptionally high, too – the hours spent by web designers and programmers far outstripped the creative hours spent on catalogs. Wasn't the business of web design (and later, web advertising) a separate business?

Traditional (TV, radio, print) advertising agencies were quick to judge that the digital revolution was another specialty that would be handled by specialist agencies, just as direct marketing had been in the past. There was no comfortable place for programmers in the production department of an ad agency. Traditional advertising creatives could do the concept work for the look and feel of web pages, but the downstream execution, which was a digital production job, belonged elsewhere.

Technological innovation at the programming end, though, became the cart that drove the horse, and the question "What can we do with technology?" became as important a creative variable as images and sound. Digital technology did not really lend itself to a simple division of labour between creative (generating the ideas) and production (executing the ideas). In an increasing number of cases, creativity was all in the execution, especially in YouTube, Facebook and Twitter.

Balkanization in the advertising industry limited the technical development of individual agencies and hobbled the intellectual growth of senior client service people. The downside of this was that each specialty became less important for clients within their growing need for a mix of specialties, and that senior agency people had not grown intellectually to keep up with the changing needs of their clients. Advertisers today, requiring traditional advertising, direct marketing, PR, customer relationship management (CRM), events/sponsorship, social, digital, etc., have had to engage a broader number of advertising agencies. Each specialized agency in a manner of speaking has "lost share" within each client relationship, and each senior agency client head has lost influence with their client, as well.

Who, then, has stepped into the gap to manage these integrated needs?

- In many cases, clients have become their own integrators. This is the most logical outcome, since clients are dealing with increasing complexity as a matter of course, and this is simply one more of the many complexities. Self-integration is probably the right course for clients, but the practice is bad for the agencies; they are on the receiving end of directives rather than taking control and offering initiatives. Self-integration makes clients stronger and more self-sufficient, while it makes agencies weaker and dependent.
- In a few cases, clients have turned to lead agencies and asked them to be the "brand navigators," managing the loose network of diversified agencies on behalf of the client. This was P&G's solution for the past decade or so, appointing brand account leaders (BALs) like Saatchi & Saatchi, Leo Burnett, Publicis USA and Grey to manage all the other agencies on a BAL brand (Pampers, Charmin, Tide and so on). Other advertisers have tried to emulate this structure with varying degrees of success.
- In a number of well-known cases (Ford, J&J, Bank of America), clients have entered into holding company relationships, but this means that all of the agencies come from a single holding company. It is not necessarily true that the holding company or a lead agency actually runs the integration, although this is the expectation.

- Finally, in very few cases, clients have required their agencies to expand their capabilities to cover a broad range of services, from traditional to digital advertising. Toyota and Lexus are two examples of advertisers who have gone relatively far in this direction with Saatchi & Saatchi and Team One, for example. In 2004, Toyota turned to its traditional (and virtually captive) agency, Saatchi & Saatchi Los Angeles, and encouraged the agency to hire digital specialists and to increase the proportion of digital executions within the marketing mix. From 2005 onwards, Saatchi & Saatchi invested in this capability, funded by fee levels that allowed them to do so, and by 2018, the amount of digital work was significantly more than 50% of the total agency's marketing work. Ironically, though, this development within a single office did not spill over to other offices within the Saatchi & Saatchi network. It was an isolated instance of the agency responding to the request of an individual client, and its successful response did not lead the way for other such responses in other offices – mainly because other clients were not making the same kinds of demands or providing appropriate levels of fees.

The Saatchi & Saatchi Los Angeles example proves that Balkanization need not be the only outcome – agencies can become integrated across disciplines. However, integration is certainly the exception rather than the rule.

Balkanization of the industry has been the default outcome, driven by the agency belief that each agency discipline belongs in a separate house. Strategically, we can see that this belief has been shortsighted, having contributed to a loss of influence by individual agencies and an overall strengthening of clients in the relationship. The decline in agency remuneration, it can be argued, is one of the many consequences of the Balkanization of the industry.

CHAPTER 9 – MEDIA AGENCY MANSLAUGHTER: THE MEDIA REBATE BACKLASH

"Well, gentlemen, there's your problem."

Credit: Mick Stevens / The New Yorker / The Cartoon Bank. With permission.

The years 2015 through 2018 will surely be characterized by historians as years of conflict and polarization, not only in politics, but in other fields, as well. The media industry has not escaped, as we shall see.

Polarization in politics intensified with the Trump presidency and Trump's unprecedented use of Twitter to broadcast his opinions to the global public. According to the fact-checkers at *The Washington Post*, Trump's opinions included more than 5,000 false or misleading claims by the 601st day of his presidency in September, 2018.[1]

This was not only a disturbing innovation in the use of person-to-person media communications, but it was also an assault on the concept of truth. Advertising practitioners now had another major worry on their hands: could an advertising claim have any credibility, or would all claims risk being perceived as "fake news?" The distinction between "real" and "fake" was muddied by Trump. Would this be a permanent phenomenon or a one-off during his presidency?

The media world experienced an early version of Trumpist invective when Jon Mandel, the former CEO of Mediacom, launched a blistering attack on media agencies, using the March 2015 Association of National Advertisers (ANA) Media Leadership Conference in Hollywood, FL, as his platform:

Some agencies have arrangements in place with media sellers that reward them [agencies] for their spending. If those agencies choose to direct more of their clients' budgets to specific vendors, they might be given lower ad rates, free ad space or even cash in return. Clients may not be made aware that these relationships exist. There are cases where there are rebates that should be going to clients that are instead going to agencies.[2]

Rebates, 'kickbacks' and other incentives for agencies that are at least potentially adverse to client interests are happening virtually everywhere in the US media landscape, including TV. Have you ever wondered why fees to agencies have gone down and yet the declared profits of these agencies are up? Advertising spending broadly has long stayed within a narrow band of 1% to 1.25% of gross domestic product globally. So if agencies are growing at a higher-than-GDP basis, the money is coming from somewhere. Most of the rebates and other nontransparent dealings occur at the holding-company level, where it's harder to track or audit.[3]

There was nothing subtle about the attack. Mandel was accusing media agencies of dishonesty, if not outright theft.

The following month, in April 2015, the ANA held its Advertising Financial Management Conference in Phoenix, AZ, where the already-high tensions from "Rebategate" received an additional jolt from an ANA study of "Client/Agency Relationships 2015," which could have been entitled "I'm OK; you're not OK." The findings related principally to relations between advertisers and their creative agencies.

The executive summary showed the following:

* A majority (58%) of advertisers said that they provide "clear assignment briefs" to their agencies, while less than half that number (27%) of agency executives agree.
* A majority (54%) of advertisers believe that the ad approval process works well, while only 36% of agency executives agree.
* Just under half of clients (47%) feel that procurement adds value, while only 10% of agencies agree.
* Regarding compensation, 72% of advertisers believe that agency compensation is fair, while only 40% of agency executives agree.[4]

Post-conference, the trade press was filled with charges, counter-charges and self-justifying explanations about the rebate accusations and the sources of client/agency relationship problems. Joint action from the two trade associations would not be long in coming, but the initial focus would be on "media transparency" (the Orwellian renaming of the rebate/kickback issue), rather than on the myriad client/creative agency relationship problems outlined at the ANA Financial Management Conference.

JOINT TASK FORCE

In April 2015, the American Association of Advertising Agencies (4As) and the ANA announced that they were taking decisive action to address concerns about media transparency.

Bringing together industry leaders from the marketer and agency communities, the two parties the accuser and the accused – established a task force to "identify material issues and to address them with constructive dialogue and pragmatic courses of action."[5]

Although creative agencies were not directly involved in this effort, they were holding their breath, because in one way or another, they were going to be affected by it. They knew that media agencies were "cash cows" within their holding companies, and that any adverse developments that affected media agency profitability would have knock-on effects for them. If rebates or other forms of opaque sources of media agency profits were found to exist, client procurement departments would make short work of them, eliminating them with the stroke of a pen, which would lead to even greater profit pressures for the creative agencies.

Further, the rebate issue eroded trust between clients and all their agencies, and trust was already in short supply. A further erosion of trust would lead to more aggressive fee negotiations, further marginalization of agency stature in the eyes of their clients, and – who knows? – more agency reviews and relationship instability.

The 4As knew this as well, and as participants on the Joint Task Force, they were back on their heels, hoping to neutralize or minimize Mandel's accusations about US rebates and kickbacks.

From afar, the Joint Task Force looked like it would have about as much success as a save-the-marriage therapy session involving an adulterous spouse who does not want to admit adultery.

TASK FORCE PRIORITIES

The Task Force began its deliberations in mid-2015, and one goal, among many, involved developing a set of guidelines and best practices to create transparency in media planning and buying.

The ANA hoped that guidelines and best practices would provide a basis for creating standardized contract language that could be used uniformly by advertisers and agencies alike.

Uniform language would knock the rebate issue on its head and ensure that transparency was established on an industry-wide basis.

The 4As had no interest in handcuffing its member agencies in this way – seeking instead to protect agency freedom to negotiate client contracts in individual/ad hoc ways, using 4As' "guidelines" to inspire the drafting and negotiation of contracts. This voluntary guideline approach was consistent with the way 4As thought about its responsibilities on behalf of its members. 4As develop guidelines and surveys in many areas, but its members are free to use the guidelines as they wish. (Despite these well-meaning efforts, though, agency members have been losing the battle with clients over several decades, and 4As' guidelines have done little to halt Madison Avenue's manslaughter). A sample of 4As guidelines and best practices is shown below:

- Best Practices: Guidelines for Digital Media Audits
- Best Practices: Guidelines for Local TV Media Audits
- Best Practices: Guidelines for Local Radio Media Audits
- Best Practices: Guidelines for National TV Buying and Stewardship Audits
- Guidelines on Client-Agency Relations and Best Practices in the Pitch Process
- Agency Search Consultants List
- Management Benchmarks & Financial Barometers Survey Series – Phases I & II
- Client Compensation Consultants Use of Surveys, Benchmarks and Definitions
- Labour Billing Rate Survey Report 2015
- Position Paper on Agency Compensation
- Advertising Agency Overhead
- Client Compensation Best Practices Dos and Don'ts
- Pricing Continuum
- Scope of Work—The Revenue Driver[6]

THE BREAK-UP

As much as the two parties claimed to be seeking common ground, they were really acting independently on behalf of their respective members. The working relationship was not helped by ANA's separate decision, in October 2015, to hire two investigative companies – K2 Intelligence and Ebiquity/FirmDecision – to conduct an outside investigation into industry transparency issues, including rebate allegations. 4As would not be involved with this investigation.[7]

Knowing where these investigations might eventually lead, and unhappy with ANA's goal of developing uniform contract language, 4As took early unilateral action at the end of January 2016, publishing 4As' "media transparency guidelines" independently of the Joint Task Force. "The most important thing here is that agencies have [already] been operating under a code of transparency with clients, and now we're making it public," said Nancy Hill, president and CEO of the 4As. "Agencies and clients now have a heightened awareness when looking at contracts.[8] We'll continue to have conversations with the ANA and their members."[9]

ANA, angry about the 4As' preemptive guidelines release, was quick to respond: "4As' guidelines are premature and continued attention is needed to address lack of industry transparency that the ANA has highlighted for the last four years. Unfortunately, the guiding principles issued by the 4As fail to fully or adequately reflect the best interests of marketers."[10]

So much for the joint efforts to increase trust.

The industry was back to square one, with K2 Intelligence and Ebiquity/FirmDecision yet to complete their investigations and publish their reports on rebates and kickbacks within the industry.

THE K2/EBIQUITY/FIRMDECISION REPORT

The 62-page investigative report was published on 7 June 2016. It was an absolute bomb, confirming Jon Mandel's accusations. The Executive Summary included the following:

> ➤ *Within the sample studied by K2, nontransparent business practices were found to be pervasive. Of the 150 sources interviewed by K2, 117 were directly involved in media buying in the US market. Of those 117 sources, 59 reported direct experience with nontransparent business practices, including rebates (34 sources) and principal transactions that enabled potentially problematic practices (33 sources).*

> ➤ *K2 found substantial evidence of nontransparent business practices in Agency Holding Companies, as well as in certain independent agencies.*

>   • *K2 found evidence of nontransparent business practices across digital, OOH, print and television media.*

>   • *K2 found evidence that senior executives at agencies and Agency Holding Companies were aware of and even mandated some nontransparent business practices, suggesting high-level buy-in.*

>   • *K2 found evidence of nontransparent business practices in the US market arising from agencies holding equity stakes in media suppliers. Several former senior level agency employees reported that they felt pressure from the senior executive level of Agency Groups or Agency Holding Companies to direct spend to companies in which the agency or holding company held an equity investment.*[11]

The K2 report went beyond the identification of "non-transparent practices" and attempted to identify the factors responsible for them. These factors included pricing pressure from advertisers, mandatory cost reductions as part of media pitches, the increased role of procurement, client-driven "extended payment terms" (up to 150 days before agency invoices are paid), a new culture of expecting agencies "to do more with less, every year" and so forth.

The ANA/Ebquity/Firm Decisions portion of the report (published separately) acknowledged that advertisers were partly responsible for rebate/kickback practices, in that "client pricing pressure may be exacerbating media agency non-transparent business practices – a number of sources independently cited advertisers' efforts to drive down agency fees as a reason why agencies are seeking additional sources of revenue beyond commissions."[12] The report encouraged advertisers to look at their own practices, particularly with respect to compensation and payment terms.

This admonishment did little to mollify 4As and its supporters. Critics of the K2 report found fault with the anonymous nature of the interviews, insisting that it was impossible to assess the credibility of the assertions. No specific agencies were identified with the taking of rebates, or if rebates were taken, whether they were kept by the agency or funneled back to the client.[13] Defenders of the media rebates and kickbacks pointed out that most existing client/agency contracts do not prohibit the practices, and that agencies that obtain rebates are technically complying with the terms of their contracts.

To counter this, critics of rebates invoked a higher standard of agency behaviour, asserting that agencies are morally responsible to operate in the best interests of their clients, and nontransparent practices clearly fall outside of this standard.

Irwin Gotlieb, global chairman of GroupM (up to 2018, when he retired), WPP's giant media agency, dismissed the K2 report in its entirety, charging at a digital media industry conference in October 2016 that the entire [K2] effort was a "business-development effort" by K2 and Ebiquity to "stoke their own prospects for forensic investigation and auditing. The ANA allowed themselves to be part of a third-party's business development," charged Gotlieb.[14]

EROSION OF TRUST: THE DENTSU OVERCHARGING SCANDAL

A further industry bomb exploded in mid-2016, when Toyota complained that Dentsu, its media and creative agency in Japan (and elsewhere), had been overcharging for media services. Dentsu, investigating its own practices, uncovered more than 633 cases of overcharging involving 111 of its clients. The overcharging, according to Dentsu, was due to "deliberate, human-caused errors" where fees were charged when online ads had been placed for a shorter-than-expected period – or not placed at all. Dentsu refused to name any of the clients affected by the improper transactions, other than Toyota, which had already received a formal apology from the advertising agency.[15]

FACEBOOK'S OVERSTATED VIDEO METRIC

In September 2016, Facebook disclosed in a post on its "Advertiser Help Centre" that its metric for the average time users spent watching videos was artificially inflated because it was only factoring in video views of more than three seconds. This vastly overestimated average viewing time for video ads on its platform for two years.

Publicis Media was told by Facebook, after further investigation, that the overestimate was between 60% and 80%.

The overall disclosure was a huge embarrassment for Facebook, which has been touting the rapid growth of video consumption across its platform in recent years.[16]

Later, between September 2016 and December 2016, Facebook would own up to three additional admissions of inaccurate viewing metrics for its clients. On top of this, Facebook was embroiled in post-election claims that it acted as a distributor of (principally) anti-Hillary Clinton "fake news" during the election cycle, helping to tip the balance towards Donald Trump. Critics called on Mark Zuckerberg, Chairman and CEO of Facebook, to clean things up.

WHERE DOES THIS LEAVE THE INDUSTRY?

The rebate and kickback scandal, as charged by Jon Mandel and documented by K2, and the unresolved conflicts between ANA and 4As, as well as the evidence of overcharging and metric mismeasurement, leave the industry more tattered than before. ANA and 4As are further apart than they were before the crisis erupted, and the Joint Task Force has amplified, rather than resolved, the issue of trust that has so long divided the industry.

The ID Comms 2018 Global Media Transparency Survey found that just 10% of advertisers rate levels of trust with their agency partners as high or very high. By contrast, the number who believe that trust is low has shifted from 29% to 40% (from 2016), while the number who believe it is average has fallen by 12%.[17]

In 2018, a study by McKinsey & Company, presented to the ANA Financial Management Conference in May 2018 by McKinsey's Sarah Armstrong, looked at the impact of the ANA investigation into rebates and media transparency, concluding that although 500 media contracts were reviewed in the past three years, and contracts have been rewritten, and media audits have skyrocketed, the impact on unsavory practices was underwhelming. "Nothing has changed" except for the adverse effect on media agency compensation and holding company share prices, which were down by double digits since the K2 report was first published. McKinsey recommended that advertisers hire "rebate specialists" whose responsibility is to track rebates and other forms of incentives to agencies – hardly a return to "trust" between the two parties. ANA, for its part, strongly disputed the McKinsey findings that "nothing has changed."[18]

Some months later, in October, 2018, the FBI entered the fray, reaching out to the ANA seeking its help – and that of its membership – with an investigation the Bureau and the US Attorney's Office for the Southern District of New York are conducting into potentially fraudulent media-buying practices.

The FBI outreach to the ANA was made via contact with its outside counsel, Reed Smith LLP.

The ANA confirmed the FBI reach-out in a letter to members from the ANA's CEO Bob Liodice.[19]

The starting point of the investigation, per the ANA letter, is to identify advertisers they believe may have been defrauded. The association is urging such advertisers to retain counsel, review their media-buying history and contracts, perform audits and then get advice on their options.

ANA maintained pressure on ad agencies over the "production transparency" issues by forming a Production Transparency

Task Force in August 2016 and issuing a report one year later on 6 August 2017.

The report concluded that there were, indeed, problems in the way production bidding and execution was handled – this was affirmed by 11 out of 12 experts convened by ANA – and that advertisers could bring this under their control through an improved focus on disciplines, accountabilities and controls. The report made ten recommendations that fell into the category of "trust, but verify," assuring that this would be a subject that ANA would continue to focus on.[20]

At the end of 2016, the Department of Justice announced that it was launching an investigation into whether ad agencies had been unfairly directing production business to their in-house production departments (or to their holding company owners) over independent shops. Later, DOJ subpoenaed Interpublic Group, MDC, Omnicom, Publicis Groupe, WPP and the records of K2 Intelligence. The suspected practices, if true, would have required collusion among various production bidders to engineer the desired pattern of winning and losing bidders. However, by November 2018, DOJ cleared all the holding companies, informing them that DOJ was no longer investigating any of their subsidiaries as part of their probe into commercial production practices and possible bid-rigging.

With all the conflict and speculation, it's Madison Avenue manslaughter on steroids, and the recent scandals have only accelerated the unfavourable trends that have been developing at a steady pace over the past several decades.

Looking ahead, it is not clear whose guidelines will be used in future contracts, although any realistic person should bet on the continued dominance of ANA and its members, who continue to hold the purse strings.

It looks as though there will be a lot of future negotiations. According to a report by international consultancy R3, new business revenue is up 36%. The report tallied an increase from $691 million in the first half of 2017 to $1.09 billion in the first half of 2018 due to a total of 3,401 agency new business wins from over 700 agencies globally, according to R3, up 3% from the first half of 2017.

"2018 has been a big year for creative wins globally – which are up 57% with some big alignments from Nestle, P&G and others," R3 principal and co-founder Greg Paull said in a statement.[21]

Let's be clear about what this means. If "new business revenue is up" in an industry whose fees are not growing, then it's due to agency relationship changes. You wouldn't use Elizabeth Taylor's eight marriages to seven different husbands to make any generalizations about the growth rate of marriage in the country between 1959 and 1991.

Not surprisingly, ad industry morale is down. Campaign US, which has surveyed morale for 2015 and 2016 , reports that morale has declined by 36%. Nearly half of industry employees said that they suffer from low morale. Nearly two thirds of respondents with low morale said they were actively job hunting.

"Poor leadership" is a major cause of job dissatisfaction and low morale. More than half of those with low morale rated the leadership at their company as "inadequate."[22]

SECTION II –
CONSEQUENCES

"Acceptance of what has happened is the first step to overcoming the consequences of any misfortune."

William James

"Have you always felt like a victim?"

Credit: Drew Dernavich / The New Yorker / The Cartoon Bank.

T he big agencies had quite a ride during the 50 years from the Creative Revolution to the lean times of today. They survived the energy crises and related recessions of the 1970s, 1980s, and 1990s, cushioned by media price inflation. They went public and were snapped up by the marketing services holding companies, who began to hold them accountable for improved margins. They absorbed the early changes in remuneration from media-based commissions to labour-based fees by cutting back on their staffing levels. They had significant staff surpluses from the high-paying commission days when the use of multiple creative teams on client briefs was routine, so the first few years of resource cuts were not terribly painful – there was plenty of "fat."

Client globalization, the fragmentation of media and the rise of procurement departments were more complicated to deal with, since they weakened the agency grip on their clients and created internal management complexities, but agencies soldiered on after the millennium, cutting headcounts and holding the line on salaries to match fee cuts. SOWs, though, continued to grow.

After 2004, a line was crossed, when fees, resources and workloads were out of balance – fees were inadequate, workloads were excessive and surplus resources were gone, so the work had to be handled by stretched, cheaper people. For the next decade, the gap between workload and resources only widened, bringing us up to date with the highly stressed situation of today.

The documentation, tracking, and negotiation of workloads never became an agency priority despite the growing gap between workload and resources. The business-as-usual practice of offering unlimited service – or at least not complaining about clients' service expectations – continued, not only because that was the way things had always been done, but also because agencies were afraid to upset the apple cart – to become more demanding with clients would have seemed suicidal, and few agency executives were prepared to take the risk.

The agency profit-equation was a complicated one: agencies had to earn 15-20% profit margins for their holding company parents, but a significant percentage of advertiser contracts generated less than this, with many of them at the 10% profit margin level.

The gap between holding company needs and advertiser contracts was relatively wide. Agencies knew full well that client contracts constrained their profits. The holding companies knew this as well, but their targets of 15-20% were non-negotiable, and agencies were expected to generate these higher targeted returns, no matter how difficult or impossible they might seem. Profit management was a senior executive responsibility at the ad agencies

– perhaps the most important responsibility of all, if job security was at all important.

WPP's share price declined substantially as a result of poor 2017 results. By the second quarter 2018, Mark Read, the new CEO, had to report disappointing results: "The advertising giant's second-quarter results showed a weak performance in North America as the company's stable of creative agencies – from J Walter Thompson, Ogilvy & Mather and Young & Rubicam – struggled. Like-for-like net sales – a figure closely watched by analysts to measure the company's underlying performance – dropped 3.3% in North America over a three-month period ending 30 June. Shares fell as much as 8% in early trading before recovering slightly."[1]

Increased agency growth used to be touted as the usual solution for closing the profit gap. As one holding company finance director wrote to me on this subject: *"There are always ways [for the agencies to generate the required margins] but most agencies need growth to deliver. It is getting much more difficult. In markets where there is no growth, this is a serious problem."* More recently, particularly in 2018, holding companies are talking about consolidating their portfolios to reduce complexity and and the number of agencies who work on client business.

Growth from new business was not a realistic solution, since there was very little net new growth for an agency when new clients were won. The predominant agency belief that new clients were "incremental" to what they already had ignored the fact that clients in their portfolio tended to disappear routinely. Newly won clients replaced newly lost clients, and the new clients usually paid at lower rates than existing clients. Furthermore, agencies invested millions of dollars in the new business pitching process. Pitching, which was the principal high-status activity of senior agency executives, was a high-cost activity that generated low or zero profits for the first few years. Profits from new clients were illusive, and new clients did little to close the gap between holding company profit expectations and actual agency profits.

Since growth was not an immediate answer, agencies dealt with profit problems through cost-reduction programmes, hiring freezes and fourth quarter downsizings. They laid off a percentage of their people when all else failed.

As with all service firms, agency assets "ride up and down the elevator every day," as the cliché goes. With a reliance on hiring freezes or downsizings to make up for profit gaps, there were fewer people riding up and down, and with the long-term growth of workloads, these people were doing more and more work. They were increasingly junior, too – senior expensive talent was much less affordable.

One example of this is shown by the New York agency home office of "The Cassandra Agency" (disguised name). This agency office illustrates the workload, fee, resource and profit issues of the industry.

Let's look "under the hood" of The Cassandra Agency New York to see how management dealt with its challenges.

CHAPTER 10 –
THE CASSANDRA AGENCY (NEW YORK): IMPLEMENTING A SCOPE OF WORK DIAGNOSTIC AND REVIEW

"I'll be leaving now, Williams... I've finished downsizing for the day."

Credit: Mick Stevens / The New Yorker / The Cartoon Bank.

The Cassandra Agency is owned by XLS Ltd, the British marketing services holding company (see Appendix A) that owns, as well, Icarus Advertising Agency (see Appendix B) and more than 100 other marketing services companies – creative advertising agencies, media agencies, market research firms, brand strategy firms, specialized consulting firms, database providers and many others. Cassandra, like Icarus, is based in New York City, and Cassandra NY serves as the headquarters office for the modestly sized Cassandra Agency global network. Cassandra and Icarus compete with one another in the marketplace, particularly during new business pitches, but they cooperate and jointly provide expert resources for XLS's "holding company relationships," organized for certain large XLS clients by Rupert Rogers-Smith, XLS's ever-aggressive and commercially minded CEO. Each agency is "on the hook" to deliver growing sales and profit margins annually via budgets agreed with XLS.

Cassandra NY, like many agency offices in the XLS family of agencies, has had a tough time meeting the margin targets dictated by XLS's Chief Financial Officer, James Donovan. During the past five years, Cassandra NY has downsized by 8-10% per year to close the annual profit gap, and this has brought the New York office down from 175 FTEs in 2012 to 113 FTEs in 2017. Among the 113 current FTEs, 94 FTEs are billed directly to clients through labour-based fee contracts, while the other 19 FTEs are "overhead people" in finance, human resources, security, building and administration. They are included in the "overhead pool" of overhead costs.

Cassandra NY operates like most creative ad agency offices. It has a client portfolio of ten major clients, some of whom have been with the agency for many years and others recently won in client pitches. Fee income from these clients is $33.5 million, varying from a high of $9.098 million for Cassandra NY's largest client, *SportsShoe*, to a low of $831,848 for *OnlineBank*, a major financial client for whom Cassandra NY does a small amount of work. Cassandra NY conducts annual fee negotiations with these clients and, for the most part, Cassandra NY accepts the fee levels that its clients dictate, even though some of these fees are inadequate and too many of them decline from one year to another.

Cassandra NY's Chief Financial Officer, Robby Ferguson, is involved in these negotiations, along with the office's client heads, and he tries to play "bad cop" when sitting across from client procurement executives, defending the agency and the "excessive hours"

Cassandra spends on client business, arguing for higher fees and taking the position that any proposed fee cuts would be "unfair" and "one-sided". He knows that he is partly play-acting, though, because Cassandra NY can ill afford the loss of any client. Client fees cover salaries, overhead costs and profits. If a client is lost, and even if all the people who work on the lost account are let go, overhead costs and profits will remain uncovered. Robby has to deliver revenues and profits to XLS as part of his responsibilities on behalf of Cassandra. There is a limit to how far he can go during the fee negotiations – he needs revenue, even if it is less than it should be. Cassandra's clients know the nature of the game and the relative power they have over Cassandra, so Robby's bad-cop bluster is whimsically accepted but has little actual influence over the outcome. If a client decides to cut fees, fees are cut.

Scopes of works (SOWs) are talked about during these negotiations – SOWs are changing, becoming more digital and social, and clients are concerned about agency capabilities to handle the changing mix of work. SOW size, though, is not a topic for clients or for Cassandra NY. SOWs are sometimes documented by clients in SOW software packages like Decideware or in project management systems maintained by agency project managers. However, these systems and their data are relatively invisible to Cassandra NY's top management, even during fee negotiations. As far as top management is concerned, the SOWs are part of the process responsibilities of the project managers and client heads, and that is the end of it. SOW data do not provide rigorous metrics for Cassandra's fee negotiations. More often, timesheet data are used by client heads and CFOs like Ferguson to make various points about the efforts of agency resources and the inadequacy of fees.

AN UNEXPECTED EMAIL
I was surprised one day to receive an email from Robby Ferguson, whom I did not know, expressing curiosity about Farmer & Company's SOW practice and asking if we could speak by phone. Most agencies like Cassandra do not have SOWs that are written down,

but this is not a problem that keeps finance directors up at night. The lack of SOWs is simply a fact of life, no more unusual than scruffy beards or untucked shirts in the creative department.

As I later learned, Robby was concerned about the upcoming fee negotiations with *ChemicalCompany*, an industrial client that paid Cassandra NY $1.6 million in fees per year. These fees were inadequate, Robby thought, and there were strong hints that the client was thinking about taking 10-15% out of the next year's (2018) fees.

One of Robby's young financial analysts had recently attended an industry conference where I spoke about SOW issues, and she encouraged Robby to bring me in to talk with him about a new way of negotiating fees with *ChemicalCompany* by documenting its SOWs.

A PILOT PROJECT

Thus began the process by which we agreed to work with Cassandra NY to document and measure *ChemicalCompany's* 2016 and 2017 scopes of work, and to use the insights from this analysis to show that SOW workloads and fees were out of balance with one another. Robby used the SOW data to negotiate unchanged fees for 2018 and to get the client's approval for a proposed re-engineering of the SOW to make it less executional and more strategic, focused on strengthening brand equity and improving the efficiency of new customer acquisition. This process is described later in this chapter.

The insights from using SOW data on *ChemicalCompany* motivated Robby to commission the documentation and measurement of all of Cassandra NY's SOWs. The office-wide SOW diagnosis was completed in late 2017 and early 2018. The remainder of this chapter describes how the SOW diagnosis was conducted and what it showed about the state of Cassandra NY's ten major clients.

SOW DOCUMENTATION AT CASSANDRA NY

Cassandra NY did not document or measure the SOWs for each of its clients. Its clients kept track of SOWs, at least well enough so that they could brief Cassandra NY on what work to do during the year, but Cassandra NY did not have an agency-wide or office-wide system to keep track of these SOWs. In fact, during my 25 years of consulting with creative advertising agencies, I have yet to find an agency or office that documented or maintained SOWs in a uniform agency-wide or office-wide system. (This is much less true for direct marketing agencies or digital agencies, which tend to be paid on a per-project basis and have more detailed records about the projects they have completed.)

The SOW documentation problem I've observed is chronic among traditional ad agencies, even those that have evolved and added direct marketing and digital/social capabilities to their product lines. Although agencies have other software systems – agency-wide finance and HR systems to document costs, revenues and personnel information – they do not have systems to document and measure the work they do for clients.

Consequently, the relevant agency executives who are affected by SOWs – client heads, office heads, finance directors, regional executives and CEOs – don't have much information about what kind of work is going on for any client, much less *how much work it represents*. Questions from senior management, like: "What kind of work are we doing for Client A?" can only be answered in the most general way, such as "Well, we're doing some traditional work, including TV, along with growing digital and social as they shift their marketing in a digital direction. We're handling it."

This kind of answer is meant to be reassuring, showing that "we're being relevant by being more digital," and "we're still in the creative game by doing TV." But that's about as far as it goes with scopes of work. The harder questions, like "Are we doing the right kind of work for Client A?" or "Are we being paid the right amount of money for the work we do?" are not being asked and cannot be answered without detailed SOW documentation and measurement. This documentation does not exist.

If you cannot measure it, you cannot manage it, goes the business meme – and because SOWs are not documented or measured, SOWs are not being managed.

I've always found this curious – I can't think of another industry in the world where a company's outputs are not known or measured by management. Imagine, if you will, Apple not knowing how many iPhones they produce or sell in a given year, or GM not knowing how many automobiles roll off its assembly lines. Apple is in the iPhone business, GM is in the automobile business, and ad agencies are in the "ad business", broadly defined. Yet, agencies are more likely to define themselves as being in the "big ideas" or "creative" business than in the "ad" business. This is a crippling myth that goes back to the Creative Revolution days, and it stands in the way of SOW documentation and measurement. I can't tell you how many times I've been told by agency executives, "You can't measure what it takes to create a big idea," or "Creativity can't be quantified." This argument is meant to justify why agency SOWs are not documented or measured.

Too often, I believe, SOWs are seen by agency executives as trappings that allow them to develop *big ideas* and be *creative*. SOWs are thus seen as an administrative means to a greater end – and they don't need to be taken seriously. If they believe this, agency executives are fooling themselves. Agencies are actually paid to develop, create and generate ads; the ads are expected to improve shareholder value for clients; and the number and type of ads can be counted, measured and used as the basis for agency remuneration. Agencies are *creative*, of course, but so is Apple and so is GM. Complex products like iPhones and Cadillacs cannot be developed without *creativity*. *Creativity* is a business requirement for nearly every business, but *creativity* is not a business in itself, and *creativity* does not improve shareholder value. It takes *creative deliverables* to improve shareholder value.

SOW DELIVERABLES AND THEIR CLASSIFICATION

Gathering SOWs for the first time is a challenging exercise for agencies, especially since SOWs need to be documented *by deliverable*, not simply by *campaign*. As useful as *campaigns* can be for thinking about marketing programmes ("*we're developing four new campaigns for Brand X in 2018*"), they're not very useful for SOW measurement purposes. SOWs are made up of individual deliverables, and it's the number and type of deliverables that we need to know in order to measure SOW workloads and compare SOWs across brands, clients and offices.

Deliverables must be classified along a number of dimensions to help us determine the *size of each deliverable*[1]. TV origination deliverables are larger than TV adaptation deliverables; there is a large variety of print deliverables that vary by size (from brochures to newspaper ads to point-of-display materials); Facebook and Instagram posts are tiny among all deliverable types, but numerous in today's SOWs.

There has been a veritable explosion in the number of deliverables in today's SOWs. Back in 1992, when we analysed our first SOWs for Ogilvy UK, which had 26 creative teams in its Creative Department (52 creative FTEs), we counted 363 deliverables for the year. These involved TV, print and radio deliverables, nearly all of which were originations. Fifty-two creatives completed 363 deliverables – about seven deliverables per creative per year, or one deliverable every seven-and-a-half weeks. Those were the days when the creatives could sit around and mull over brand positioning, market segmentation and creative possibilities, ad by ad.

By contrast, in 2017, the Cassandra agency had a very different mix of work. Along with its TV, print and radio deliverables, Cassandra (as we will see) completed an extensive mix of brand concepting, creative ideas, and direct, digital and social deliverables – including online videos, Facebook posts, Twitter posts, email marketing and more. The 2017 deliverable count was 10,859 deliverables. Granted, the 2017 deliverables were each "smaller" than the 1992 deliverables, but the output per creative skyrocketed – from seven deliverables per year to 287 deliverables per year, leaving very little time for "*creative thinking*". We'll examine the 10,859 deliverables later in this chapter.

THE SCOPEMETRIC® SOW CLASSIFICATION SYSTEM

In the ScopeMetric® system developed by Farmer & Company, deliverables are classified along four dimensions:

1. **Deliverable type** (i.e., TV, strategy, social media, website, etc.), which has 19 categories;
2. **Deliverable detail** (i.e., TV:30, competitive analysis, Facebook posts, landing page, etc.), which has 211 categories;
3. **Origination or adaptation**, with 6 possible dimensions[2]; and
4. **Creative complexity** (low, average, high).

In addition, we gather the "number of deliverables" of each type.

See Appendix C for a full description of this classification scheme.

In Excel format, a SOW template with this classification scheme looks like the following (see Table 10-1).

TABLE 10-1: THE CASSANDRA AGENCY NY – SCOPE OF WORK CLASSIFICATION SAMPLE 2017

Client	Campaign Name	Project Name	Deliverable Type	Deliverable Type Detail	Project Type	Creative Complexity	Number of Deliverables
SportsShoe	<Fill in Campaign Name>	<Fill in Project Name>	TV	TV:30	Adaptation	Low	14
ClothingRetailer	<Fill in Campaign Name>	<Fill in Project Name>	TV	TV:30	Adap-Prod only	Low	2
OnlineBank	<Fill in Campaign Name>	<Fill in Project Name>	TV	TV:20	Origination	High	1
RentalCar	<Fill in Campaign Name>	<Fill in Project Name>	TV	TV Tag	Orig-Crtv only	Average	1
OnlineBank	<Fill in Campaign Name>	<Fill in Project Name>	Print	Print Ad Page	Origination	Average	2
ChemicalCompany	<Fill in Campaign Name>	<Fill in Project Name>	Print	Print Ad Insert	Adap-Crtv only	Low	1
RentalCar	<Fill in Campaign Name>	<Fill in Project Name>	Print	Print Ad Gatefold	Orig-Crtv only	Low	1
SportsShoe	<Fill in Campaign Name>	<Fill in Project Name>	Print-BTL	Brand Book	Adaptation	Low	1
KitchenEquipment	<Fill in Campaign Name>	<Fill in Project Name>	Print-BTL	POS/POP	Origination	Average	5
ClothingRetailer	<Fill in Campaign Name>	<Fill in Project Name>	Print-BTL	Catalog	Adap-Crtv only	Low	1
SportsShoe	<Fill in Campaign Name>	<Fill in Project Name>	Print-DM	Brochure	Adap-Crtv only	Low	1
SportsShoe	<Fill in Campaign Name>	<Fill in Project Name>	Website	Content Update	Adap-Crtv only	Low	1
SportsShoe	<Fill in Campaign Name>	<Fill in Project Name>	eDM	E-mail-HTML	Adaptation	Low	4
SportsShoe	<Fill in Campaign Name>	<Fill in Project Name>	Online Video	Video:30	Adaptation	Low	1
SportsShoe	<Fill in Campaign Name>	<Fill in Project Name>	Ad Unit/Banner	HTML5	Adaptation	Low	1
SportsShoe	<Fill in Campaign Name>	<Fill in Project Name>	Print-DM	Self Mailer	Adap-Crtv only	Low	2
PensionFund	<Fill in Campaign Name>	<Fill in Project Name>	OOH	Airport Poster	Adaptation	Low	2
ChemicalCompany	<Fill in Campaign Name>	<Fill in Project Name>	OOH	Dgtl Billboard	Adaptation	Low	2
KitchenEquipment	<Fill in Campaign Name>	<Fill in Project Name>	Social Media	Facebook	Adaptation	Low	40
KitchenEquipment	<Fill in Campaign Name>	<Fill in Project Name>	Social Media	Twitter	Adaptation	Low	20
KitchenEquipment	<Fill in Campaign Name>	<Fill in Project Name>	Social Media	Community Mgmt	Origination	Average	1
KitchenEquipment	<Fill in Campaign Name>	<Fill in Project Name>	Social Media	Social Presence	Origination	High	10
ClothingRetailer	<Fill in Campaign Name>	<Fill in Project Name>	Social Media	Instagram	Origination	Low	84

When we work with agencies like Cassandra to reconstruct their SOWs for the first time, we train executives in the use of this classification scheme. Deliverable type and deliverable detail are fairly straightforward. Origination/adaptation and creative complexity are somewhat more complicated.

"Originations", for example, apply to deliverables whose work is genuinely *original* – the ideas behind the deliverables are developed from scratch. Ongoing or long campaigns require a number of originations, each based on original ideas or executions, but after the originations have been developed, what follows is a succession of *adaptations* based on the origination ideas.

This is especially true in multidisciplinary campaigns, where TV or print originations establish the campaign themes, and executions in a variety of other media are adapted from them. Consequently, in a typical SOW, we expect to see a limited number of originations and a larger number of adaptations based on the originations.

THE "OVERCLASSIFICATION" PROBLEM

Creative agencies often believe that all their work is "original", and if you ask agency client teams to classify a list of deliverables, you'll find that they classify most of their work as "originations". It takes some effort to "talk them down" to classify their work more realistically – to show a mix of few originations and numerous adaptations.

The same problem exists with the classification of creative complexity. *High creative complexity* originations are reserved for the once-in-a-blue moon efforts to develop ads for new products, entirely new campaigns, line extensions, products in new markets and so on. Creative complexity for the remaining deliverables tends to be average or low, and many of them are more appropriately classified as adaptations in any case.

Creative agencies tend to classify much of their work as "high creative complexity" when the bulk of it falls into lower complexity classifications. This is understandable. Agencies claim that it is difficult to get client approvals for their work, and the complexity of the ad approval process colours agency perspectives about the creative complexity of their deliverables. We counsel our agency clients to think about the "creative complexity associated with cracking the brief", not the complexity of the client's ad approval process.

Why does this matter? Well, when we're trying to determine the amount of work in a SOW, it's important to get the classifications right, since classifications drive workload values. A SOW that is overclassified with too many "origination-high creative complexity" deliverables is going to have very high workload values, and high workloads require a high number of agency FTEs. These high headcounts require high levels of fees. The agency tendency to overclassify drives up calculated workloads to unrealistic levels, making the current staffing and fees look woefully inadequate. Agencies that do this appear to have inadequate fees for their SOWs, along with severe understaffing for the amount of work.

It's very important to eliminate overclassification problems. Our experience with agencies shows us that we will go through three rounds of rework on the classification exercise before we've eliminated the overclassification of deliverables.

Advertisers, by contrast, have a completely different bias when classifying SOWs. Advertisers underclassify deliverables, routinely classifying most of them as "adaptations" of low or average complexity. Advertisers have a bias to see SOWs as much simpler than they really are, just as agencies tend to see them as much more complex than they actually are.

Agencies and advertisers are two parties with diametrically opposite biases, and this is why the two parties need to get together to talk through proposed SOW deliverables and *their classifications*. Out of this will emerge a greater clarity of understanding about what each side believes the other is thinking. Agencies will avoid overinvesting in certain deliverables when they know that their client sees them as adaptations rather than originations. Advertisers will have a better understanding of what kinds of deliverables require original creative thinking when they have a firm list of originations before them.

The absence of discussion about a clear list of classified deliverables can only lead to misunderstandings that can have dire consequences. Yet, this is how the industry typically operates today.

CASSANDRA'S 2017 SCOPES OF WORK FOR TEN CLIENTS

We worked with Cassandra in early 2018 to document its 2017 scopes of work for the New York office, and we went through three rounds of rework before the overclassification problem was sorted out. In the end, though, we and Cassandra were satisfied that the SOW data-gathering exercise had been done correctly, and that the deliverables were correctly classified. All the classifications of the deliverables for each client was "pressure-tested" through discussion and debate. What remained was to review the client-by-client outcomes. How much work was being done for each client? What were the associated fees and agency resources? Were workloads, fees and resources in balance with one another?

Let's look first at each client's fees, deliverables, ScopeMetric® Units and price per SMU (see Table 10-2).

TABLE 10-2: THE CASSANDRA AGENCY NY – CLIENT WORKLOADS

Client	Fees	Actual SOW Deliverables	Calculated SMUs	Calculated Deliverables per SMU	Calculated Price per SMU
SportsShoe	$9,098,247	1,843	33	56	**$277,696**
KitchenEquipment	$3,595,325	568	14	39	**$249,659**
RentalCar	$4,112,545	186	26	7	**$160,191**
OnlineBank	$831,848	77	5	15	**$159,454**
BeerCompany	$1,576,227	350	12	29	**$132,265**
High Priced Clients	**$19,214,191**	**3,023**	**90**	**34**	$213,560
TravelAgent	$2,316,516	1,315	22	60	**$105,703**
ClothingRetailer	$4,291,190	4,174	41	102	**$104,549**
ChemicalCompany	$1,614,227	204	21	10	**$77,356**
PensionFund	$2,003,362	480	27	18	**$75,203**
MovieStudio	$4,077,965	1,663	57	29	**$72,086**
Low Priced Clients	**$14,303,258**	**7,836**	**167**	**47**	$85,629
Total ten clients	**$33,517,450**	**10,859**	**257**	**45**	$130,414

As you can see, there are very large differences among the clients. What's striking is the large range of *workloads relative to fees*. *SportsShoe* has fees of $9 million, 1,843 deliverables (for 33 SMUs) and a price per SMU of $277,696. We could call this "high fees, low workloads", and this would explain the high price per SMU.

MovieStudio, at the other end of the spectrum, has much smaller fees at $4 million, but with 57 SMUs, it has 72% more work. It's a "low fee, high workload" client, and this is reflected in its low price per SMU of $72,086.

There is a four-fold difference in price from the best client, *SportsShoe*, to the worst client, *MovieStudio*. None of these ten clients had SOWs that were thoughtfully documented, negotiated or used to determine fees. We could safely say that workloads were random relative to their fees – and that this randomness explains the differences in prices among the clients.

The ten clients can be divided into two groups of five clients each on the basis of price. The top high priced clients, *SportsShoe* through *BeerCompany*, accounted for $19 million of Cassandra's $33.5 million in income – 57% of the total. However, these high-priced clients accounted for only 90 SMUs out of Cassandra's 257 SMUs of work – 35% of the total. With 57% of the fees and only 35% of the workload, it's understandable that this group of five clients had a high average price of $213,560.

At the other end of things, the low-priced clients were represented by *TravelAgent* through *MovieStudio*, and they accounted for only $14 million of Cassandra's $33.5 million of fee income (43%), while their workloads were 167 SMUs out of the total of 257 – 65% of the total. With 43% of the fees but 65% of the workloads, the low-priced clients were condemned to an average price of only $85,629 per SMU.

We can use the aggregate data of SMUs and deliverables to make other observations about the ten clients in Cassandra's portfolio. Look at the column entitled "Calculated Deliverables per SMU", which is derived by dividing the number of deliverables by the SMUs – giving us a quick view of the "average size of the deliverables" for each client.

RentalCar, for example, had 186 deliverables that calculated to 26 SMUs, or about seven deliverables per SMU. These are "big" deliverables, probably mostly originations in broadcast.

ClothingRetailer, by contrast, had 4,174 deliverables that calculated to only 41 SMUs, or 102 deliverables per SMU. We are sure to find that these are mostly adaptations in digital/social.

SportsShoe (the best client with a price of $277,696) and *MovieStudio* (the worst client with a price of $72,086) each completed 1,600-1,800 deliverables. *MovieStudio's* deliverables were each nearly *double the size of SportsShoe deliverables* – at 29 deliverables per SMU for *MovieStudio* versus 56 deliverables per SMUs for *SportsShoe*.

There is a dramatic difference among the fees, deliverables, SMUs and price from the best to the worst clients.

Arguably, the five low-priced clients are underperforming clients for Cassandra NY, in that their SOWs are being underpaid. If the low-priced clients, who are currently earning $85,629 per SMU, could be managed upwards over the next several years, realizing higher prices for their work, then the profit potential is staggering. If these clients could achieve the current (and depressed) market price of $132,628 per SMU, then *each SMU* would generate an additional $46,999 of income. For 167 SMUs, that would be a significant $7.8 million in additional income for Cassandra NY, or 23% of today's $33.5 fee income.

Cassandra NY is underperforming by $7.8 million or 23% of total income.

While it may not be realistic to assume that Cassandra can drive up its pricing performance by 23%, it would not be unrealistic for its management to begin looking for 10% improvements or more through better pricing negotiations based on scopes of work.

Pricing is not the only problem that Cassandra endures through its failure to document and manage scopes of work. Low prices lead to understaffing, and understaffed clients have unhappy, stretched agency people who generate sub-quality work.

What do Cassandra's ten clients look like from a staffing and productivity standpoint? See Table 10-3, below:

TABLE 10-3: THE CASSANDRA AGENCY NY
– CLIENT WORKLOADS AND CREATIVE OUTPUTS

Client	Contract Fees	Calculated SMUs	Calculated Price per SMU	Contract FTEs	Creative FTEs	SMUs per Creative
SportsShoe	$9,098,247	33	$277,696	30	8.8	3.7
KitchenEquipment	$3,595,325	14	$249,659	11	3.1	4.6
RentalCar	$4,112,545	26	$160,191	10	5.1	5.0
OnlineBank	$831,848	5	$159,454	2	1.1	4.7
BeerCompany	$1,576,227	12	$132,265	8	2.2	5.4
High Priced Clients	$19,214,191	90	$213,560	61	20.3	4.4
TravelAgent	$2,316,516	22	$105,703	10	2.6	8.5
ClothingRetailer	$4,291,190	41	$104,549	14	4.7	8.8
ChemicalCompany	$1,614,227	21	$77,356	5	1.7	12.1
PensionFund	$2,003,362	27	$75,203	6	2.2	12.0
MovieStudio	$4,077,965	57	$72,086	17	6.4	8.8
Low Priced Clients	$14,303,258	167	$85,629	52	17.6	9.5
Total ten clients	$33,517,450	257	$130,414	113	37.9	6.8

There is an approved staffing plan for each client – it's part of how fees are calculated. Cassandra NY has 113 FTEs assigned to its ten clients; creatives account for 37.9 FTEs of this total (34%). The creatives are principally responsible for doing the creative development and creative supervision of produced deliverables. The number of SMUs per creative is an important productivity measure.

When we developed the SMU, we established a "standard productivity metric" of 4.1 SMUs per creative as the correct value. (See Chapter 13 for a explanation of the reasons for 4.1 SMUs per creative.) That number has increased to 5.0 by 2017, so that a figure of 4.1 to 5.0 SMUs per creative per year is an appropriate value and represents good practice.

At Cassandra, the top five clients achieve a creative productivity level of 4.4 SMUs per creative, and this is great – but it requires an average price of $213,560 to achieve it, and this is *significantly above* the industry price of $132,628 today.

The bottom five clients show what happens when price is low, like $85,629 – it leads to inadequate creative staffing, with each creative having to generate 9.5 SMUs per creative per year.

The average for Cassandra NY is 6.8 SMUs per creative per year, which is 36% higher than today's standard of 5.0 – not a good thing.

Cassandra's overall creative department is being stretched, and it's the result of inadequate prices for the work Cassandra is doing.

There is, in fact, a relationship between price and creative output for Cassandra NY (and every other agency we have ever analysed). See Table 10-4.

TABLE 10-4: THE CASSANDRA AGENCY NY CREATIVE OUTPUT PER YEAR VERSUS PRICE PER SMU

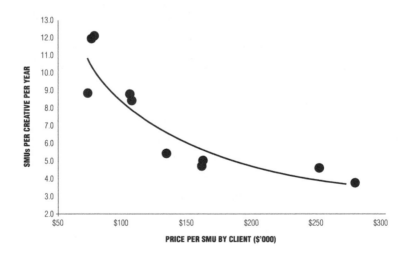

High-priced clients are characterized by high fees and modest workloads. High-priced clients have a surplus of creative resources relative to the SOW workload, and the creative output per year in SMUs per creative per year is mathematically low.

Low-priced clients, by contrast, are characterized by low fees and high workloads. Low-priced clients have a deficit of creative resources relative to the SOW workloads, and the creative output per year in SMUs per creative is mathematically high.

We have evaluated this hundreds of times during the past 25 years, and the graphic pattern shown in Table 10-4 is absolutely consistent.

The failure to document and negotiate agency workloads from SOWs has led to price declines over 25 years, and these price declines have inevitably driven up creative outputs per year. As long as creative output per year does not exceed 5.0 SMUs per creative per year, there's nothing wrong with this. However, declining pricing trends are pushing creative productivity levels *above* 5.0 SMUs per creative per year, and we are seeing agency offices that average (like Cassandra NY, for example), output rates well in excess of 5.0 SMUs per creative per year. This is, indeed, unhealthy.

At Cassandra NY, there is too much work for low fees, and the low fees lead to inadequate agency resources.

Before Cassandra NY can decide what to do about this general problem, we need to look at the nature of its SOWs. What kind of work is Cassandra NY doing? Where are the opportunities to change the nature of the work and to reduce the SOW workloads by client?

Let's take a look at Cassandra's scope of work mix.

OFFICE SCOPE OF WORK MIX

The total office, we recall, had 10,859 deliverables or 257 SMUs among the office's 10 clients.

1. What was the office's mix of work by *deliverable type*?
2. What was the mix of work by *deliverable complexity* (from the most complex, "origination high creative complexity") to the least complex, "adaptation low creative complexity")?

Table 10-5 and the accompanying breakdown (next page) give the picture of the office as a whole.

TABLE 10-5: THE CASSANDRA AGENCY NY MIX OF SMUs BY *DELIVERABLE TYPE AND COMPLEXITY/SIZE* 2017

Distribution of Deliverables						
	Broadcast	Print/ OOH	Print/ BTL	Print/ DM	Digital/ Social	Strategic/ Research	Total # Deliverables
Adaptation – Low	83	3,607	302	1,366	2,002	502	7,863
Adaptation – Average	14	77	66	12	419	154	742
Adaptation – High	–	–	6	14	10	17	46
Origination – Low	55	26	49	30	590	138	890
Origination – Average	42	14	8	–	906	98	1,068
Origination – High	12	–	–	–	130	108	250
Total Deliverables	207	3,724	431	1,422	4,058	1,017	10,859

Distribution of SMUs						
	Broadcast	Print/ OOH	Print/ BTL	Print/ DM	Digital/ Social	Strategic/ Research	Total # SMUs
Adaptation – Low	4.7	40.4	5.7	41.9	16.7	10.4	119.8
Adaptation – Average	1.0	4.1	2.4	0.5	5.1	4.3	17.5
Adaptation – High	–	–	0.4	0.7	0.2	1.5	2.8
Origination – Low	4.5	1.4	2.8	3.4	12.4	6.6	31.1
Origination – Average	15.9	5.3	1.6	–	26.4	5.2	54.3
Origination – High	12.5	–	–	–	8.8	10.2	31.5
Total SMUs	38.5	51.2	12.9	46.6	69.6	38.2	257.0

Distribution of SMUs by %						
	Broadcast	Print/ OOH	Print/ BTL	Print/ DM	Digital/ Social	Strategic/ Research	Total % SMUs
Adaptation – Low	2%	16%	2%	16%	6%	4%	47%
Adaptation – Average	0%	2%	1%	0%	2%	2%	7%
Adaptation – High	–	–	0%	0%	0%	1%	1%
Origination – Low	2%	1%	1%	1%	5%	3%	12%
Origination – Average	6%	2%	1%	–	10%	2%	21%
Origination – High	5%	–	–	–	3%	4%	12%
Total % of SMUs	15%	20%	5%	18%	27%	15%	100%

Cassandra NY's mix of work includes 1,017 "strategic/research" deliverables that account for 38.2 SMUs, or about 15% of the total office workload (see above). This somewhat understates the amount of strategic work being carried out by the office, since the origination deliverables in the scopes of work each include some portion of up-front strategic work. On the whole, we believe that Cassandra's total strategic workload is somewhere between 15% and 20% of the total work done by the office, with all of this work supporting the remaining creative and production deliverables.

The creative and production work includes the following (see previous page, Table 10-5):

- **Broadcast** (207 deliverables, 38.5 SMUs)
- **Print/Out of Home** (3,724 deliverables, 51.2 SMUs)
- **Print/Below-the-Line** (431 deliverables, 12.9 SMUs)
- **Print/Direct Marketing** (1,422 deliverables, 46.6 SMUs), and **Digital/Social** (4,058 deliverables, 69.6 SMUs)

What is striking about Cassandra NY's overall workload is the degree to which small deliverables have taken over the mix of work, with the adaptation deliverables accounting for 8,652 deliverables for 140 SMUs – 55% of the total workload. These adaptations are small; it takes 62 deliverables to make up one SMU.

By contrast, Cassandra NY is carrying out 2,207 origination deliverables for 117 SMUs, and these originations account for 45% of the total office's workload in SMUs. It takes 19 origination deliverables to make up one SMU.

Cassandra NY's creative legacy was in TV and traditional print. Over the years, though, Cassandra has been driven by its clients' SOWs to do more adaptations and to become more digital and social, and small deliverables now dominate the total number of deliverables and the SMU workload.

It's rather extraordinary that the origination/adaptation workload mix is 45/55. This is one of the monumental changes that has occurred in the industry since the media commission days, when nearly 100% of an agency's work was pure origination.

Cassandra NY is being overwhelmed by the logistics of handling nearly 11,000 deliverables, and the office does not have the necessary resources to deal with a workload of this magnitude.

Cassandra NY's top management concluded, from the office data, that "we're doing too much executional work for our clients – too many low-complexity deliverables, too many SMUs. We need to "upgrade" our SOWs wherever possible to do higher complexity work that has a greater chance of growing our clients' brands. At the same time, we need to reduce the amount of total work in the SOWs, since we think that it is unlikely that we can negotiate larger fees for the existing work. Consequently, the challenge we face is "how to re-engineer our SOWs to end up with a lower quantity and more effective mix of work."

INDIVIDUAL CLIENT SCOPE OF WORK MIX

Management concluded that they would first focus on improving four of the five underperforming clients, all of whom have low prices per SMU, high creative outputs per head, a relatively high percentage of adaptations in their SOWs, and a relatively high number of small deliverables in their SOW mixes (see Table 10-6).

TABLE 10-6: THE CASSANDRA AGENCY NY FOUR UNDER-PERFORMING CLIENTS (EXCLUDES CHEMICALCOMPANY 2017)

Client	Contract Fees	Calculated Price per SMU	SMUs per Creative	% Adaptation SMUs	Actual SOW Deliverables	Calculated Deliverables per SMU
TravelAgent	$2,316,516	$105,703	8.5	25%	1,315	60
ClothingRetailer	$4,291,190	$104,549	8.8	66%	4,174	102
PensionFund	$2,003,362	$75,203	12.0	46%	480	18
MovieStudio	$4,077,965	$72,086	8.8	94%	1,663	29

Let's take these four clients one at a time and see what Cassandra NY's management was considering negotiating with clients to re-engineer the scopes of work (see Tables 10-7 through 10-10).

TABLE 10-7: TRAVELAGENT SCOPE OF WORK 2017

TravelAgent						
Distribution of Deliverables						
	Broadcast	Print/ OOH	Print/ BTL	Print/ DM	Digital/ Social	Strategic/ Research	Total # Deliverables
Adaptation – Low	–	–	–	–	600	–	600
Adaptation – Average	–	–	–	–	120	–	120
Adaptation – High	–	–	–	–	–	–	–
Origination – Low	–	–	–	–		–	–
Origination – Average	–	–	–	–	576	–	576
Origination – High	–	–	–	–	–	19	19
Total Deliverables	–	–	–	–	1,296	19	1,315
Distribution of SMUs						
	Broadcast	Print/ OOH	Print/ BTL	Print/ DM	Digital/ Social	Strategic/ Research	Total # SMUs
Adaptation – Low	–	–	–	–	5.3	–	5.3
Adaptation – Average	–	–	–	–	0.2	–	0.2
Adaptation – High	–	–	–	–	–	–	–
Origination – Low	–	–	–	–	–	–	–
Origination – Average	–	–	–	–	15.1	–	15.1
Origination – High	–	–	–	–	–	1.3	1.3
Total SMUs	–	–	–	–	20.6	1.3	21.9
Distribution of SMUs by %						
	Broadcast	Print/ OOH	Print/ BTL	Print/ DM	Digital/ Social	Strategic/ Research	Total % SMUs
Adaptation – Low	–	–	–	–	24%	–	24%
Adaptation – Average	–	–	–	–	1%	–	1%
Adaptation – High	–	–	–	–	–	–	0%
Origination – Low	–	–	–	–	–	–	0%
Origination – Average	–	–	–	–	69%	–	69%
Origination – High	–	–	–	–	–	6%	6%
Total % of SMUs	0%	0%	0%	0%	94%	6%	100%

TravelAgent uses Cassandra NY to generate ideas for social presence and then to carry out a high volume of executions. This is shown in Table 10-7, above, where 576 deliverables, all of them **creative-only originations of average creative complexity**, account for 15.1 SMUs and 69% of the total SOW workload.

For this SOW of 1,315 deliverables (21.9 SMUs), TravelAgent pays Cassandra NY $2.3 million, which calculates to a low price of $105,703 per SMU that requires the 2.6 creative FTEs to generate 8.5 SMUs per head.

After a period of reflection about the SOW, Cassandra NY concluded that there was little likelihood of getting higher fees from the client. The agency also concluded that it was unlikely that they could cut the workload *and* achieve a higher origination mix within the SOW – the origination mix was already very high at 75%, and so was the SOW workload.

What was wrong was the way Cassandra NY was handling idea generation, treating idea-generation deliverables as "creative-only originations" in an effort to be "creative" and to wow the client with the originality of its work in social media. This was a self-generated problem; it was not due to the client insisting that Cassandra generate so many original ideas.

Peter Smith, the *TravelAgent* account head, explained it this way: "We've been reluctant to see this client for what it actually is, which is an adaptation client requiring a few original ideas. We've been overinvesting in idea creation for the social platforms. We have to cut back and downgrade the way we work to get a better balance of workload and resources. We've since discussed this with the creative director and the assigned creatives, and instead of trying to generate 576 semi-original social ideas, we need to scale back our approach. We're going to lighten the workload without any client discussion by doing fewer originations – changing the mix of work. The battle will be won in our own heads. The number of deliverables will stay the same, but the SMU count will go way down for next year."

TABLE 10-8: CLOTHINGRETAILER'S SCOPE OF WORK 2017

ClothingRetailer							
Distribution of Deliverables							
	Broadcast	**Print/ OOH**	**Print/ BTL**	**Print/ DM**	**Digital/ Social**	**Strategic/ Research**	**Total # Deliverables**
Adaptation – Low	15	3,240	143	–	8	84	3,490
Adaptation – Average	2	12	43	–	44	18	119
Adaptation – High	–	–	–	–	2	1	2
Origination – Low	–	–	24	–	514	10	548
Origination – Average	1	–	–	–	2	7	10
Origination – High	–	–	–	–	–	4	4
Total Deliverables	**18**	**3,252**	**210**	**–**	**569**	**124**	**4,174**
Distribution of SMUs							
	Broadcast	**Print/ OOH**	**Print/ BTL**	**Print/ DM**	**Digital/ Social**	**Strategic/ Research**	**Total # SMUs**
Adaptation – Low	0.2	22.0	2.3	–	0,1	–	24.6
Adaptation – Average	0.1	0.5	1.4	–	0.3	0.1	2.4
Adaptation – High	–	–	–	–	0.0	0.1	0.1
Origination – Low	–	–	0.9	–	11.8	–	12.7
Origination – Average	0.1	–	–	–	0.0	0.8	0.9
Origination – High	–	–	–	–	–	0.3	0.3
Total SMUs	**0.4**	**22.5**	**4.6**	**–**	**12.3**	**1.2**	**41.0**
Distribution of SMUs by %							
	Broadcast	**Print/ OOH**	**Print/ BTL**	**Print/ DM**	**Digital/ Social**	**Strategic/ Research**	**Total % SMUs**
Adaptation – Low	0%	54%	5%	–	0%	–	60%
Adaptation – Average	0%	1%	3%	–	1%	0%	6%
Adaptation – High	–	–	–	–	0%	0%	0%
Origination – Low	–	–	2%	–	29%	–	31%
Origination – Average	0%	–	–	–	0%	2%	2%
Origination – High	–	–	–	–	–	1%	1%
Total % of SMUs	**1%**	**55%**	**11%**	**0%**	**30%**	**3%**	**100%**

ClothingRetailer is an adaptation-focused client with print and digital/social deliverables. It is fairly classified as an "execution" rather than "strategic" client, and its scope of work is more of the "grind-it-out" variety than one that can be credited with moving the brand. Cassandra NY is not the only agency working on the account's brands; it is, though, one of the agencies that is working more at the executional end of things.

This might be okay if the economics of the client made sense, and if the agency people on the account were not being stretched so severely – but in reality, *ClothingRetailer* is paying only $104,549 per SMU, and the creatives are cranking out 8.8 SMUs per head. These are small deliverables – it takes 102 of them to make up one SMU.

However, *ClothingRetailer* pays Cassandra NY $4.3 million in total fees, and of this amount, roughly half contributes to overhead and profits, so *ClothingRetailer* is certainly not to be sniffed at as a client.

Cassandra NY needs to try to propose a higher value SOW with a greater mix of originations designed to influence brand performance. At the same time, though, the overall workload needs to be reduced.

Robby Ferguson, the office's finance director, asked Sarah Greenwood, the *ClothingRetailer* account head, to organize an effort to propose an improved SOW – probably to be implemented in 2019 – for an unchanged fee. Sarah followed through with her client, letting them know that Cassandra NY was reviewing all of its client SOWs, asking for a meeting to discuss a fundamentally restructured SOW for Cassandra's forthcoming work with *ClothingRetailer*.

Her request for this meeting was successful, and a few weeks later, Sarah was able to table a higher-value SOW with a lower workload, making an argument, supported by customer data, that the improved SOW would have a positive impact on store visits and would do a better job of stimulating *ClothingRetailer*'s sales.

The client reacted positively to Sarah's proposal, and this began a dialogue that would continue throughout 2018 and eventually lead to a revised SOW and improved creative mission for Cassandra NY.

Sarah was thrilled with the results. *"Without the SOW diagnosis, we never would have thought to open up the subject of the work we were doing – all our previous efforts were designed to get more money from the client, and this never worked. The new approach gave us a different kind of dialogue, and it certainly will lead to a healthier relationship and a better mix of work."*

TABLE 10-9: PENSIONFUND'S SCOPE OF WORK 2017

PensionFund						
Distribution of Deliverables						
	Broadcast	Print/ OOH	Print/ BTL	Print/ DM	Digital/ Social	Strategic/ Research	Total # Deliverables
Adaptation – Low	26	58	39	–	37	1	161
Adaptation – Average	6	8	20	–	130	10	173
Adaptation – High	–	–	5	–	8	5	18
Origination – Low	2	–	1	–	–	49	52
Origination – Average	13	1	3	–	10	2	28
Origination – High	–	–	–	–	2	46	49
Total Deliverables	46	67	68	–	186	112	480
Distribution of SMUs						
	Broadcast	Print/ OOH	Print/ BTL	Print/ DM	Digital/ Social	Strategic/ Research	Total # SMUs
Adaptation – Low	1.9	3.6	1.3	–	0.4	–	7.2
Adaptation – Average	0.4	–	0.9	–	2.8	0.4	4.4
Adaptation – High	–	–	0.3	–	0.2	0.1	0.7
Origination – Low	0.4	–	0.1	–	–	1.6	2.0
Origination – Average	2.3	0.4	0.6	–	0.7	0.1	4.0
Origination – High	–	–	–	–	0.4	7.9	8.3
Total SMUs	4.9	3.9	3.3	–	4.4	10.2	26.6
Distribution of SMUs by %						
	Broadcast	Print/ OOH	Print/ BTL	Print/ DM	Digital/ Social	Strategic/ Research	Total % SMUs
Adaptation – Low	7%	13%	5%	–	2%	–	27%
Adaptation – Average	1%	–	3%	–	10%	2%	17%
Adaptation – High	–	–	1%	–	1%	1%	2%
Origination – Low	1%	–	0%	–	–	6%	8%
Origination – Average	8%	1%	2%	–	3%	0%	15%
Origination – High	–	–	–	–	1%	30%	31%
Total % of SMUs	18%	15%	12%	0%	17%	38%	100%

PensionFund offers a number of financial products to its customers. Cassandra NY completes a substantial volume of original thinking for the products, as evidenced by 38% of the workload in strategic/research (above). Concurrently, Cassandra carries out a broad range of creative development and production work across broadcast, traditional print, out-of-home, print below-the-line and digital/social – it is very much a fully integrated offering.

What is surprising is the low fee ($2 million), the meagre resources (6 FTEs, of which 2.2 are creatives) and the high workload (480 deliverables for 26.6 SMUs), leading to a very low price ($75,203 per SMU) and high creative output (12 SMUs per creative). Clearly, this is a case where the high volume of separate strategic work is destroying the economics of the business.

Cassandra NY obtained the agreement of the client to re-engineer the SOW by cutting back on the 112-separate strategic/research deliverables and "embedding" the required strategic work in the individual broadcast, print and digital/social deliverables. In doing so, Cassandra was able to reduce its total SMU workload by more than 20% while retaining the same fee – thus improving its economics substantially.

TABLE 10-10: MOVIESTUDIO'S SCOPE OF WORK 2017

MovieStudio						
Distribution of Deliverables						
	Broadcast	Print/ OOH	Print/ BTL	Print/ DM	Digital/ Social	Strategic/ Research	Total # Deliverables
Adaptation – Low	–	180	66	1,337	–	46	1,628
Adaptation – Average	–	–	–	–	–	–	–
Adaptation – High	–	–	–	–	–	–	–
Origination – Low	–	–	–	30	–	6	35
Origination – Average	–	–	–	–	–	–	–
Origination – High	–	–	–	–	–	–	–
Total Deliverables	–	180	66	1,366	–	51	1,663
Distribution of SMUs						
	Broadcast	Print/ OOH	Print/ BTL	Print/ DM	Digital/ Social	Strategic/ Research	Total # SMUs
Adaptation – Low	–	10.2	1.0	41.5	–	0.3	53.0
Adaptation – Average	–	–	–	–	–	–	–
Adaptation – High	–	–	–	–	–	–	–
Origination – Low	–	–	–	3.4	–	0.2	3.5
Origination – Average	–	–	–	–	–	–	–
Origination – High	–	–	–	–	–	–	–
Total SMUs	–	10.2	1.0	44.8	–	0.4	56.6
Distribution of SMUs by %						
	Broadcast	Print/ OOH	Print/ BTL	Print/ DM	Digital/ Social	Strategic/ Research	Total % SMUs
Adaptation – Low	–	18%	2%	73%	–	0%	94%
Adaptation – Average	–	–	–	–	–	–	0%
Adaptation – High	–	–	–	–	–	–	0%
Origination – Low	–	–	–	6%	–	0%	6%
Origination – Average	–	–	–	–	–	–	0%
Origination – High	–	–	–	–	–	–	0%
Total % of SMUs	0%	18%	2%	79%	0%	1%	100%

MovieStudio is a high-volume, low-fee client for Cassandra NY. The work principally involves creative development of low creative complexity adaptations, like direct mail kits (over 1,300 separate deliverables) and a number of outdoor billboards and posters. The agency also supervises the production process for the high volume of produced deliverables.

All in all, the workload is high for the meagre fee of $4 million, covering the efforts of 17 FTEs, of which 6.4 were creatives. Price was only $72,086 per SMU, and the creatives were each generating 8.8 SMUs per head during the year.

Cassandra's management reasoned that they were "killing their people" for an "inadequate fee" and a programme of work that "had no chance to move the client's brands" in a positive direction. Cassandra was really acting like a production studio rather than a strategic partner. Furthermore, their analysis of *MovieStudio* showed that their client was losing share in its marketplace rather than strengthening its position.

Cassandra NY prepared a detailed strategic analysis of *Movie-Studio's* strategic performance – something it had never done in the past – and showed that the agreed scope of work was a low-value effort from which neither *MovieStudio* nor Cassandra NY benefitted. Cassandra was invited to submit its thoughts about a "more substantial SOW" for the coming year, and this was done and approved, leading to a modest reduction in the fee but a substantial reduction in low-end deliverables. Morale on the agency team increased substantially, as the agency was able to carve out some TV and print originations to replace a high percentage of the direct mail kits – some of which the client took in-house and the rest went to a low-cost studio owned by XLS.

Cassandra NY attributed its success in renegotiating its relationship on its strong strategic analysis of MovieStudio's situation and on its longstanding creative reputation in TV and print.

SUMMARY

On the strength of its negotiating successes with its weak clients, Cassandra NY fully committed to a programme of reviewing its SOWs on a routine basis and using the data from ScopeMetrics® to engage clients in discussions designed to improve SOW quality – believing that this would lead to healthier relationships and improved economics for the agency.

In short, Cassandra NY's commitment to improved SOW management opened the door to becoming a more engaged, strategic partner with its clients, seeking to enjoy the improved relationship and economic benefits that such engagement would permit. Henceforth, as a matter of operational policy, Cassandra NY's account heads would take the initiative to propose annual SOWs to its clients, showing how the proposed SOW would help the client achieve its brand performance objectives within a fee framework affordable for the client and fair for Cassandra NY.

When the proposed SOWs exceeded the client's fee budgets, the two parties negotiated cut-down SOWs with fewer deliverables and fewer SMUs, rather than resorting to the previous practice of cutting down on the seniority of the staff or reducing the allocated headcounts. This step went a long way towards assuring both sides that SOW size, appropriate fees and thoughtful allocations of agency people, conducted in a fully transparent way, would safeguard the quality and effectiveness of the agency's annual work.

CHAPTER 11 – THE UNDERMANAGED ADVERTISING AGENCY

"Remember, 'accounting' and 'accountability': nothing in common."

Credit: Leo Cullum / The New Yorker / The Cartoon Bank.

Cassandra New York muscled its way into improving its client relationships in 2017 and 2018, documenting scopes of work and engaging in vigorous client discussions about the amount and type of SOW work needed to improve client performance. SOW data was used internally to document the health or sickness of individual clients. Underpaid and understaffed clients could be clearly identified, and corrective action plans developed and put in place. Management reviewed the agency's performance as a business and enlisted client heads to become more accountable, client by client, to improve agency health.

Before the SOW diagnosis, Cassandra NY had been a victim of chronic fee reductions and arbitrary SOW growth. It had become a commodity-like supplier, fighting for scraps of new business that were paid at rock-bottom prices. Now, though, Cassandra NY felt more like its destiny was in its hands. The agency was committed to actively manage its business. With improved SOW information, and a commitment to improve prices and productivities, Cassandra NY fought its way back into strategic partnerships with its clients and developed pride for its own managerial activism.

Cassandra NY, though, is an anomaly in the industry.

Most advertising agencies are chronically undermanaged, and the degree of undermanagement is serious, leading to a liquidation of agency capabilities and a substantial deterioration in business health. There may be cultural and historical reasons for this undermanagement, but the reasons explain rather than justify inadequate management practices.

WHAT IS "UNDERMANAGEMENT" OF AN AD AGENCY?

An ad agency is a *sport* and a *business*, much like a professional athletic team. The sport is about being *creative and competitive on the playing field*, having fun, beating competitors for new clients, and getting clients to agree to mind-stretching creative concepts. Having the right talent is absolutely critical, along with a bench of up-and-coming players who can be mentored, seasoned and prepared for larger roles.

Agencies love the sport of the advertising business – the incalculable joy of being creative with client brands, the elation of winning new business and awards, and exultation from the industry recognition that goes with winning. The Cannes Festival of Creativity *and* the Super Bowl define peak moments in agency life, one in June and the other in January/February. Between these peaks is the hard work of responding to pitches, negotiating fees and dealing with day-to-day clients and their ongoing issues.

The business of advertising is another matter. It's the logistical end of things, involving fees, costs, profits, headcounts, owners, offices and organization. It's the superstructure on which the agency is built, permitting the sport of advertising to be played comfortably and profitably.

Businesses do not manage themselves. They are affected by the same laws that govern the physical universe, where *entropy increases*, and everything moves towards disorder unless other forces intervene. Unmanaged or undermanaged businesses decay and fail. Competitors steal market share; products lose their edge; prices and fees decline inexorably[1]. Machines run down or wear out; technologies become obsolete; bicycle tires deflate on their own.

What's special about business is the constant addition of management energy into business affairs, designed to halt disorder, oil the machinery (or invent new machines), pump up the leaky tires and keep the enterprise going against all odds. Owners expect management to increase shareholder value every year, without interruption. Management organizes itself to succeed.

Peter Drucker, who made his academic career and professional reputation by defining the *science of management*, described what managers have to do:

- *Business management is no different from the management of other institutions:* it has to manage. And managing is not just passive, adaptive behaviour; it means taking action to make the desired results come to pass.
- *A manager sets objectives.* He or she determines what the objectives should be. She determines what the goals in each area of objective should be. She decides what has to be done to reach these objectives.
- *A basic element in the work of the manager is measurement.* The manager establishes targets and yardsticks – and few factors are as important to the performance of the organization and of every person in it. He or she sees to it that each person has measurements available that are focused on the performance

of the whole organization and that, at the same time, focus on the work of the individual.

- **The manager analyses, appraises, and interprets performance.** *As in all areas of this work, he or she communicates the meaning of the measurements and their findings to subordinates, superiors and colleagues.*[2]

When we examine the business management practices of advertising agencies, we see how short of the mark they fall.

- Most agencies do not document, measure or track the amount and type of work they do.
- Most agencies do not measure or know the price of the work they carry out. (*This is unique among industries in the world, apart from the legal profession.*)
- Most agencies do not measure or know the productivity of their people – how much work each of them actually does.
- Most agencies do not have standards for price or productivity or know in what direction price and productivity are moving.
- Most agencies do not establish measurable objectives for their key executives – other than profit margins. A margin objective can lead to dysfunctional outcomes, like understaffing low-fee, high workload clients in order to hit margin targets.
- Most agencies do not have a culture of management accountability, either within offices or across offices within the agency network. Without accountability, there is no genuine business management.

Kevin Roberts, CEO of Saatchi & Saatchi from 1997 to 2016, described his management philosophy to me during a private meeting in his office in 2014. I was working with Saatchi & Saatchi New York at the time, and with the agency's data in hand, I was making a case for tighter management of SOWs, fees and resources in a management transformation to be led by Kevin and his top management team.

Kevin strongly disagreed with my proposal, and for emphasis he wrote down 112 words, quoted below, which he provided for *Madison Avenue Manslaughter* (which I was then writing). "I'll look like a complete Neanderthal to your readers," he said, "but it will be good for your book."

"We don't believe that anyone can run a first-rate creative shop with organizational diagrams and spreadsheets. That kind of Bain-and-McKinsey stuff would kill our creative capability. A creative agency needs to operate like more like an ant colony, where every ant knows its job and has the freedom to do it. As long as we hire and inspire the right people, to do the right thing, to build our clients' business and market shares, our agency should grow, and our creativity should flourish. If we take another approach, like a typical command-and-control company, we'll end up in the dustbin of mediocrity. I still believe in hiring Mad Men rather than Math Men."

This was a philosophical statement about the *sport of advertising*, not about the *business of advertising*. Kevin believed that *winning at the sport of advertising* would translate into *winning at the business of advertising*. According to this theory, if you foster creativity, and if you succeed in being creative, then you will grow and become profitable. Management's job is to foster creativity. Creativity requires organizational freedom. Consequently, senior management must step aside and focus on getting new clients, leaving others *to define their jobs and use their organizational freedom to do these jobs as they see fit.*

He is certainly not alone in this belief. My experience with the industry confirms that Kevin's "ant colony" management philosophy is an industry standard, not its exception.

Sadly, though, ant colony management has the opposite effect, leading to agency disorder and decay. It's a loser's strategy. An organizational free-for-all and lack of relevant SOW measures lead to a loss of control over pricing and productivity.

Client heads cave in to client demands and agree to do vast quantities of unpaid, out-of-scope work. Creatives are saddled with unmanageable deadlines and volumes of work. "Sorry," they're told, "we don't have enough budget to put more people on the account. You know what procurement is like."

When workloads, prices and productivities are not managed, agencies maintain profit levels through cost reductions and downsizings, and this means getting rid of the senior people who are needed to win at the creative game. Lack of management leads to a liquidation of agency capabilities.

THE AGENCY BUSINESS TRIANGLE

There are three key dimensions in every business – outputs, income and costs. For ad agencies, the outputs are strategies, deliverables and SMUs; the income is fee income from clients (however calculated); the key costs are FTE salaries for client-facing people. All three dimensions need to be understood by agency executives, and from the three dimensions they can derive the three Ps: *Price, Productivity, and Profitability*[3] – that need to be managed proactively. Business management at ad agencies requires price management, productivity management and profitability management.

TABLE 11-1: THE AGENCY BUSINESS TRIANGLE AND THREE PS

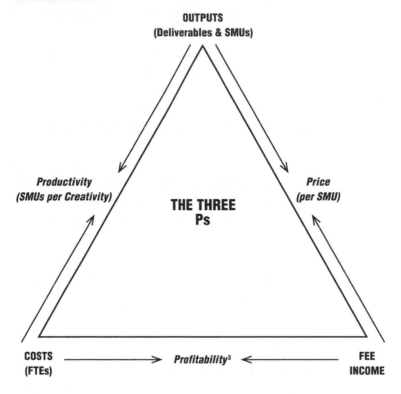

At any point in time, the three dimensions must be in balance. Total costs must be less than income – that's how profits are generated. If fee income is weak, then costs and outputs must be scaled back.

Agencies, as we know, do not have information about outputs (SOW workloads), and consequently, price and productivity cannot be known. Agency executives know client fees and timesheet hours/costs/headcounts (even though timesheet information is at least 30% incomplete or inaccurate). By knowing fees and timesheet information, agency executives can measure client profitability, and client profitability is the single measure that they care about. They are satisfied when they earn 15% operating margins, ignoring the fact that this margin might be generated through serious understaffing of certain clients. Ignorance is bliss, at least for a while.

As long as workloads grow faster than income (or income grows slower than workloads), price will decline. Thus, there is both a "workload imperative" (*get workload under control*) and an "income imperative" (*get paid better for all the work that is done*).

These are not easy problems to solve. *Workload growing faster than income* is the default industry condition:

1. **Advertiser marketing experimentation with new media will continue**. As effective as mass advertising media have been – and nothing has ever matched TV for its ability to reach large audiences – digital media promises mass customization, permitting the possibility of reaching a large number of individual consumers with tailored messages at lower cost with less waste. The hope is that improved targeting will be more effective, leading to improved brand growth. With increased innovation and the evolution of digital technology, experimentation is the name of the game for advertisers. Consequently, marketers will continue to experiment with digital advertising and social engagement programmes without making compensating and equivalent cuts in their traditional media spend. This tendency will drive continued workload growth.

2. **Aggressive procurement practices will continue, and fees will be cut accordingly**. Procurement departments live and breathe cost reduction. They're inclined to see marketing expenditures as *costs* rather than investments. Procurement worships the god of shareholder value. Procurement believes that agencies are fat and profitable. *Overall, procurement is motivated to drive down agency fees and income*. No effective argument has been posited by agencies to neutralize procurement's behaviour. Agencies have not, for example, shown that greater investments in marketing would give

disproportionately greater returns to their clients. Few agencies have made persuasive arguments about the mismatch of fees and workloads. Consequently, procurement's attitudes are set, and they are reinforced at industry conferences. It will take a large effort to change their attitudes and behaviour.

3. **The agency self-image as a *"provider of creativity"* will continue**. The *creativity paradigm* leads agencies to focus on "creativity" as their relevant output rather than on the growing tangible volume of work that they actually produce. If agencies could see themselves instead as *"creative developers and producers of marketing deliverables,"* they might have a greater sensitivity about workload volumes. Instead, they are allergic to the idea that they are "delivering measurable stuff." As a result, they don't measure how much stuff they commit to or how much stuff they do. Continuation of the allergy will surely favour the continued growth of agency workloads faster than income. It will take not only executive energy but a change of mindset to reverse this trend.

Agency turnaround plans must be developed by agency top management teams and carried out with vigor throughout their agencies, with a goal to develop the full support and engagement of client heads and their client service teams. This will not be easy, since these plans will require an executive leadership style that has little precedent in most agencies' history. The requirement for senior executives to *manage agency operations* with a tougher mindset is inconsistent with the laissez-faire style associated with *agency self-organization*, which has been the traditional way agencies have been run to date.

Leadership style is not the only challenge. There is a "followership" challenge as well, in that agency people are used to being unmanaged rather than being reviewed and held accountable. Agency executives may initiate a new style of leadership, but getting agency people to follow will be difficult. The most important required followers are client heads and their client

147

service teams. Today, these folks have a lot of latitude to do whatever they want and define their jobs in whatever way they wish, subject only to client requirements. They will resist management efforts. The resistance will be partly intellectual (*tight management will kill our creative culture*) and mostly self-serving, since they will not like the prospect of being managed. They're quite prepared to be managed by their clients, and to salute when a client needs something, but they can be expected to resist when their own executives try to tighten things up.

Let's not, then, view this as an easy turnaround. Agency executives will have their hands full. They will need to charge ahead without wavering, reward those who follow, and deal with those who resist in a firm way.

THE HEAVY LEGACY OF BILL BERNBACH

The agency allergy to measuring work has a long history, but we only have to go back to the early 1960s to find a grand figure who not only wrote about it but may have influenced several generations of agency executives.

The grand historical figure is none other than Bill Bernbach.

Bill Bernbach (1911-1982), the renowned founder of Doyle Dane Bernbach (DDB), has a special place in industry history for his creative innovations on behalf of Volkswagen, Avis and Alka-Seltzer – ads that were the backbone of the Creative Revolution, described in Chapter 2.

He is also remembered for his quotations, which surely helped to establish the *culture of creativity* that continues to dominate agencies today:

- *"Properly practiced creativity must result in greater sales more economically achieved. Properly practiced creativity can lift your claims out of the swamp of sameness and make them accepted, believed, persuasive, urgent."*
- *"Nobody counts the number of ads you run; they just remember the impression you make*[4]*."*

The 1950's and 1960's world of Bill Bernbach no longer exists, but the Creative Revolution still shapes agency thinking even though *creative* advertising is no longer the novelty it was 50- to- 60 years ago. TV advertising is just as likely to be skipped as ignored by today's ad-weary consumers. Agency prices are only 25% of what they were during The Golden Age; doing unlimited work is no longer economically feasible.

The fact that nobody counts the number of ads that an agency completes is regrettable. One can't really blame Bill Bernbach for this – what he meant was obvious and relevant for the Creative Revolution time period. However, the advertising industry has since moved on, and the fact that ads are not counted or measured is now a major strategic problem.

ADVERTISER VS. AD AGENCY MANAGEMENT CULTURES

The enemy is *"workload growing faster than income."* The advertisers' teams are well-organized and relentless. Among other things, marketing and procurement executives get together at ANA conferences and share *"best practices."* These *best practices* focus (in part) on cost-reduction subjects, including how to reduce agency fees, what kind of benchmarks to use, whether or not to establish internal ad agencies, whether or not to take production responsibilities away from agencies, and many others. The discussions certainly have the effect of stiffening the backbones of marketing and procurement executives, making them stronger and tougher when they think about negotiating with their ad agency partners. Furthermore, these executives work and operate in cost-conscious, performance-focused corporate cultures where accountability is a fact of life, and reviews of performance are routine. A certain amount of tough-mindedness flourishes in corporate settings.

This does not mean that advertisers are well-organized and disciplined in their day-to-day dealings with agencies. On the contrary: advertiser briefing and ad approval processes are often very poor, and SOW planning processes are almost non-existent. Months can pass before contracts are signed, and out-of-scope deliverables pop out of nowhere, like dandelions on an uncut lawn.

This kind of disorganization should not fool agencies into thinking that advertiser cultures are disorganized and undisciplined. To the contrary, there's a lot of corporate backbone throughout the marketing and procurement organizations. Client disorganization, such as it is, allows clients to get something for nothing. There's more method to madness in their disorganization.

Agencies' organizations and cultures could not be more different from their clients'.

Accountability for agency operations is fragmented. Each office in a network is a separate profit centre. Each department in an office self-defines its missions. Creative heads focus on creativity; finance directors focus on headcounts, overhead and budgeted/actual costs and profits; client heads manage the service that they provide to their 'disorganized' clients and keep them coming back for more. (Despite this, there seem to be very *few* happy clients.)

Managing service levels means a number of things: obtaining internal or freelance resources when workloads require additional capacity; rescheduling deliverables; handling rework; agreeing to new client SOW priorities, including new or repositioned work – but client heads do not really manage SOWs in a proactive way. They do not, as a rule, hold the line on scope creep. They respond. They mobilize their teams to deliver whatever they have to deliver. For many client heads, this is the essence of their job: appeasing their demanding, disorganized and grumpy clients. The miracle is that they achieve this in the face of resource constraints. The downside of the miracle is that their success is killing their own agencies.

Their "bosses" – the agency, regional and office CEOs – leave them alone, for the most part. They do not review their performance. They do not discuss SOWs. For the most part, their bosses are out in the marketplace, drumming up new business, seeking new clients as a way to shore up growth and deliver promised revenue and profits to the holding company.

Who is responsible for an agency's operational response to growing workloads and declining fees? In today's agency culture, it's everyone ... and no one. The agency management culture is fragmented and divided. Everyone does their own thing. An integrated counter-attack is hard to organize, and in practice, it simply does not happen. At the end of the year, the finance director has the ultimate responsibility to deliver the agency's profit margin, and this is often done through cost reductions – a blunt instrument, indeed, but the laissez-faire culture does not allow for much fine-tuning during the year.

The agency management culture is a barrier to change.

It is virtually unchanged from the management culture of more than 50 years ago, reinforced by the Creative Revolution, when the agencies were rich and the creative departments accepted no masters. Agencies could operate as businesses without much active management as long as they could keep their commission-paying clients and add a few new ones every year.

Agencies retain a perverse but understandable pride in the unmanaged culture that is associated with "being creative."

Although agencies have seen considerable changes in their operating environments – the rise of holding companies, the change from commissions to fees, the empowerment of procurement, the globalization of client relationships, the development of new digital and social media and the fragmentation of their client relationships – they have been constant in their commitment to self-organizing management cultures that celebrate creative departments and allow other individuals to define their own rules and priorities.

How does self-organizing actually work in the typical agency? We know what the creatives and production people do. What do the other "ants" do?

CLIENT HEADS AND CLIENT SERVICE TEAMS

Collectively, client heads and client service executives are the custodians of 100% of agency income. They approve 100% of the agency's strategic and creative workloads, and they use 100% of the billable capacity assigned to them.

Client heads have vague and unwritten job descriptions. This was not the case during the commission era, when a client head's clear mission was to get the client to spend large amounts of money on commission-paid media. The change from commission-based remuneration to fee-based remuneration change was momentous for client heads – they ceased to be media salesmen on behalf of the agency. Today, it is assumed that client heads understand their revised responsibilities, which can be described as *"please your clients, hang on to client income, and do the best you can to deal with client demands and disorganization."*

This definition captures what has been a long, slow decline in agency responsibilities for client heads. Client heads and their client service colleagues were previously the activist and aggressive "owners" of their commission-paying clients during The Golden Age, fighting off all client attempts to cut media spend or bring in other agencies. Since then, client heads have lost a lot of their aggression, and since the change from commission-based to fee-based remuneration, no one has quite redefined what their new muscular roles ought to be.

Furthermore, client service responsibilities have become divided, especially after 1980, first through the widespread adoption of a British innovation, "account planning". Agencies created "account planners," who were tasked to do a better job of bringing consumer insights into advertising – a role in which client service people were deemed not to be sufficiently expert. Account planning (today called strategic planning) was brought to the US by Jay Chiat in the 1980s and spread throughout the industry. Strategic planners number approximately 20 FTEs for every 80 to 100 client service FTEs. The strategic planning innovation reduced the responsibilities of client service executives and put strategic planners at centre stage with respect to advertising development.

More recently, client service responsibilities have been divided again through the creation of agency project managers, who are believed to do a better job "project-managing client work through the agency." Project managers were a recent (post-2000) response to the chaotic and costly way that client work was being shepherded through agencies' creative and production departments. This type of coordination used to be solely the responsibility of client service people, and it gave them bully rights over the creative and production departments – account managers were the guys and gals who pushed the work through these overworked departments.

No more, at least at this writing. Agencies hope that project managers and project management systems will bring some order to the flow of workload through the agency (the jury is out on this issue, as best I can tell – project managers have even less accountability than client service people).

Client heads and their client service teams, then, have been downsized and downgraded over the past decades – responding to changes in remuneration and to perceptions that their generalist skills were not quite good enough to deal with advertising research and project management.

In the current era of big data, the perception that client service people are not quite up to the analytical task has a new twist. At the March 2014 4A's conference in Los Angeles, advertisers and agencies sparred over agency access to clients' brand data. Clients expressed concerns that agencies "could not be trusted" with this sensitive data. Others expressed concerns that agencies were insufficiently analytical. "It's not the data itself that's the advantage," said a Google executive. "It's the insights." That only works if agencies have the skills to derive insights from data. "My challenge to agencies is to say, 'Use my data to be proactive,'" said one CMO. "But I struggle and worry you don't have the talent." (Marketers, Agencies, Google Spar Over Brands' Precious Data, 2014)

What client heads and their client service teams are left with today is "servicing the client and responding to demands," doing their best to manage client expectations and needs for creative and analytical work.

It is assumed that "doing their best" will generate profits, but client heads and their teams are under no "do or die" imperative to ensure that profits are 15% or greater. Each client head can make excuses for why targeted profits cannot be earned:

- *The fee was set by the holding company or the CEO. I can't do anything about it.*
- *The contract profitability is for 10%, not 15%. I can't change the contract.*
- *The client will only pay for an agency team of 15 FTEs, and that's it – they won't pay for the 20 we need.*
- *My job is to get the work done within these limits.*

Clients put unmanageable constraints on agency performance, acting like spoiled children at a party. Agency client heads are like nannies or babysitters who believe that the brats and the party are beyond saving. It's easier to give in than to fight. It's also less risky. Who wants to lose a client over an argument? Who wants to lose a job?

Each client head has fully delegated authority to manage his/her clients in any way that he/she sees fit. Each can approve out-of-scope work, whether or not it is paid for, and use agency resources, whether or not their costs are covered by client fees. They can plan SOWs or let their clients plan them for them. They can negotiate aggressively or simply give the client the service that the client wants. They can manage their resources tightly or loosely.

In the meantime, in background, strategic planners go about their job, helping to bridge the gap between clients and agency creatives on consumer research matters, while project managers help to schedule and push the workload through the various agency departments.

However client heads handle their client situations, they can be sure that what they do today will be relatively invisible to senior agency executives.

The way that client heads go about their management job is not measured or reviewed. There are no metrics other than profit margin to differentiate between who is doing a good job and who is not. There are no standards for the client head. There is no defined "*Agency Way*" for managing clients. The job is left up to the individual initiatives of the client heads, who carry out their responsibilities without a rule book, set of standards or measures.

Client heads are responsive to clients and generally unresponsive to agency initiatives that interfere with their freedoms. Client heads are not interested in transparency. They do not want their actions exposed and visible. They simply want the freedom to act and service. If they do a good job keeping the client on board, they create job security for themselves.

This is the agency culture, developed and reinforced for more than 50 years. Client heads each "run" part of the agency, and the total agency is simply the sum of their actions, whether or not the actions are known and whether or not the actions are strategically good for the agency. Client heads do not wish to make trade-offs or to say "no" to their clients in order to promote agency interests. To do so would represent a major change in attitude and a shift in the centre of gravity away from client interests towards agency interests.

No one is telling them that this is what must happen.

CHAPTER 12 –
THE RESULTS-FOCUSED AGENCY

"Good news—I hear the paradigm is shifting."

Credit: Charles Barsotti / The New Yorker / The Cartoon Bank.

D uring the Creative Revolution in the 60s and 70s, highly creative agency work was designed to drive client product growth rates, and to do a better job than the hard-sell 'unique selling proposition' (USP) ads that had been current in the industry.

This strategy was successful and agencies were well-rewarded for their efforts – clients spent growing amounts on media, and agencies reaped growing income from their 15% media commissions and from winning new clients. All the evidence from this period, about 50 years ago, suggests that the Creative Revolution was successful in delivering results and rewarding agencies at the same time. New highly-creative agencies like Wells Rich Green (1966) entered the market and took clients away from their less creative competitors; industry growth rates were strong, driven by higher client media spends, and during this period, many agencies went public, based on strong and growing top and bottom lines. Creativity was unique and highly visible; agencies perceived as highly creative were "hot" and in demand.

However, the worlds of 1960 and of 2019 are very different. We've had nearly 60 plus years of these *creative* ads; the originality of this type of creativity is long since gone. What might have been seen to be "edgy" and creative in the 1960s would be "ho-hum" today. In the current era, too, the media mix is much more diverse, and the amounts spent on creative experimentation – mostly through social and digital media – are very large and diffuse. The volume of creative output has grown exponentially. We're well beyond the time when pure creativity could be focused on television advertising and deliver dramatic changes in brand results. It's now harder to assess the impact of creative efforts; creativity is one of many factors that drives success. Advertisers are increasingly concerned about the need to identify *all* the factors that drive marketing ROI. The development of tools to measure ROI is a current preoccupation, and the large investment in digital marketing has both accelerated the preoccupation and provided hope that through the magic of "big data" ROI solutions can and will be found.

The corporate obsession with "shareholder value" is a major factor, and it gives further urgency to the quest to find marketing ROI solutions. Advertisers want to make sure that marketing expenditures contribute to the realization of increased shareholder value. John Wanamaker's observation that *"Half the money I spend on advertising is wasted; the trouble is I don't know which half"* begs, with increasing urgency, for the need to find and eliminate the non-value-adding half. Procurement ignores the theoretical 50/50 split between wasted and non-wasted expenditures and attacks, with vigor, all fee expenditures, particularly the expenditure on agency fees. Procurement defines agency fees as "non-working costs," along with the out-of-pocket spend on production costs. The only marketing costs defined as "working costs" are media costs – the spend on media designed to reach consumers. Working costs are better than non-working costs, in their view, but all marketing costs are suspect.

Procurement people are skeptical about current levels of marketing costs – they believe, as an article of faith, that all marketing expenditures are chronically inflated and excessive. Supporting their skepticism is a belief that agencies have done very little to provide results-based arguments to defend the effectiveness of agency contributions and the reasonableness of agency fees.

Traditional agencies (in particular) continue to highlight *creativity* as their most distinguishing characteristic. Since this speaks less to client concerns, their bragging about creativity is really an inwardly focused narcissistic exercise that distracts agencies from more relevant client priorities. We've discussed this subject in previous chapters. Our argument is not over the need for creativity in agency work. Creativity is to ads as product quality is to cars, airplanes and electronic equipment – it's absolutely necessary, and it needs to be built-in to the product, but it is not the only factor that matters, and it hardly provides sustainable differentiation from one agency to another. True, one agency will be "hot" for a given period and will grow and win business, but then the wheel turns, and the hot creative agencies of today become targets for other upstarts – like Droga5, 72andSunny, or Anomaly – and are eventually superseded in the same way that professional tennis stars are eventually vanquished at the US Open or Wimbledon. The great bulk of the actual creative work in the industry is done by non-hot agencies, in any case, and hot agencies are more notable for the amount of trade-press ink that is devoted to their hotness than for their actual impact in the marketplace.

Agencies need to refocus on their clients' needs and acknowledge that the creative paradigm does not deliver the same kind of dramatic brand results that it did 60 years ago. Its value has declined substantially if we measure it by the average price that clients are prepared to pay. If pure creativity continued to deliver the kind of results that it did in the past, then agencies would be paid much more than they currently are – improved client results would most certainly justify higher agency fees.

Agencies need to refocus their thinking and *to organize themselves to maximize the probability that their work will generate improved results for clients*, aligning themselves with their clients' preoccupation with *increased shareholder value*. We believe that this will require a very substantial change in the way agencies organize and think about themselves, particularly in the way that senior agency executives define their roles and the way that client heads and their colleagues in client service employ their skills and carry out their responsibilities, particularly with respect to SOW matters. It means that "creativity" can no longer serve as the rallying cry or key factor by which agencies identify themselves to clients, potential clients and their own people.

What does it mean for agencies to *organize themselves to maximize the probability that their work will generate improved results*? It's one small step short of organizing themselves to *guarantee* results, because guarantees are simply not possible. It's a giant step away from thinking only about being a good service provider and being creative. Instead, it's a giant step towards creating intimate strategic partnerships with each client, basing them on mutual commitments to seek improved results and increase shareholder value.

Agencies need to initiate the creation of *marketing and strategic performance partnerships* that see themselves and their clients as co-equal partners, each with specific responsibilities and roles, each of them committed to finding successful, results-generating marketing paths for the advertisers' brands.

Shared commitment. The commitment is best captured in a short document that could be called "principles of a relationship between [agency] and [advertiser]" (fill in the appropriate names) and signed by the two parties to indicate that it is a contract of mutual expectations. The document should be structured around a number of key governing assumptions:

1. **Focus on results**. The relationship is designed and structured to bring about improved market performance for advertisers relative to their current and potential customers at the expense of their competitors. This means, in the most general terms, improved growth and profitability, gains in market shares and strengthened brand equities.

   Some baseline brand strategic analysis is required at the beginning of a results-focused relationship, answering the following kinds of questions:

   - Why are our brands performing the way they do today? What is the source of business? Customers' perceptions? Competitors' strengths and weaknesses? What explains our current performance?
   - How much better could the brands perform if certain things happened? If we penetrated new segments or new markets? If we developed new products? If we had a different media mix and spend level? If our scope of work was constructed differently?
   - What would it cost to go down the new path? What could be achieved at lesser levels of spend?
   - What plan should we jointly commit to?

2. **Become a partner**. In these relationships, ad agencies are the advertiser's "marketing and strategic performance partners," expected to propose, deliver and execute marketing communications that have the highest probability of achieving agreed performance-improving goals.

3. **Make a mutual commitment**. Each party has an expectation that their relationship will become a committed, long-term relationship that will endure by virtue of the value and satisfaction that it generates for both parties.

4. **Structure for flexibility**. The relationship will be structured for flexibility and experimentation. The route to marketing success in today's environment involves thoughtful judgments about what *should* work, with ongoing experimentation and constant adjustment to exploit what can be learned. As a result,

the relationship must be structured to permit fast, flexible and committed adjustments to agreed marketing plans.

Respective and joint responsibilities. In addition to accepting these key assumptions, agencies and their clients need to clarify their respective and joint responsibilities. A non-exhaustive list might look like the following:

1. *Joint development of an understanding of the strategic and operational situations (positions) of brands and products.* Advertisers and agencies must develop a shared, equal and transparent understanding of the current strategic and operational situation of the advertisers' brands and products. These strategic and operational situations define the starting point for marketing performance improvement programmes.

    Advertisers need to involve agencies in the development of brand marketing analyses and plans, and to share, on an ongoing basis, the content of their final brand strategic and operational plans. It is within these documents that advertisers document and communicate to *their top management* what their brand situations are and how management intends to work its way out of them through investments in marketing and sales. An unfortunate trend during the past decade has been "keeping agencies in the dark" and dealing with them at arm's length about a number of key things, like brand strategic analyses and operational plans. Today, this tendency manifests itself in a number of ways, like not sharing customer "big data" with ad agencies, either on the assumption that agencies cannot be trusted with this confidential data or that they are not sufficiently competent to use it and add value with it. The lack of trust is only understandable in an environment where advertisers change agencies with greater frequency and more whimsically than they did in the past. In our proposed scheme, agencies are changed only if there is a significant failure in the relationship, so the notion that confidential information cannot be exchanged is moot.

2. *Joint development of high-probability action plans for brands and products.* Advertisers and agencies must jointly develop and agree on proposed action plans for each brand and product. These proposed action plans should have, in the shared judgment of the advertiser and agency, the highest probability of delivering marketing success. The plans, of course, will need to be tried out in the marketplace and adjusted on the basis of market feedback and actual experience. Action plans can include the development of new products, new pricing strategies, expanded distribution, new messaging to consumers, revised media mixes, or a host of other marketing possibilities. *"What actions will best drive improved growth and profitability?"* ought to be the dominant question.

Key phrases are "shared judgment" and "highest probability." Marketing involves an expenditure of today's dollars for an uncertain future outcome, just like any other business investment. How should marketing dollars be spent? What data, experience and judgment can be brought to bear to increase the odds of success? What is the expected outcome? On what key assumptions does an improved outcome rely? Advertisers and agencies bring different perspectives and skills when addressing these questions. Better that each party work with the other to resolve the uncertainties than for each to work independently, or even worse, for the advertiser to work solo on the problem and then direct the agency to execute.[1]

3. *Joint development of relevant SOWs for brand action plans.* Advertisers, of course, ultimately approve and fund fiscal year SOWs involving media costs, agency fees and production budgets. Their own budgetary processes require them to do this *before* the beginning of their fiscal year – in October and November for fiscal years that begin on January 1, for example. All too often, agency fee and production budgets are determined by advertisers *before* detailed SOW campaigns and deliverables are planned for the year. Detailed SOW planning is completed *after the fact*, tailored to fit the advertiser's agreed budget figures, rather than the other way around.

Agencies complain, nearly halfway through a fiscal year that *"We have still not signed a contract with the client, and it's already May!"* This is not because there are no client budgets. The budgets exist. The unsigned contracts are a symptom that the SOWs have not been planned in detail – they're being handled on an ad hoc basis. The agency is supposed to show its flexibility by reacting to any and all SOW initiatives as they come up. The result is unfunded scope creep, workloads that stretch agency resources, agency resentment and below-standard creative work.

These are not circumstances that drive the development of high-quality SOWs or, for that matter, high-quality relationships. Ad hoc SOW planning puts an advertiser in a dominant, 'superior' position and its agency in a submissive, victim-like role. The resulting work is less effective than it could be, and resentments build up in both parties. Agencies in this situation await the day when their clients will "finally get their act together," but they wait in vain.

Instead, agencies need to play an active role and work on an early, joint basis to propose SOWs that they believe will make a difference to brand performance. The time to do this is long before advertisers begin their internal budgeting deliberations over media costs, agency fees and production costs. To do this well requires agency sophistication and in-depth understanding of the client's brands' competitive and marketplace dynamics, derived from an immersion in consumer, market and competitive data. It's the kind of analysis that used to be done routinely by senior agency client service executives during the media-commission days, when the clear market imperative was increased media spend – clients who outspent their competitors saw increased sales and market share gains. Since then, though, as the marketplace has become significantly more complicated and the commission system dropped, agency account executives have ironically retreated into more passive "servicing roles," and their analytical capabilities have withered on the vine. Analytical and planning capabilities can and must be rekindled.

The principles of a relationship document ought to specify that agencies be responsible for proposing relevant annual SOW deliverables for an agreed media mix. The SOW should be first prepared on a budget-blind basis, as if there were no realistic budget constraints – the focus should be more on "what kind of returns might we expect if we carried out this proposed SOW at this proposed cost." The proposed SOW should be designed to "implement the agreed action plans" through carefully-tailored mixes of marketing communications deliverables across media disciplines. Later, if budget constraints require a more modest programme, the SOW can be cut down to size.

4. *Calculating agency staffing and fees for SOWs.* Agencies should propose appropriate, skilled and sufficient staffing headcounts and seniority mixes by department for the proposed SOWs, using agreed and transparent "resource standards" for each type of project in the SOWs, taking into account the total volume of work proposed. SMUs must be the key driver of agency resources on the basis of clear, transparent and jointly-agreed metrics.

Once agency resources are proposed, appropriate fees can be calculated.

Determining agency headcounts and fees from SOWs turns on its head the current practice where clients first establish agency fees and thus dictate agency headcounts without first establishing the quantity and type of work to be done. This practice, as we showed with The Cassandra Agency, sees agencies "staffing to fee" rather than "staffing to workloads," leaving them with inadequate resources to handle growing workloads.

5. *Tracking SOW adjustments throughout the year.* SOWs will be adjusted during the year as advertisers and their agencies receive market feedback and adjust and optimize marketing communications to improve results. The greater proportion of digital marketing in the SOW mix should put SOW development on a more experimental basis. Even though a great deal of thought may have gone into the original SOW planning, the

marketplace harbours mysteries and uncertainty, as consumers themselves adjust and evolve their purchasing behaviour in line with the evolution of new marketing technologies. The marketplace needs to be learned and relearned as it evolves. Social and mobile marketing are, at this time of writing, still relatively unproven, but with the passage of time, increased effectiveness can surely be expected. Increased experimentation across all marketing technologies will yield insights into what works best, and SOW development will become an ongoing process of planning, measuring and adjusting.

SOW changes will need to be tracked and measured, and the associated changes in agency resources and fees can then be made on a regular (say quarterly) basis. New deliverables will be added or changed; selected planned deliverables can be dropped. SOWs can be handled in a very dynamic way without changing overall fee budgets if the sum of all added and changed work is matched by the sum of all cancelled or dropped work. The more robust the tracking and measuring process, the more dynamic this process can be.

What inhibits experimentation today, at least from an agency perspective, is the underlying belief that SOW changes are synonymous with unpaid scope creep, which is detrimental for agency performance. Agencies will be unenthusiastic and passive participants in the SOW-experiment game as long as they feel as that they are carrying the costs and receiving no benefits. By contrast, the joint use of a robust SOW tracking system brings courage and commitment to SOW experimentation, and agencies, rather than passively resisting experimentation, can become enthusiastic participants.

6. *Eliminating process inefficiencies and non-value-added costs.* Both parties must commit to running a lean and efficient relationship with a minimum of unnecessary rebriefing, rework and other related inefficiencies that raise costs and undermine the ability of the relationship to perform as required to deliver improved results. Metrics like "mutually acceptable rework rates" and

"number of ideas to be generated (for this type of brief)" and "number of creative teams to be used" need to be developed, agreed and used to measure relationship efficiencies on an ongoing basis.

Often, the source of process inefficiencies lies with the advertiser, who may have poor briefing and hierarchical ad approval processes. Poor briefings lead to off-brief work and rework; hierarchical ad approval processes involve delays and high levels of rework as each "approver" up the chain of command adds individual changes to submitted creative work. High rework rates, of course, add a creative burden to already-stretched agency creative resources and, in the end, foster lower rather than higher creative quality.

Procurement departments understand, in general, the deleterious effects of process inefficiencies, and in their usual professional dealings with manufacturing and distribution suppliers, they work diligently to eliminate inefficiencies. Somehow, though, this particular discipline did not migrate to advertiser-agency relationships when procurement first became involved, and both advertisers and agencies continued to live with one another in a way that tolerated if not exalted the reworking and continued reworking of creative work to "get it right." As laudatory as it is to be committed to overworking creative work until it is "exactly right," how much better to be committed to "getting it right and approved as soon as possible" and have an open dialogue with advertisers about what is required to bring this about.

Procurement departments, instead of investing in an effort to understand the "advertising process" and finding ways to eliminate relationship waste, fall back on pure fee-cutting, on the assumption that if agencies have less in the way of fees, agencies themselves will find ways to become more efficient. What this ignores, though, are two things: 1) agencies are absolutely terrible at managing their own processes, having no leadership, experience or capabilities to do so, and 2) the existence of briefing and ad approval process inefficiencies within advertisers' own marketing departments, which are invisible because SOW deliverables are not documented, tracked or measured. Fee-cutting does not reduce process inefficiencies; instead, it simply stretches resources further as workloads grow.

Briefing and ad approval inefficiencies are not the only inefficiencies that exist. Most agency contracts are written as labour-based contracts, which means that fees are calculated on the basis of a certain number of agreed agency man-hours for the fiscal year. In fact, agency man-hours are what advertisers are contractually buying rather than brand strategic studies and advertisements. As a reflection of this, many if not most advertiser-agency contracts are written as "reconcilable contracts," meaning that agency man-hours are audited, usually by the advertisers' internal audit departments, and if agencies deliver *fewer* man-hours than contracted, for whatever reason, they have to refund a portion of their fees; if agencies deliver *more* man-hours than contracted, they are entitled to more fees. This latter case is often not respected, though, since advertisers often argue that time sheet hour overage is simply due to agency "inefficiency." The agency process of delivering correct time sheet information and justifying overages or underages is extremely time-consuming for both parties. In the end, no one is satisfied with the results, because the principal argument, *"we did more/less work than forecasted"* falls on deaf ears when there are no specific workload measures.

The auditing of time sheet hours is a time wasting process that can be eliminated if contracts focus on paying agencies for deliverables rather than for man-hours.

7. *Mutual support of the relationship.* A relationship focused on achieving results requires strong leadership from both parties. Relationships of this nature are negotiated at very high organizational levels, but the troops below the generals don't always get the word, and it is a normal feature of organizational life that junior people on both sides of the divide find ways

to engage in conflicts and torture one another in minor and annoying ways. Leadership is required to ensure that petty conflicts or the pursuit of selfish interests from within their respective organizations are not permitted to interfere or sabotage the joint aspirations and goals of the relationship.

Within advertisers, this will require a balancing of the sometimes-competing interests of marketing and procurement, on the one hand, and between corporate marketing and local marketing organizations, on the other hand. The competing interests of marketing and procurement are easy to identify – marketing wants agencies to do more work at no extra cost, and procurement wants agencies' fees cut on a regular basis. Part of what has made advertiser-agency relationships increasingly dysfunctional over time has stemmed from this dynamic, which has led to agencies doing more work for less money with fewer resources. The resentment that this generates is incompatible with the needs of a performance-focused relationship. Marketing and procurement need to eliminate their inherent conflicts by changing the way agency contracts are structured, focusing on deliverables rather than hours.

The competing interests of corporate marketing and local marketing are of an entirely different nature, but they can severely sabotage the results-focused relationship. The conflict is over relative power. The type of advertiser-agency relationship we envision puts relatively more power in the hands of central marketing departments, since they have a larger say over agency SOWs, particularly for global relationships, and in global relationships this means "*more originations developed in the centre (rather than locally), with adaptations handled locally.*" The relative power of local marketing organizations to direct agency ad origination is diminished, inevitably. In the worst cases, local marketing organizations refuse to play under the new rules, insisting on their right to direct local agency operations and to ignore centrally generated advertising work that they do not feel is appropriate for their markets.

Local agencies are all too willing to get sucked into this power-play, since they have many of the same resentments about being consigned to second-rate status by the agency centre. There are few compromises that can satisfy the bruised egos that are created when the centre takes more responsibility and power. Corporate and agency senior leaders must clearly communicate to their local operations that there is a new way of playing the game, and that instances of non-compliance will not be tolerated. Eventually, the new roles will become the old rules, and a new equilibrium can be established.

Agencies have built-in conflicts of their own. Agencies are organizationally federations of individual profit-centre offices rather than portfolios of clients that happen to be served by multiple offices. Office heads and office finance directors seek to maximize office profit margins as a first priority; being "good global client providers" is farther down the list. Offices understandably find it hard to make financial sacrifices for global clients that they merely service rather than run. Within agencies, leadership is required to ensure that the sometimes-selfish profit-centre motives and behaviours of individual offices within the network are subordinated to the needs and interests of results-focused relationships. Strong leadership from agency CEOs on this issue needs to be made for the record and reinforced on an ongoing basis.

Finally, the senior leaders of advertisers and agencies have a responsibility to ensure the success of one another in their joint efforts to make these types of relationships a success. Conflicts must be smoothed out; junior executives and local organizations must be brought into line; procurement and marketing must find a way to work together to ensure relationship efficiency and fair compensation; and agencies must focus their creative efforts on advertising that works in the marketplace for the benefit of their clients.

CHAPTER 13 –
MEASUREMENT OF
SCOPES OF WORK

A Critique of Pure Reason

This is boring.

PAUL NOTH

Credit: Paul Noth / The New Yorker / The Cartoon Bank.

I have not yet discussed where SMUs come from – how they were developed in the first place, and how agencies and advertisers can use them on their own to develop SOW management disciplines and create improved relationships.

HISTORY

An early ad agency consulting assignment was in 1992, when Farmer & Company was asked, in its capacity as a strategy consulting firm, to help determine why Tea & Crumpets UK (T&C),

the London office of a (disguised name) major global advertising agency, had rather suddenly become unprofitable. The CEO responded to the profit problem with a number of extraordinary steps, including moving T&C's office to a new, low-cost location, while reducing overheads and freezing salaries and bonuses. Still, operating margins hovered at 5%, which was then half of the desired level. Something in T&C's internal operations was awry, and the CEO thought that a strategy consultant might help to uncover the reasons.

After some initial interviews and a review of industry and agency data, we learned that our client had enjoyed a long period of media price inflation from about 1975 to 1990, and that the increased revenues from inflating media prices allowed the office to invest in additional costs to provide increased services for clients, like strategic planning and research services – in the hope that these increased services would somewhat mollify client resentment over the "free revenue ride" the agency enjoyed from media price inflation.

By 1990, fee-based remuneration was replacing media commissions, and this drove revenue downward. Logically, T&C's managing director could have reduced costs and services at a fast rate to match the reductions in revenue, but he found that cost and service *reductions* were a lot harder to implement than cost and service *increases* – services for clients could not simply be turned off like a faucet. Furthermore, he was not sure that his problem was chronic and long term. He did not want to take draconian cost reduction steps at a time when his profit problem might disappear as mysteriously as it appeared. Consequently, the steps he took to reduce costs and services lagged his revenue reductions, and office margins were squeezed.

This was our hypothesis about the situation, and in graphic form it looked like Table 13-1, next page.

TABLE 13-1: THE CHANGING PRICE AND COST PATTERNS

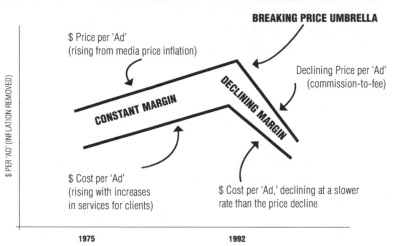

This generic pattern of price and cost behaviour had been char-acterized as the "*breaking price umbrella*" by The Boston Consult-ing Group in one of Bruce Henderson's "Perspectives" in 1968.[1]

If our hypothesis was right – that this was an example of a breaking price umbrella – then T&C had few remedies other than accelerated cost reduction. The challenge would be to determine how this could be done without crippling agency operations.

The hypothesis could be verified if the right price and cost data could be gathered and analysed. The *right data*, though, was *unit price data (price per ad)* and *unit cost data (cost per ad)*, and this required an understanding of the *number of units (number of ads)* being developed and produced by the agency. We couldn't simply count up the TV, radio and print ads for each year, since each type of ad was unique in its own way. A TV ad was not the same as a print ad in terms of the amount of work (man-hours) involved in its development and production. TV ads were "bigger" than print ads. In addition, each ad in each medium was either an original piece of work or an adaptation of previously developed work, and within these two categories there were at least three different levels of creative complexity (low, average and high) based on how original the work needed to be. High creative complexity ads were 100% original and took more time and used more creative resources than low creative complexity ads, which were based on ideas from existing ad campaigns.

TABLE 13-2: CREATIVE COMPLEXITY DEFINITIONS ORIGINATIONS AND ADAPTATIONS

	Originations	Adaptations
High Creative Complexity:	Associated with new strategic briefs, requiring many (3+) new creative routes as outlined in a new creative brief. Typically this is for a new product, a launch, a relaunch or a line extension. These could be characterized as "here's something entirely new and original."	Complete change to two thirds of script/sound/copy, storyboard/layout, or footage/image.
Average Creative Complexity:	Secondary/ongoing deliverables from an existing strategic brief, but involving a new creative brief requiring at least 1-2 creative routes. These could be characterized as "something new, but in line with what has been done previously."	Complete change to one third, or minor changes to two thirds of script/sound/copy, storyboard/layout, or footage/image.
Low Creative Complexity:	These involve a single creative route, from an existing strategic and creative brief, with very little need for new creative thinking. These could be characterized as "more of the same, but different in some minor way."	Minor change to one third of script/sound/copy, storyboard/layout, or footage/image.

We needed to find a way to develop a "unifying workload metric" for a highly diverse mix of briefs. We reasoned that it was like trying to evaluate a basket of fruit containing a number and mix of fruits. How could you evaluate it so that you could compare it to another basket of fruits? You'd have to find a "unifying metric," like *weight* (you'd weigh and compare the baskets)

or *caloric content* (using weight and caloric values per gram for each type of fruit, and then compare the calories per basket).

SOWs presented us with the same type of problem. Let's say, for example, that one client in T&C had a SOW with a mix of 50 various TV and radio briefs, and another client had a mix of 75 print ads. Which advertiser had the larger SOW? Which advertiser required the greater number of creative and production resources? By how much? It was not possible to know by simply counting the briefs.

We reasoned that *creative man-hours* for each type of brief *at a standard level of resource,* which we defined as *one creative team, with zero rework,* would be like *weight* or *caloric value* for a basket of fruit.

The use of creative man-hours for each type of ad would allow us standardize SOWs across T&C's clients and arrive at a unit price (fee divided by workload) and unit cost (cost divided by workload). Once we had this, then we could analyse and diagnose T&C's price and cost behaviour.

Our plan was to build a database of T&C's creative briefs, with the actual number of creative teams used on each brief and the actual rework rates incurred by brief, to be called the "T&C actual brief database" – and then work with the creatives to develop what we called "T&C creative day standards" to answer the following question.

- For each type of brief (*by media type, by origination/adaptation, by creative complexity*), working under ideal productivity circumstances (*no exceptional internal delays or client-driven rework delays*), how many full working days would it take one creative team, on average, to do the following:

1. *Creative days in creative development.* Complete the creative development work on each type of brief, including reviewing the work internally and then with the client to gain client approval, *and*

2. *Creative days in production.* Oversee each brief's creative content through the production process to the air/insertion date.

We reasoned that once we had the T&C actual brief database and T&C creative day standards for each type of brief, we could use these two sources of data to calculate the *actual number of creatives required* for the T&C SOWs. This ought to come very close to the *actual number of creatives in the T&C office working at standard billability.* After sick days and holidays, standard billability (utilization) was 86.5%, or 225 working days (1,800 hours) per creative during the year. Thus, 52 creatives or 26 creative teams ought to complete 11,700 creative days (93,600 billable hours) working on creative deliverables.

If our T&C actual brief database was correct (there were 363 various briefs), and the T&C creative day standards for each type of brief were accurate as well, then if we multiplied each actual brief by its appropriate creative day standard and summed up the total for all of the briefs, we would have total creative team-days required for the office's SOWs, taking into account the usage of multiple teams and the actual rework rates.

It took a number of iterations to micro-adjust each of the T&C creative day standards so that their final values would generate 11,700 creative days for 52 creatives from the 363 briefs in the T&C actual brief database, but after some careful adjustments, we found the right set of values.

Summary of the office. For the 363 briefs completed during the year, according to our analysis, the *average* number of creative teams per brief was 2.3 (varying from a high of six teams per brief to a low of 0.5 teams per brief), and the *average* number of full reworks was 2.6 reworks per brief. This was an exceptionally high number of average creative teams per brief and rework rates across the SOW. The T&C CEO was upset with the way the two executive creative directors were lavishly allocating creative teams to the office's work. *"Here we are,"* he said, *"struggling to make a profit, and the creative directors are acting as if creative resources are unlimited and free. No wonder they keep asking for more people! They are totally undisciplined and out of touch with our financial situation."*

A more efficient scenario. The CEO asked us to model a more efficient scenario, using the actual briefs and seeing how many creatives would be required if creative resources were allocated in a different way. We established, with the input of various people in the agency, what came to be called "T&C Gold Resource Standards" that had the following structure:

TABLE 13-3: AGREED T&C GOLD RESOURCE STANDARDS FOR CREATIVE TEAM ASSIGNMENTS 1992

GOLD RESOURCE STANDARDS						
	Originations			Adaptations		
	Low	Average	High	Low	Average	High
Number of Creative Teams	1	1	2	0.5	0.5	0.5
Expected Rework Rate	0.5	1	2	0.25	0.5	0.5

No brief was expected to be given more than two creative teams and to incur more than two rounds of rework. The *typical* brief would have about one creative team (or less, for adaptations) and about one rework or less.

We modeled the office's 363 briefs at gold standard, and instead of requiring 52 total creatives (at an average of 2.3 teams per brief with 2.6 average reworks per brief) the new T&C gold standard allocation required 35 creatives (at an average of one team per brief and one rework per brief). This was one third less than the current creative staffing. Furthermore, the expected reduction in coordination activities associated with creative reviews and rework at the client could lead to a reduction in client service personnel from 65 FTEs to 44 FTEs while maintaining a ratio of 1.25 client service FTEs per creative FTE.

Our SOW analysis and subsequent discussions at T&C concluded with the following summary:

- *T&C profitability was depressed by a 30% over-allocation of creative resources across the SOW, on the one hand, and the provision of a large number of client service personnel to handle the high coordination needs associated with high rates of rebriefing, reviews, and rework.*
- *While this level of over-allocation of resources might have made sense and was affordable during the media commission days, it was no longer affordable in the expectation of further fee cuts in a fee-based environment. New rules for the allocation of resources needed to be established and used.*
- *A more rational allocation of creative resources, using T&C gold resource standards to limit creative teams to one creative team per brief (except for high creative complexity briefs), leading to fewer client reviews and lower rework rates, would not only reduce creative costs but also permit a reduction in client service staffing.*

T&C took on board these advised recommendations and then proceeded as follows for 1993:

1. Every client head was required to forecast his/her 1993 SOW, using "Farmer format:" media type, origination/adaptation, and creative complexity (low, average, high).
2. The SOWs were modeled, using T&C gold resource standards, to determine the appropriate gold standard creative staffing for each client.

3. The CEO and his executive team conducted "live SOW reviews" with each client head, reviewing the proposed SOWs for each client and ensuring that the client head understood and accepted the revised creative staffing on the account.

4. The creative staffing for all accounts was summed up, and an additional 10% headcount cushion was added for new business and other contingencies, leading to a proposed T&C creative staffing level of 39 creative FTEs, down from 52 creatives during 1992. Client service headcounts were similarly reduced, to 49 FTEs, down from 65 during 1992.

5. The two executive creative directors, whose management of creative staffing was partly responsible for the office's profit problem, decided to resign rather than work under more tightly managed circumstances, and they were replaced by a new executive creative director who was prepared to work with the CEO to improve creative quality within the more tightly managed creative capacity constraints at the same time.

6. The T&C profit margin increased from 5% to 14% in 1993, and the new SOW forecasting and management system was adapted on a permanent basis.

This work for T&C identified a cost management problem that was depressing profitability – creative costs were being managed according to old rules developed during the more lavish media commission era. The need for a more stringent resource management approach was not recognized until profits were at a very depressed level. Measurement of workload and the adoption of new resource management standards were required.

Over the next decade, until 2003, Farmer & Company worked with T&C's offices and with other global advertising agencies, taking our SOW analyses from one office to another. We reconstructed traditional advertising SOWs (TV, radio, print), documented the number and type of briefs, determined the number of creative teams and the actual rework rates by brief, modeled the actual brief databases and found over-allocations of creative and client service resources. The problem seemed endemic at the 30 agency offices we diagnosed over this ten-year period. Our findings were certainly consistent with the existence of breaking price umbrellas and lagging cost management practices. Routinely, we found surplus creative and client service resources that accounted for the depressed profitability that agency offices were experiencing between 1993 and 2003.

We were reassured that our traditional advertising SOW resource model seemed to work well in different agency offices in the US, Europe and Asia – accurately calculating the number of actual creatives in an office from the actual brief databases and the creative day standards. Ad agencies, we learned, worked in the same way around the world, taking the same amount of time per creative team to develop and produce ads. Agency offices varied from one another only in the degree to which they used multiple creative teams and incurred rework – and in the salary levels they paid their people. Agency offices were otherwise uniform in the way they used creative resources for the basic business of creating and producing traditional ads.

THE SCOPEMETRIC® UNIT (SMU)

We reasoned that a standardized unit of work for a SOW could be based on creative man-hours for a given creative deliverable at an appropriate level of creative staffing and productivity. A TV origination ad of high creative complexity could be valued at X units of work (based on the creative man-hours required for two creative teams and two reworks for this category of ad) while a TV adaptation ad of low creative complexity could be valued at Y units of work (based on 0.5 creative teams and 0.25 reworks for this category of ad).

The unit of work needed to be simple and easy to communicate. I remembered something David Ogilvy wrote about creative productivity in *Ogilvy on Advertising*: "*The average copywriter gets only three commercials a year on air.*" (Ogilvy, 1983, p. 20).

If creative productivity for traditional advertising had improved modestly by (say) 1.5% per year since David Ogilvy's 1983 assertion of three commercials per creative, then by 2003 the "*average creative would complete to 4.1 ads per year.*"

If we modeled all types of creative deliverables, one at a time, using our proven creative day standards and gold resource standards, then our resource model would tell us how many creative FTEs would be required to take each deliverable through creative development and production.

TABLE 13-4: CREATIVE FTES AT GOLD RESOURCE STANDARDS FOR A SELECTION OF BRIEF TYPES (CREATIVE FTE = 1,800 HOURS)

	Low Creative Complexity	Average Creative Complexity	High Creative Complexity
Full-Up Originations	Creative FTEs Rounded	Creative FTEs Rounded	Creative FTEs Rounded
TV/Cinema	0.10	0.15	0.35
Print/Poster	0.06	0.11	0.27
Radio	0.08	0.10	0.23
Adaptations			
TV/Cinema	0.02	0.03	0.04
Print/Poster	0.01	0.02	0.02
Radio	0.01	0.02	0.03

If we took these FTE values and multiplied them by 4.1 then we would have SMU values for this sample of briefs:

TABLE 13-5: SMU VALUES FOR A SELECTION OF BRIEF TYPES
(BASED ON A CREATIVE PRODUCTIVITY LEVEL OF 4.1 SMUS PER CREATIVE PER YEAR)

	Low Creative Complexity	Average Creative Complexity	High Creative Complexity
Full-Up Originations	SMUs	SMUs	SMUs
TV/Cinema	0.40	0.62	1.43
Print/Poster	0.25	0.43	1.09
Radio	0.32	0.43	0.93
Adaptations			
TV/Cinema	0.09	0.13	0.15
Print/Poster	0.05	0.07	0.10
Radio	0.05	0.08	0.11

A number of key generalizations can be made from the simple SMU table above:

- High complexity originations are about 2.3 times as large as average complexity originations;
- Average complexity originations are about 1.5 times as large as low complexity originations;
- Adaptations, in general, are between 1/5th and 1/10th the size of comparable originations.

In 2004, once we developed the SMU, we set about to gather and create SMU values for briefs in direct marketing and digital media. We were fortunate in this respect, because we were working with a number of direct marketing and digital agencies whose SOWs were in these areas, and they had a keen interest in developing workload and resource values, using our methodology.

By 2018, we had 4,014 different types of projects in our SMU database. The SMU database became a unique analytical resource, permitting us to determine how much work was involved in any given SOW. The projects covered a wide range of areas – see below.

TABLE 13-6: SCOPE OF WORK PROJECT CATEGORIES AND NUMBER OF PROJECTS IN FARMER SCOPEMETRIC® DATABASE

	Project Type by Category	Number of Projects in Category	Total SMUs in Category**	SMU Average Size Ranking (Large to Small)
	Project Categories with SMU Values			TV Index = 100
1	TV	288	75	100
2	Print	288	58	78
3	Video	246	29	45
4	Online Videos	180	16	35
5	OOH	417	37	34
6	Print - BTL	432	32	28
7	Print - DM	306	20	25
8	Radio	252	15	23
9	Creative Development	108	6	21
10	Applications	72	3	16
11	Website	234	6	10
12	Ad Unit - Banners	126	2	7
13	Social Media	165	3	7
14	Production Management	144	2	4
15	eDM	90	1	3
	Total with SMU Values	**3,348**	**306**	**35**
	Project Categories without SMU Values			
16	Account Management	162	–	–
17	Coordination	90	–	–
18	Planning	108	–	–
19	Research	90	–	–
20	Strategy	216	–	–
	TOTAL	**666**	**–**	**–**
	Grand Total	**4,014**	**306**	**N.A.**

Armed with the SMU, we revisited the SOWs and resource plans of all our clients since 1992. We were interested in answering two questions:

What was the Price per SMU paid to our clients for their SOWs? Price was defined as fee income divided by workload in SMUs. We removed inflation by using published GDP deflators, and we used the then-current exchange rates so that our analysis would be in constant dollars.

What was the creative productivity over time, and how had it changed? Creative productivity was total number of SMUs per year divided by the number of creative FTEs.

We have described in previous chapters the two displays that answer these questions, but it is instructive to repeat them here.

TABLE 13-7: PRICE CURVE 1992-2018
(PRICES IN CONSTANT DOLLARS PER SMU)

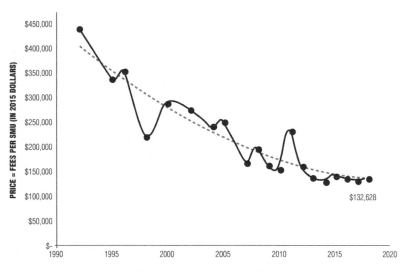

Source: SMU = ScopeMetric® Unit, a uniform measure of scope of work workload developed by Farmer & Company

TABLE 13-8: INCREASE IN CREATIVE PRODUCTIVITY
(1992-2018 IN SMUS PER CREATIVE PER YEAR)

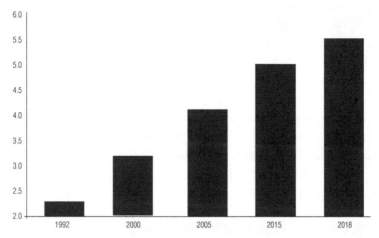

Source: Farmer & Company client data

Creative output had been 2.3 SMUs per creative per year in 1992 for our clients, even less than the three ads per year described by David Ogilvy[2], but with the continued deterioration of client fee levels, and the growth of workloads, our clients had been downsizing and driving creative output levels upwards.

Today (2018), the average level of creative output is about 5.5 SMUs per creative, and it is rising. This is not a healthy trend. Creatives are being increasingly stretched.

SUMMARY

It took us many years to develop a database of workload values.

Once this was done, we had all the elements we needed for a SOW diagnostic system. We could review industry pricing behaviour over time. We could examine changes in creative output. We could take apart a SOW and determine the degree to which agency clients were overstaffed or understaffed. We could pick apart the operations of an agency office, as we did with the Cassandra Agency.

We did all of these things over many years, and they told us a story about what was happening in the industry. Workloads were growing; fees were flat or declining; prices were falling; creative resources were being stretched – and these problems were continuing, principally because agencies were not documenting, tracking or negotiating their workloads with their clients. Management priorities were, instead, focused on new business development, although this was not solving the problem.

In the end, this "workload story" describes the unhappy circumstances that define agency life. The story has not yet come to an end, since each year brings greater workloads, lower prices and fewer resources, but the inevitable consequences can surely be predicted. Sooner or later, for one agency or many, the promised level of profit margins will not be generated, and this will affect holding company performance. The superior margins from media operations will no longer mask the weaker margins from ad agency operations, and embarrassing questions will be asked about the earnings quality of the holding company portfolio.

CHAPTER 14 –
PRODUCTION, CLIENT SERVICE AND STRATEGIC PLANNING RESOURCES

Credit: Tom Cheney / The New Yorker / The Cartoon Bank.

T he previous chapter described the origin and basis of the SMU and focused on the variability of creative resources and costs relative to workload. In fact, the variability is so predictable that we can use calculated creative resources (at gold resource standards) as the basis for defining the SMU. Accordingly, we pegged the SMU as *"4.1 times calculated creative FTEs for a given creative deliverable (brief) at its relevant gold standard determined resource value."*

What about the other key resources, like production, client service and strategic planning? How do these resources vary with the work in agency SOWs? More to the point, how do these resources vary with the workload as defined by SMUs?

Broadly speaking, all agency resources are variable with workload. Creative, production, client service and strategic planning resources increase with increases in SMUs, and they decrease with decreases in SMUs. However, there are some additional unique factors that influence the degree of variability of these resources, and these unique factors must be taken into account when using SMUs to calculate resource requirements.

Let's look at the variability of resources, department by department.

PRODUCTION RESOURCES

As with creative resources, production resources vary directly with SMUs, but the variability of production resources is a function of the media type as well.

Certain types of media are more "production intensive" than other types of media. To illustrate, I've taken the Farmer & Company database of brief types and looked at one uniform category: the 116 briefs that are classified as "full-up originations of average creative complexity among 10 sclected media categories." For briefs in this uniform category, average production resources vary from a low of 0.08 production FTEs per SMU (print - traditional) to a high of 0.24 FTEs per SMU (email - dDM) within the ten media types shown below in Table 14-1 (next page). That's more than a 3:1 difference in production intensity for a uniform type of brief that varies only by media.

TABLE 14-1: PRODUCTION FTES PER SMU AND PER CREATIVE FOR VARIOUS MEDIA TYPES

	Media Type*	Number of Briefs in our database in this category	Average Number of Production FTEs per SMU in this category	Production Ratio: Production FTEs per Creative FTE in this category
1	Print	16	0.08	0.41
2	Social Media	9	0.15	0.73
3	TV	16	0.10	0.50
4	Online Videos	10	0.10	0.52
5	Applications	4	0.13	0.67
6	Ad Unit – Banners	7	0.15	0.75
7	Radio	14	0.16	0.79
8	OOH	23	0.17	0.86
9	Video	13	0.22	1.11
10	eDM	5	0.24	1.19
	Total	**117**	**0.13**	**0.65**

*FULL-UP ORIGINATIONS OF AVERAGE CREATIVE COMPLEXITY

Media type and brief classification drive the production resources per SMU. If both are known, then with our SMU database, production resources can be determined easily, using an SMU and resource look-up table.

Within these media types as shown above, the weighted average production resource for full-up originations of average complexity, is 0.13 production FTEs per SMU, or 0.65 production FTEs per creative FTE . For a more typical mix of briefs across all media types and across all classifications (originations and adaptations of all creative complexities), the average production resource is 0.14 production FTEs per SMU, or 0.7 production FTEs per creative FTE.

For a traditional-only mix of briefs, the average production resource is 0.12 production FTEs per SMU, or 0.62 production FTEs per creative FTE. These are, of course, averages based on certain SOW mix assumptions rather than benchmarks that can be used in a general way.

The fact that certain media types have a higher intensity of production resources than others should be self-evident. All media are not created equal with respect to production.

The ratio of production FTEs versus creative FTEs per brief ("production ratio") is a useful metric, showing the "production intensity" of a given brief type relative to its creative requirement. In Table 14-1, above, I've shown production ratio in the final column, which is determined by dividing the production FTEs for a given brief category by the Creative FTEs for the same category. The production ratio varies from a low of 0.41 production FTEs per creative for print to a high of 1.19 production FTEs per creative FTE for eDM.

Armed with our database of production resources per SMU by media type, we can calculate an agency's need for production resources, based on a properly structured SOW as the input. Conceptually, we can say that "production FTEs vary both with SMUs and media type." Graphically, it looks like Table 14-2, below:

TABLE 14-2: PRODUCTION FTES VARY WITH SMUS AND MEDIA TYPE

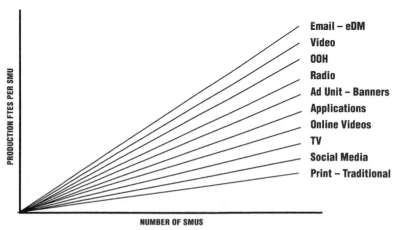

CLIENT SERVICE AND STRATEGIC PLANNING RESOURCES

Client service people have the responsibility to manage client relationships, to ensure that there are clear brand strategies to guide creative work, to handle the briefing of creative teams for new creative work, to handle the planning, coordination and approval of creative work at their clients (including coordinating rework), and to see that production work is done on time to meet media deadlines. When their clients are global clients, additional senior client service executives will oversee and coordinate SOW and resourcing activities on behalf of the client for several agency offices throughout the network. If the agency is a "brand navigator" or "brand account leader" or "integrator" of a number of agencies for the client, then additional senior client service executives will be responsible for global brand strategies as well as SOW and resourcing issues on behalf of the client for these related or unrelated agencies.

In the name of client relationship management, client service executives provide ongoing services and hands-on help – by writing presentations for client executives, completing competitive analyses, providing briefings, dealing with budgetary and SOW changes, and generally doing everything they can to ensure that operations between the agency and the client run smoothly. Creating good will is high on the list of any client service executive's priorities.

Brand strategic planning based on consumer insights was once exclusively in the hands of senior client service executives, but the creation of the separate strategic planning department with specialized strategic planners changed this. Despite the existence of these specialists, though, brand strategic planning remains under the general executive responsibility of senior client service executives, so as a rule we think of client service and strategic planning as a *single agency resource*. Hereinafter, I will refer to this single agency resource as "CS&P resources" or "CS&P people."

Despite our best efforts over the years, we have been unable to directly model an agency's need for CS&P resources based on the various activities that these individuals engage in. That's because their activities are an absolute hodge-podge of services that vary significantly by client and by circumstances. A list of what CS&P people do on behalf of their clients would be staggeringly long, and none of the services could be seen as uniform in any way. This stands in direct contrast to the general uniformity of what agency creatives or production people do when making different types of ads.

Uniformity is not the case for CS&P people. More accurately, their work is varied, and for them as for many others, *"work expands so as to fill the time available for its completion,"* in the memorable words of Cyril Northcote Parkinson.[1] For a given number of CS&P people, a unique mix of client services will be carried out that consumes the billable capacity of the individuals. It's probably fair to say that even if the number of individuals on a client account were increased by (say) 50%, their collective client service work would expand by 50%, as well.

One challenge about CS&P services is to know how much "capacity" to assign to manage the various CS&P responsibilities of relationships. Whether the "capacity" is small or large, the assigned CS&P people will be 100% busy.

How much, then, is "just right?"

We've observed how agencies have handled this over the years, and we've developed a pragmatic way of thinking about CS&P headcounts:

CS&P headcounts vary in proportion to SMUs, on the one hand, and to relationship complexity, on the other hand.

Thus, CS&P headcounts vary in proportion to creative headcounts, with the proportion varying up or down depending on relationship complexity:

TABLE 14-3: CS&P HEADCOUNT
PER CREATIVE HEADCOUNT

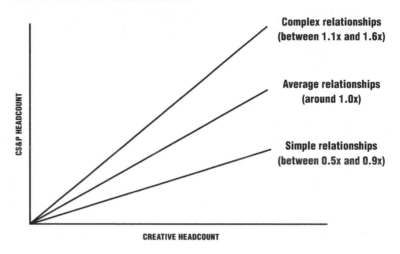

The proportion of CS&P headcounts to creative headcounts can be expressed as a CS&P ratio which varies with relationship complexity. The ratio is the CS&P headcount divided by the creative headcount. If there are, for example, ten CS&P full-time equivalents and ten creative full-time equivalents, then the CS&P ratio is one (or 1.0x), and so forth. Simple relationships have a CS&P ratio of between 0.5x and 0.9x; average relationships have a CS&P ratio of about 1.0x, and complex relationships have a CS&P ratio of between 1.1x and 1.6x headcounts per creative. The CS&P ratio has been in decline over the past decade. Just as creative headcounts have declined per SMU under the pressure of declining prices, so has the proportion of CS&P resources relative to creative resources. Typical or average relationships used to have CS&P ratios of 1.5x during the years 1990 to about 2004, but since then, CS&P ratios have declined to 1.0x.

Complexity of a relationship defines the magnitude of the CS&P ratio. Normal responsibilities include carrying out brand strategic work, coordinating the briefing and ad approval processes between a client and the creatives and managing the relationship for budgeting and planning purposes. Highly complex relationships include some or all of the following CS&P tasks that are in addition to normal CS&P responsibilities:

- Integrating the strategic and creative operations of numerous agencies across geographies or media disciplines;
- Managing global operations out of a single agency office, including conducting global brand strategies and all global brand creative work;
- Managing exceptionally high levels of brand strategies and other types of strategic work;
- Managing exceptionally inefficient processes, like inefficient brief approval or ad approval processes;
- Managing exceptionally high rates of rework associated with these processes;
- Managing an exceptionally complicated SOW planning and budgeting or fee-setting process.

It is fair to say that the advertisers are responsible for many of the factors that drive up CS&P ratios, particularly when the high ratios are due to process inefficiencies involving brief approval, ad approval, rework rates and SOW planning or fee-setting. Agencies know this, of course, and try to staff up accordingly rather than work with the client to make relationships more efficient. In the particularly fraught fee-setting environment of today, agencies will happily accept any inefficiencies in a relationship if the inefficiencies justify additional headcount and billable hours.

This is, of course, unfortunate – but labour-based fees encourage rather than discourage relationship inefficiencies, and as long as agencies are paid for these inefficiencies, they are hardly motivated to develop the skills or put in the effort to eliminate them.

CHAPTER 15 – MANAGING SCOPES OF WORK AND PREPARING CLIENT RESOURCE PLANS

"Obviously, some people here do not appreciate the gravity of our situation."

Credit: Frank Modell / The New Yorker / The Cartoon Bank.

I f you've read this far, you'll recognize that all the elements are in place for knowing how an ad agency can go about managing its SOWs, client by client, and determining the appropriate resources and fees for its relationships, using the various principles and metrics outlined in this book.

SOWs need to be documented in the format described previously, and the SMU workloads calculated by an SOW model that uses the SMU database (like Farmer & Company's ScopeMetric® model).

First, then, creative headcounts can be calculated from the SMU count, using a productivity metric like "5.0 SMUs per creative per year." For a SOW with (say) 1,000 deliverables and 20 SMUs, there will be a need for 4.0 creative FTEs.

Second, the production resources can be calculated by the model, given the number of SMUs and the particular media mix of the SOW. If the SOW has a typical media mix (like the one shown in Table 14-1), there will be 0.13 production FTEs per SMU. For a 20-SMU scope of work SMU scope of work, this will require 2.6 production FTEs, or 0.65 production FTEs per creative FTE.

Third, we can calculate the requirement for Client Service & Planning Resources, using the CS&P Ratio. Let's assume that the client relationship has "normal and typical" complexity, so that there is a need for 1.0 Client Service & Planning FTEs per creative FTE. There are 4.0 creative FTEs, so the relationship requires 4.0 CS&P FTEs (which is probably made up of 3.2 client service FTEs and 0.8 strategic planners, since there is usually a 80%/20% mix between the two departments).

In summary, with 4.0 creatives, 2.6 production FTEs and 4.0 CS&P FTEs, the resource plan would have 10.6 FTEs. For 20 SMUs in the SOW, this would calculate to an allocation of 0.53 FTEs per SMU, which is a fairly typical ratio.

If the average salary and benefits of an FTE on this account were (say) between $106,000 and $107,000, then 10.6 FTEs would have a cost of $1,128,750, and if the agency was charging these FTEs out at an average multiple of 2.35x (for a 15% margin), then the fee would be $2,652,562, or $132,628 per SMU for the 20 SMUs. That works out to only $139 per hour per FTE for the 10.6 FTEs, using 1,800 hours per FTE.

That's roughly where the US market is in 2018. The depressed price per SMU of $132,628 allows for an agency team with salary levels of only $106,000 to $107,000 per FTE, which is probably less than half the salary levels of the typical management consulting team.

Surely, depressed and declining prices per SMU are driving down agency salaries and making agencies non-competitive in the industry. Ideally, of course, SOW management will be done in sync with engaged clients with whom an agency has previously established *Marketing and Strategic Performance Partnerships* as outlined in Chapter 12. These partnership clients are more likely to pay fairly for agency workloads and resources, believing that agencies are critical partners who contribute in a major way to the achievement of brand growth and profitability. SOW planning and agency resourcing decisions are critical processes in planning for improved performance.

There's a chicken-and-egg problem with clients, though. There are few clients who have these kinds of partnerships with their agencies. Client relationships have been deteriorating for more than a decade, as fees have declined faster than agency workloads, and agencies have been treated more like commodity suppliers of creative execution services than as strategic partners. Clients work with strategic management consultants on issues they deem fundamental and important. Clients have beefed up their own capabilities and lowered their expectations for their agency relationships. Associated with this has been the agency practice of downgrading the cost and seniority of their own resources in response to unfavourable relationship economics. There are many reasons for this, and they have been discussed in previous chapters, but the effect has been a deterioration of relative agency capabilities at a time when their clients face unprecedented difficulties in achieving growth and profitability in the dog-eat-dog competitive world brought about by online commerce.

Agencies have to dig themselves out of the hole they have dug for themselves over the past decade. Their situation is a bit like being on a losing football team, behind in the fourth quarter and needing some last-minute team heroics to come out winning. It's a situation that calls for entirely new strategies: *new ideas and leadership from the top,* bringing fundamental changes in agency management style, operational direction and nitty-gritty attention to detail, uncomfortable as this might be for those more used to the casual, hands-off management culture of ad agencies.

Glorification of past leaders and their management styles is a distraction. Today's conditions require new approaches and an abandonment of the belief that there is any possibility of returning to a time when agencies were exceptionally well-paid for carrying out what was, then, a relatively simple creative business involving TV, print and radio.

Office heads are the essential, key executives for bringing about effective management of scopes of work, whether they be called office president, chief executive, managing director or something else. Traditionally, office heads were once high-status agency executives responsible for new business development, recruiting and client problem-solving in key agency offices (New York, Chicago, London, Paris, Frankfurt, Tokyo, etc.). Office heads needed Mad Man skills to deal with clients during the commission era, but with the evolution of remuneration to fees and the increased importance of global clients in an office's mix of clients, the job has become increasingly managerial and custodial in nature as they struggle to balance fees and resources to achieve holding company margins. The office head is no longer today quite the local god he or she used to be, and with an increasing percentage of global clients, office heads have less control over clients than was the case in the past. Although the office head job is increasingly managerial, *it is not managerial enough.*

The office head can have a greater influence over client operations, influencing client scopes of work and agency resource plans. Office heads have the potential authority to provide and impose standards on client heads. This is not an authority that has been used to any great extent in the past. In point of fact, office heads have left client heads alone to handle their clients as they best saw fit, rarely looking very closely at what client heads were doing on a day to-day, month-to-month or quarterly basis.

The office head has the singular authority to establish processes and standards for each client head, and it is office head *leadership at the office level* that is required today. Of course, office heads are unlikely to step up to these responsibilities unless they are required to do so by agency chief executives, so it's critical for CEOs to understand the office-level need for increased management and to direct the agency's office heads to begin the process, as described below.

Office head authority should be used in the following way:

1. **SOW forecasts as a matter of policy.** Office heads must establish a policy that each client head must forecast his/her SOW 'by deliverable' for the office's/agency's fiscal year. If the fiscal year is January through to December, then this must be the period for the client head's SOW forecast, even if his/her client's fiscal year is structured differently – July through June, April through March or on some other basis[1]. Forecasted SOWs represent a stake in the ground: *"This is the work we should do or will be required to do for each client in our coming fiscal year."*

2. **SOWs in a uniform format, permitting calculation of SOW workloads in SMUs.** There has to be a uniform model for the SOWs, even if individual clients of the agency specify *their own* unique format for *their* SOWs. Uniformity within the agency is an absolute requirement. At Farmer & Company, we provide our clients with the Farmer ScopeMetric® Model, which outlines the projects by media type, by media detail, by origination/adaptation and by creative complexity (low, average, high). Additionally, the model specifies if an individual project is creative only, production only or full-up. What's important is that the relevant detail be provided to permit SMUs to be calculated across clients for comparative purposes.

3. **SOWs diagnosed for their "state of health."** The forecasts of SOWs in a uniform format with SMU values permit "state of health" diagnoses to be performed. What is the price for the work in each of the SOWs (fee per SMU)? What are the creative productivities, as measured in SMUs per creative per year?

What is the ratio of production FTEs to creative FTEs (the production ratio)? What is the CS&P ratio? How appropriate are these metrics for the SOW and relationship?

4. **SOW changes tracked throughout the year.** It's one thing to get a SOW forecast at the beginning of the fiscal year and to use it for diagnostic purposes. It's another thing to see what actually happens. Office heads need to specify that SOWs will be tracked during the year and that changes will be monitored. Project management systems should be exploited to track SOWs in a uniform way, deliverable by deliverable, categorized in accordance with the format suggested in Chapter 13. Farmer & Company's ScopeMetric® database of SMU values can be used on a licensed basis and incorporated in project management systems so that SMU values can be calculated and relevant SOW diagnoses run on a an ongoing basis.

5. **Client (and client head) performance reviewed at regular intervals.** Office heads need to demonstrate their commitment to SOW management practices by sitting down with client heads, one by one each quarter (or so), and reviewing their client operations. The following kinds of questions ought to be raised during the reviews:

    • What work are we doing for your client? How does our work address the client's brand performance problems? *If not, what can we do about it?*

    • Is the client's fee budget and our SOW large enough to deal with its brand performance problems? Do we have enough share of the overall fee budget so that we are the agency that is making a difference in client performance? *If not, what can we do about it?*

    • How are we being remunerated by this client? Is workload being considered in the fee calculation? *If not, what can we do about it?*

    • How much work is in the SOW – in projects and SMUs? What is the fee per SMU? SMUs per creative? What is our CS&P ratio? *If these metrics are not acceptable (insufficient fee per SMU or stretched resources), what can we do about it?* Clients whose metrics are not acceptable are classified as "misaligned" clients: the fees, resources and workloads are misaligned with one another. There is too much work, too little fees, and too few resources for the work. Misaligned clients are a big problem – recall the Cassandra NY Office from Chapter 10, which had a majority of clients in the "misaligned" category. Misaligned clients need to have corrective action plans developed and implemented by their respective client heads.

- What improvements are you (the client head) prepared to commit to for the rest of this fiscal year? (These commitments need to be negotiated by the office head, ensuring that they are ambitious and realizable.)
- What are your three key long-term priorities for the management of this client? Where does the alignment of fees, resources and workloads fit into your priorities?

Any client head who sits through a review of this nature will have little doubt about the importance that the office head puts on effective client and SOW management. Improvements in the performance of clients within the office's portfolio of clients will be expected. Client heads will inevitably feel that they need to be more on top of their client situations, being more proactive with fees and SOW issues. In other words, they will inevitably feel *accountable* for their client and its relationship with the agency, and under management pressure to do something about existing problems.

Client reviews – or performance reviews, as they ought to be known – are a standard feature of corporate life. *Management*, it is said, is getting subordinates to do what they would otherwise not do on their own. As J Sterling Livingston pointed out in *Pygmalion in Management*, his landmark *Harvard Business Review* article of 1969 (reprinted in 2003), *"If managers' expectations are high, productivity is likely to be excellent. If their expectations are low, productivity is likely to be poor.*

It is as though there were a law that caused subordinates' performance to rise or fall to meet managers' expectations." (Livingston, 2003). The challenge, then, is to get office heads to show their expectations to client heads through the review process. The example set by office heads will raise the performance bar for client heads.

Unfortunately, the culture of the advertising agency has ratified, over many decades, a policy of benign neglect regarding client operational matters. Agency wealth, particularly during The Golden Age, was based not on how well or how closely an individual client was managed but rather on how long a client remained a client of the agency. Commission-based remuneration assured the generation of profits. Increases in agency wealth were generated through new business wins. Understandably, it was the responsibility of client heads to retain their clients, principally by offering great creativity and unrivaled and endless service, and it was the responsibility of office heads to develop new clients. If each party did what was expected, then agencies grew and flourished. This was "ant-colony" management, in the memorable words of Kevin Roberts. Each ant knew what it needed to do – and did it.

Alas, that is not the case today, and the responsibilities of office heads and of client heads have changed. It is not a natural progression for either group of executives to be effective under both the old rules and the new.

6. **Action plans designed to deal with misaligned clients.** Client reviews must lead to action plans – that's the purpose of the exercise, especially for misaligned clients whose poor economics are stressing the agency organization and compromising its ability to do first-class work. If misalignment is due to poor fees relative to workload, then efforts must be undertaken to increase the fees or reduce the workload, using the documentation of workload and SMU metrics to facilitate the discussion.

Agencies negotiate with clients all the time over fee levels, seeking remuneration for out-of-scope work, overtime for rework and annual fee increases for growing SOWs, but their usual justification is the excessive time sheet hours that they incur. Time sheet hours are easily attacked by clients, who argue that excessive hours are merely a symptom of agency inefficiency.

7. **Progress in achieving action plans – reviewed on a regular basis.** Client heads need to organize initiatives and discussions with their clients to promote the achievement of their action plans, and office heads need to inspect the results from time to time. This can take place within the context of regularly scheduled review meetings or on a more ad hoc basis. What's important is that office heads must be seen as following up with client head commitments, and learning more about the client head's capabilities and about the sources of resistance at the client if the client head constantly turns up empty-handed. Out of this process, office heads will certainly learn more about "who can deliver" improvements from their clients. The learnings can be exploited for the benefit of all if aired at routine office board meetings, where the client heads assemble with other senior office executives to discuss office operations.

8. **Best practices discussed and disseminated for training and leadership purposes.** Successful client heads should be given airtime and bragging rights at office board meetings, revealing what they went through to transform a misaligned client into an aligned client through interactions with procurement and marketing. Giving successful executives time and visibility is a way of celebrating success and reinforcing "Pygmalion-in-management practices" that encourage all client heads to strive for success with their clients. Collective experience is a powerful force, but it needs to be mobilized. Best practices are routinely shared inside consulting firms and at corporations, but they are woefully absent within advertising agency networks.

Best practices could focus on "how I used workload data and other metrics to bring about a change with my client." Everyone can benefit from hearing successful war-stories, whether the forum is within one office or across agency offices.

Best practices help to create winning cultures by exploiting and celebrating success. By contrast, organizations that fail to recognize and mobilize best practice success stories cut themselves off from a valuable asset. A worldwide ad agency, with 10-20 clients per office and 100 offices around the world has 1,000-2,000 local client heads and the wealth of experience that they represent. What would it take to mobilize and disseminate the best practices of this group of individuals and exploit them for the benefit of the agency?

9. **Rewriting advertiser-agency contracts.** Office (and global) contracts need to be upgraded on many fronts. First, contracts should be explicit about the agency role in the relationship. We believe that agencies should be acknowledged as strategic performance partners, as outlined in Chapter 12, and held to the higher standard that this implies – responsible for the joint planning of SOWs that have the highest probability of achieving improved brand results, and managing or coordinating the network of agencies that has been mobilized to provide expertise across all media types. Second, contracts need to be explicit and complete in all areas relating to SOW issues – planning, measuring, tracking, resourcing, remunerating, dealing with out-of-scope and rework issues and the like. It is not enough to declare that an agency is the advertiser's agency of record (AOR) and will carry out strategic, creative and production work in accordance with a SOW. The devil is in the detail. How is the workload of the SOW measured? By what agreed standards is the SOW resourced by the agency for relationship coordination, strategic work, creative work and production? How is the cost or the billing rates of the resources determined? What rewards exist if the agency delivers or over-delivers the expected results from the SOW programme? Ad agencies need to have "model" contracts in mind as they manage their relationships towards new contracts and new ways of working with their clients. The effort is long overdue.

FEES, RESOURCES AND WORKLOADS

The office head sets the tone through personal leadership in the office, and his/her efforts should lead to increased client head accountability for client management practices. From a practical standpoint, though, how should client heads proceed with their clients in negotiating fees and resources from the forecasted SOWs?

Agencies need a uniform way of thinking about these issues. Negotiations with clients should not be individual crap shoots by client heads. There's more to success than being charismatic and lucky. The agency needs to make the client head negotiation job easier by adopting certain concepts and approaches that each client head can fall back on, relying on an agency's values, accumulated wisdom and experience to bolster his/her negotiating skills.

Agencies should create an "agency way" as a framework. At Ogilvy & Mather, it would be called "The Ogilvy Way." At Saatchi & Saatchi, it would be called "The Saatchi Way." At TBWA, it would be called "The TBWA Way," and so on.

What are the key principles of an "agency way?" I think that they can be articulated as follows:

THE AGENCY WAY
MISSION

1. *We believe, based on our experience, that all client brands, operating as they do in competitive, complex and ever-changing environments, underperform relative to their full potential.*
2. *Our mission is to help our clients achieve the full potential of their brands.*

REQUIREMENTS

3. *Achieving this mission requires top-level strategic partnerships, along with the mobilization of our executive, strategic, analytical, creative and production resources in focused efforts designed to achieve improved brand performance.*

4. *We will seek to work exclusively in long-term committed client relationships that have improved brand performance as the overall goal.*

5. *We will take the initiative to promote these types of relationships in our new business efforts, and we will refrain from accepting work in situations where potential clients merely expect their agencies to provide short-term commodity services that are paid at commodity rates.*

6. *We will invest to develop and maintain expert resources and capabilities across all media platforms to assure that we have a credible and competitive offer for clients, permitting us to develop and maintain AOR status wherever possible.*

7. *At the same time, we will work in a strategic and effective manner with other agencies engaged by our clients to plan and carry out integrated scopes of work.*

8. *Our creative capabilities will be exploited for the benefit of improved brand performance. We will celebrate "creativity with a purpose" rather than creativity for the sake of creative awards.*

9. *Achieving our mission will permit us to create the highest levels of employee satisfaction, to be able to recruit and retain the best in the industry and to fulfil our responsibilities to increase shareholder value for our shareholders.*

PRIORITIES

10. *We, with our clients, will identify and agree on the factors responsible for brand underperformance and then organize the best mix of strategy, media, creativity, production and spend to bring about the realization of brand full potential over a defined period of time.*

11. *This effort will require joint efforts with our clients to clarify the situation of each brand relative to its full potential, to agree on strategic and creative solutions, to plan and carry out appropriate strategic and creative scopes of work within an agreed mix of media, to evaluate the results of these efforts and to adjust the efforts and the scopes of work accordingly.*

12. *A key step in our relationships will involve the planning and agreement on the scopes of work by deliverable for the coming fiscal year, quarter by quarter. We will work jointly with our clients to forecast, prepare, discuss, debate and agree on the scopes of work and spend levels that have the highest probability of achieving improved brand performance levels.*

13. *Throughout the year, we will track the completion of and changes to the scope of work to ensure that our work adjusts to changes in the marketplace and stays within agreed budgetary constraints.*

14. *We will encourage scope of work experimentation and adjustment, required to improve brand performance in today's ever-changing marketing environment.*

COMPENSATION

15. *Our compensation will be based on the amount and type of work we carry out, taking into account the number, types and billing rates of the agency people that the work will actually require, working at agreed productivity rates on the agreed scopes of work.*

16. *We will commit to improved productivity rates over time with as we and our clients jointly improve the efficiency of scope of work planning, briefing, rework, ad approval and budgeting processes.*

17. *We will calculate a long-term "rate card fee" for each type of deliverable in our scopes of work. We will agree with our clients on the workload metric (in SMUs) for each type of deliverable in our scopes of work, and on the overall Price per SMU to be applied to calculate the rate card fee.*

18. *Over time, our compensation will evolve to give greater weight to results expected and results achieved, but at the beginning of our relationships, compensation will be based on "the work we do and the resources required to carry it out," with scope of work providing the basis on which the compensation will be calculated and agreed.*

19. *As our strategic relationships progress and generate positive results, we will agree on ways that we can earn clear performance-based*

bonuses based on the achievement of specific, pre-determined and agreed-to goals, or (alternatively) on increases in the price per SMU we're paid for our SOW efforts.

Does this seem like pie-in-the-sky thinking?

Agencies complain today that they are treated like junior partners in their relationships, forced to accept excessive workloads, inadequate fees and impossible deadlines. They watch as their clients flirt with other agencies and divide relationships among an increasingly large number of agencies across all disciplines. They observe other advertisers in the industry careen from one agency to another, firing their incumbent agencies and bringing on newcomers for a short period of time before beginning the cycle over again. Agencies think "maybe I had better keep my mouth shut and do whatever I am asked" rather than *articulate requirements for a successful relationship.*

Yes, I suspect that what I have outlined above will seem like the amusing but unrealistic fantasies of a management consultant, completely out of touch with the practical realities of today's agencies, or so it would seem.

Well, maybe so, but current agency strategies of "keeping mouths shut and doing whatever asked" are leading to decay, irrelevance and disaster. That's the path. Agency senior executives owe something more to their organizations than leading them down this path – or, if this is the best they can do, then they should take big cuts in pay. Agency executives should not earn seven-figure pay packages for presiding over the progressive and inevitable weakening and decay of their organizations.

CHAPTER 16 –
TRANSFORMING
THE AGENCY

Credit: Mick Stevens / The New Yorker /The Cartoon Bank.

Strategic transformations are management's answer to a two-part question:
1. What are our most fundamental problems?
2. What do we have to do to solve them?

That may seem commonsense, but in practice, it's not that simple.

It takes discipline to think about and identify the *fundamental* problems among the range of problems with which an organization is grappling. In the agency world, there are many real problems that can be identified – some are fundamental, and others are symptoms of larger problems. Here's a short list of what is heard and written about today. Some of these are excuses designed to explain away poor performance or weaknesses in the marketplace.

1. **We're insufficiently digital.** *We'd like to be more digital, and we know that we need to be more digital, but we have too few digital people and no particular digital reputation. As a result, we have little digital work from clients and insufficient financial resources to invest in digital capabilities.*

2. **We give away our work.** *We pitch for free and give away our best ideas. We have too much unpaid work. We're paid for some of our hours, but not all of our hours, and the rate that we're paid is a commodity rate. We should be paid for the ideas that we create and sell them at a price that reflects the value of what they're worth.*

3. **Our principal problem is procurement.** *We're great partners with marketing, but our clients have been hijacked by procurement. Procurement buys agency services in the same way that they buy paper and pens, at the lowest price possible. We'd be fine if it weren't for procurement.*

4. **There's no pricing discipline in the industry.** *Our fellow agencies undercut one another to get new business. When we pitch, we're unlikely to get a fair price; there's always an agency that will price lower. It's very difficult to win new business at a fair price.*

5. **Our own organization negotiates poor contracts.** *We're stuck with client contracts with low fees negotiated by the holding company or one of our senior executives. We can't make money on many of our contracts.*

6. **Our creativity seems lackluster.** *Something is missing – our creativity is off the mark. We're not winning new business. We're losing long-term clients. We need to shake up our creativity with new leadership and new energy, and we need to look at the creative resources we currently have. Maybe they're simply not up to the mark. We need to reinvest to become more creative.*

7. **We lack project management skills.** *Our operations are chaotic, and that's costing us money. We need to invest in project management people and systems to get our operations and costs under control.*

8. **We're not as analytical as we need to be.** *The marketplace requires us to build mass brands in a personalized and fragmented world. We have to develop better analytics to put the focus on delivering improved brand results while not squandering brand equity.*

9. **We're not attracting the right talent.** *Companies like Google, Facebook and Twitter attract millennials by offering strong creative cultures, competitive compensation and the opportunity to make a difference. We're less relevant on these dimensions, especially on salary, and we're losing the battle to hire and retain the best talent.*

10. **We're not reinvesting enough in our culture.** *Ideas are the agency's livelihood and lifeblood. They need to inspire. We need to continue to invest in having the best ideas for our clients and brands. We need to be brave enough to challenge the legacy models of how things have been done to ensure we continue to set the standard for creativity. This requires a conscious investment to maintain and strengthen our culture. We need to get back to the basics of Bill Bernbach. David Ogilvy and Leo Burnett.*

I could go on with this list, but you get the idea.

Let's assume that this is a representative list of top-of-mind industry problems. Many of these are simply complaints – grumbles about an industry that is going in the wrong direction – rather than starting points for corrective action. The complaints can be summarized like this: "*We know what our problems are, but solving them either requires more money, which we do not have, or a change in attitude by procurement or our fellow agencies, which is not likely to happen. Consequently, although we're smart enough to know how we would like things to be, or how they need to be, we have no practical way to get there. We'll just have to soldier on with things the way they are, do the best we can under the circumstances and hope for the best. We'll focus on improving our creativity and winning new business."*

The complaints reflect the industry's two most fundamental problems: inadequate pricing and a lack of management confidence about solutions. Poor pricing prevents agencies from investing in digital and analytical capabilities, and from being able to hire the kind of talent that solves client brand problems in a complicated media world. No amount of investment in project management disciplines will solve these problems. Lack of management confidence condemns agencies to insufficient action and a bleak future. The best agency people will walk away, voting with their feet, making the problems even worse.

Poor pricing is the outcome of past agency decisions on a number of fronts. The agency focus on "creativity" at a time when clients began to obsess about "shareholder value" was one key factor. So was the failure to measure workloads and to accept, instead, hourly-based remuneration as the basis for fixed fees. So was the continued provision of unlimited client service, just like in the good old days, even though it was not affordable. Passivity in the face of the salary-and-overhead benchmarking consultants was an additional factor that corrupted the basis of fee calculations. The absurd notion that there are industry "benchmarked" salaries, overhead rates and profit margins should never have been accepted as a basis for serious discussion between ad agencies and their clients. Many agencies may have lower salaries, overheads and profit margins than Agency A, but this does not mean that Agency A should be compelled to use these metrics as a basis for fee negotiations with their clients. There may be market prices for diamonds, silver and gold, but Tiffany and Kay Jewelers do not charge the same prices. If you want Kay Jewelers' prices, don't go to Tiffany!

Poor pricing is the mathematical outcome of growing workloads and fixed or declining fees, and poor pricing has locked in agency weaknesses. In the many years that Farmer & Company

211

has been measuring prices for agency work (in SMUs), we've observed that the price has declined by 70% from $438,171 per SMU to $132,628 in 2018. Understandably, this has affected and weakened agency operations in a significant way.

Poor pricing has eroded agency salaries. At the the time of writing, in 2018, using available salary data from industry sources (see, for example, www.glassdoor.com) we observe that agencies pay new university graduates less than half the going rate paid by Google, Facebook, Twitter or any of the consulting firms. The higher salaries of this latter group reflect the intense competition among these firms for top-tier graduates, and they reflect, as well, the superior pricing these firms derive from their commercial operations. Taking the consulting firms as the most comparable example, the strategic consulting firms earn fees that are a five times to six times multiple on the costs of their higher-paid people compared to the typical agency multiple of 2.2 times to 2.4 times on lower-paid people. A consulting firm may receive at least $450-$500 per hour for a typical mix of its consultants on an engagement, while a comparable agency will receive $100-$200 per hour. Both types of companies, it should be noted, have to deal with procurement for the approval of their contracts and remuneration rates, so procurement cannot be fingered exclusively as the "bad guy."

The pricing problem is the root cause of the very real salary and talent problems, and unless there is a genuine commitment by senior agency executives to improve pricing, one vigorous step at a time, then there is little hope that agencies will acquire the talent to become more relevant for their clients. This is because the pricing problem leads agencies to downsize and juniorize – forms of disinvestment masked by the delivery of profit margins. Because the generation of profits is seen as a good thing – the real objective of agency operations, at least in the eyes of holding company owners – it is hard to recognize the deteriorating situation for what it is. Understandably, agencies have lost a lot of problem-solving credibility with their clients, and this puts even more pressure on pricing.

Poor pricing leads to disinvestment, and disinvestment leads to reduced problem-solving, and reduced problem-solving leads to further poor pricing. This is a classic self-reinforcing feedback loop – a doom loop for agencies – and the industry is caught in the midst of it.

Holding companies, for their part, probably understand this problem, but they are understandably reluctant to acknowledge it or to take visible steps to help their agencies fix it. First of all, any recognition or acknowledgment that their ad agencies are generating profits by squeezing resources would be a tacit acknowledgement that holding company earnings are low quality and becoming lower quality over time. This would not be the kind of information that would shore up P/E ratios or share prices. Second, holding companies are not really organized to provide much help in an operational sense. Holding companies are principally organized as financial entities, good at making acquisitions, imposing new financial controls and budgeting systems, and negotiating budget and profit targets with a huge number of independent portfolio companies. They are financially sophisticated and have grown in financial sophistication, but they are not really organized to provide hands-on operational improvements, which is what agencies need today.

Say what you will, the holding companies have brought about a remarkable change in the culture of their agencies. The unfortunate part of this is that the achievement of holding company financial targets has become a principal goal of ad agencies – a goal that trumps, on the basis of current evidence, the agencies' own strategic health.

Excess agency costs have long been wrung out. Our consulting work suggests that most agency SOWs were appropriately staffed in 2004, when agencies were being paid appropriately by their clients for the workloads then being commissioned. Resources and workloads were in balance. In previous years, agencies overstaffed their work, much like T&C Agency. The year 2004 was a brief interlude between the overstaffing of prior years and the understaffing of recent years. Holding companies always sought growing profit margins, but the profit quest since 2004 has had dire consequences. Holding company profit requirements have contributed to the agency downsizing problem – and been a factor in agency disinvestment for the past ten years.

The real agency problem is not from holding company pressures, though, but from their own managerial passivity in letting work-loads get out of control without finding a way to measure them, track them, resource for them and negotiate fees based on them.

The real agency problem resides in the C-suite of ad agencies, and it is to the C-suite that we must turn to find leadership for the required changes. This won't happen unless agency CEOs finally admit that poor pricing is the fundamental problem that must be solved. Agency CEOs have the responsibility to solve the price problem. It's time to get started.

How, then, should senior agency executives begin the process?

If you – the reader – are an agency CEO, then the only way this can get started is if you convince yourself and your agency organization that the current path is unacceptable and cannot continue – it's a dead-end. You must screw up the courage to take organizational risks in overturning the laissez-faire agency culture – a task for which you may feel unprepared. You may have little confidence in yourself about directing the transformation, knowing that uncertain risks are sure to be run. But as an historian once wrote, "A ship in harbor is safe, but that is not what ships are built for."[1] A lack of confidence tells you that you are in the right place – it's the destiny of leaders to have doubts during difficult times but to overcome them to do what needs to be done.

Lou Gerstner, who joined IBM in 1993, certainly had doubts about himself and his prospects as he considered the challenges he would face as CEO:

"IBM's sales and profits were declining at an alarming rate. More importantly, its cash position was getting scary … mainframe revenue had dropped from $13 billion in 1990 to a projection of less than $7 billion in 1993, and if it did not level off in the next year or so, all would be lost … I was convinced … that the odds were no better than one in five that IBM could be saved, and that I should never take the position … The company was slipping rapidly, and whether that decline could be arrested in time – by anyone – was at issue.

Burke [Jim Burke, an IBM board member] introduced the most novel recruitment argument I have ever heard: 'You owe it to America to take the job.' He said IBM was such a national treasure that it was my obligation to fix it.

I responded that what he said might be true only if I felt confident I could do it. However, I remained convinced the job was not doable – at least not by me" (Gerstner, 2002, pp. 15-16).

Gerstner did overcome his lack of confidence to join IBM, of course, and the transformation he affected – turning the giant computer company into an integrated consulting service provider – emerged from his efforts to uncover the reasons for IBM's sales and profit problems. He had no blueprint at the beginning. *"I simply had no idea what I would find when I actually arrived at IBM* (Gerstner, 2002, p. 21). He took the job because he relished the challenge.

To kick off the transformation, let me suggest ten steps that will start agency CEOs on a positive path. You don't have to believe in all of them at once, but if you start out believing the first one, you're well on your way:

1. **Uncover and accept the fundamental problem.** Do some due diligence, diagnosing SOW workloads, fees and resources by client. You will find that your most fundamental problems stem from declining prices (fees divided by workload), and that past management responses to this decline – cost reductions – have caused a serious deterioration in agency capabilities.

Take this one office at a time. You're likely to find that each of your offices looks something like the New York office of The Cassandra Agency (Chapter 10). In finding and admitting the price problem, you take the first critical step towards identifying appropriate solutions.

2. **Renounce downsizing and disinvestment as responses for your price problems.** Acknowledge that the downsizing and disinvesting approach is inappropriate for the future and must be abandoned. Obtain the support of your parent holding company for this. Cut yourself a deal for a year or two while you work on a transformation. Then, take a deep breath – you've abandoned the past, and it's all new territory for you and your organization from this point onwards.

3. **Commit to a programme that will realize improved pricing.** You must commit to putting a floor under agency prices and then taking the necessary steps to increase prices by getting workloads under control and paid for, and then (subsequently) enhancing the value of agency services for your clients to realize better prices for your services.

4. **Measure and track agency workloads.** You must establish a policy that *every client served by the agency will have a documented SOW in a uniform format*, permitting the measurement of workloads on a comparable basis across brands, clients, offices and regions. Your office heads must implement this on your behalf – or else. As a result of the policy, you must invest in SOW management and measurement tools, and require 100% compliance in the use of the tools by agency client heads across the agency network. This will not be an easy matter. Agency personnel are used to ignoring the centre – they've rarely been held accountable for compliance, and no one thinks they'll get fired for ignoring senior executive policies.[2] Expect this to be difficult, follow through by introducing sanctions for non-compliance, should all else fail.

5. **Establish clear accountabilities for workload management and metrics among the agency's client heads.** You must reverse

decades of loose or absent accountability practices and establish, in a way that is understandable for all concerned, that client heads will be held accountable for workload management practices, fees and resources.

6. **Establish clear review processes to be conducted by office heads.** Client heads need to be accountable to office heads. Establish a policy that office heads will review client heads on a regular basis, at least quarterly, to examine the alignment of workloads, fees and resources and the progress being achieved at eliminating misalignments among these factors. This will give office heads a new set of responsibilities, and it will significantly increase your "reach" into the organization. Office heads are your key lieutenants, and you need to have them on board for the transformation process. If certain office heads do not want to cooperate in this venture, then sack them. That will help to make it clear that you are serious about your programme.

7. **Establish, as a matter of policy, that the agency be paid for all the work it carries out for its clients.** Client heads who are managing misaligned clients will be expected to develop corrective action plans to improve fees. Renegotiations with clients will be undertaken on a serious basis. Senior agency executives will be required to provide support for fee renegotiations. It is a fundamental economic fact that there is more to be gained by being paid for all the work that is done than by attempting, against all odds, to negotiate better salary or overhead terms. Be prepared to drop clients whose fees are entirely inadequate for the work they require. Make it clear that this is the reason the client is being dropped.

8. **Acknowledge and accept that clients are governed by shareholder value concerns, and that the mission of the agency needs to be refocused on helping clients improve brand growth and profitability.** Agency creativity is a factor that contributes to delivering results, but creativity is a factor, not an end in itself. Agency creativity no longer delivers results automatically, as it did during much of the Creative Revolution.

It's time to abandon the tired *"we're creative"* marketing positioning associated with the creative paradigm, and to step up to the challenge of saying *"We're committed to delivering results."*

9. **Generate and publish thought leadership about how marketing and advertising delivers results in today's multidisciplinary world.** Agency websites are devoid of ideas. Where are the White Papers and thought pieces that give current and potential clients food for thought? Which agencies can demonstrate that they think longer and harder about the challenge of brand growth and profitability than their competitors? Which client heads and strategic planners are clear thought leaders within an agency network, as demonstrated by their authorship of insightful papers, perspectives and presentations on issues of current concern to advertisers? By what process does an agency tap into and document its own intellectual insights about marketing and advertising effectiveness for clients – and provide meaningful content for current and potential clients? You need to elevate and expose the fragmented knowledge within your network by making it visible and essential. Knowledge must replace creative awards as the focus of an agency's culture. The potential knowledge-creators, like CS&P executives, must increase their professional ambitions and become trained for the more taxing challenge of identifying client performance challenges and putting together marketing strategies and SOWs that contribute to client growth and profitability.

10. **Upgrade CS&P talent.** Recent efforts to "upgrade" CS&P by replacing a percentage of the people with project managers took agencies in the wrong direction. The upgrading process ought to be designed, instead, to convert CS&P people into business-sophisticated and results-obsessed executives who provide consultative services to clients, solving brand growth and profitability problems. Advertiser strategic needs have been growing in complexity, and the pressures of globalization, the proliferation of brands/line extensions, the growing power of the trade, increased competition, increased consumer

price-sensitivity and the growth of internet commerce have made brand growth and profitability more and more difficult to achieve. Agencies, during the past two decades of fee declines and growing workloads, have downgraded the seniority and capabilities of CS&P people because of cost pressures that affected recruiting, entry-level salaries and training. Predictably, a void in brand thought-leadership has been created in the marketplace – and filled by new competitors: MBA-trained strategy and brand consultants working in blue-chip consulting firms. Inevitably, if this direction is not reversed, then advertisers are likely to opt out of the need to pay for agency CS&P resources (other than for a minimal amount of account coordination and communication) and limit agency services to the provision of creative resources only. Agencies must re-establish themselves on the strategic playing field, and add an upgraded "strategic brand and performance consulting" capability to the front end of their resource offerings. Advertisers will always seek and find solutions for their problems. Agencies will be part of the solution only if they offer capabilities that are valued and competitive when compared to the alternatives that their clients may consider.

The effort will require intensive analysis, exceptional communications, changes in key executives and unwanted commentary from the outside world. Going through a transformation is like weathering a storm at sea – the sooner it is over, the better. Here's Gerstner again: *"I've had a lot of experience turning around troubled companies, and one of the first things I learned was that whatever hard or painful things you have to do, do them quickly and make sure everyone knows what you are doing and why. Dithering and delay almost always compound a negative solution. I believe in getting the problem behind me quickly and moving on"* (Gerstner, 2002, p. 68).

THE REAL NEED IS FOR FOCUSED CEO LEADERSHIP

The recurring theme of this book is that agencies are plagued with growing workloads and declining fees. The workloads are not measured, so the knowledge of this problem is not widespread. It is certainly not among the top 10 problems that agency CEOs would describe today.

This lack of knowledge makes it easier for CEOs to respond to agency profit problems by downsizing. If workload sizes and growth rates were known, CEOs would certainly pause before downsizing.

Agencies need strong CEO leaders who are prepared to grapple with three clear challenges:

1. **The workload challenge**. Agencies must begin to document, track and measure their workloads. This will permit their organizations to do a much more effective job negotiating fees and putting a brake on declining fees.
2. **The mission challenge**. The mission challenge involves rethinking and then repositioning the raison d'être of the agency from "creativity" and "big ideas" to "results for clients." Only through such a repositioning can agencies begin to set a course for higher fees (as measured by billing multiples) and begin to close the "value-added gap" between themselves and the management consulting firms. This cannot be done without a wholesale upgrading of skills, particularly in client service, so training is part of the required mix.
3. **The accountability challenge**. The third challenge involves running the agency like a business and creating a strong sense of accountability throughout the organization, office by office and client by client. The current loose structure, justified somewhat romantically on the basis that "this is what is required to run a creative organization," ignores the fact that creativity is being killed on a daily basis by the very lack of accountability.

These three challenges – workload, mission, and accountability – are CEO challenges. No other executive in the management structure has the stature and authority to bring about these transformations in these three critical areas.

These are "insider challenges." I rather doubt that an outsider would have the credibility to overturn the agency culture, which is what is called for here. It's an insider's challenge, and if there is a CEO or CEO candidate who can intellectually separate himself or herself from the culture that nourished his/her career, there's a big challenge ahead. Take it on! Disrupt the agency! Don't expect to be applauded! It may not be a lot of fun, but it is what is needed.

"In order to arrive there
To arrive where you are, to get from where you are not,
You must go by a way wherein there is no ecstasy."

T.S. Eliot

Take comfort in the fact that if you embark on this journey, with seriousness and commitment, you will most certainly succeed, while others – more cautious, more conservative, more wedded to the past – will surely fall by the wayside.

APPENDIX A –
XLS LIMITED, THE MARKETING COMMUNICATIONS HOLDING COMPANY: A BUSINESS CASE

Rupert Rogers-Smith, Chairman and CEO of XLS Ltd, the marketing communications holding company, was having another sleepless night, tossing and turning in the marital bed, and his wife left the bedroom in a huff to sleep in the guest room – a bad sign. He didn't really blame her – there was no point in having both of them tired in the morning, but there was always hell to pay when she left in the middle of the night. He hated having to talk about it in the morning. Sophie, his wife, was fed up with hearing about his business worries, and she had been encouraging him to retire – he was wealthy and successful, and he didn't need to fret this way, or so she thought. The subject of XLS was a sore point for the two of them.

When Rogers-Smith could not sleep (this was a frequent occurrence), and as soon as his wife departed for the other bedroom, he turned on the light and pulled out a pad of yellow-lined legal paper to jot down what was on his mind. Tonight, he was thinking about XLS's strategy for the future. He wrote cogently and completely – it was the only way he could remember his key points.

He was still smarting from an analyst's report on XLS that he had read the previous night. It was written by the industry's most prominent securities analyst, James Foresight, whose institutional investors hung on to his every word. Foresight's report was not positive about XLS or its competitors. Q3 results for 2017 had just been announced, and Foresight had taken a negative view, casting doubts on earnings and growth prospects for 2018. This would impact XLS's share price and put pressure on XLS to correct its performance – or at the least, the *perception* of its performance – and raise questions about its long-term growth and profitability.

Foresight's report (in part) read as follows:

1. *With agency holdco revenues now in for the six largest globally diversified companies, we calculate global organic growth for 3Q17 of around +0.7%. For the US/North America (including the US where the number is broken out or North America where it is not), the comparable figure is +0.7%. The trends causing a deceleration from growth levels of +4% in 2014 and 2015 are real, and are most likely driving the current results downwards.*

2. *We estimate that the six most similar holdcos – WPP, Omnicom, XLS, Interpublic, Publicis and Havas – grew organically by +0.5% globally during 3Q17, similar to trends from earlier in the year, but still slower than any other quarter since 4Q09 in the midst of the global financial crisis. Among Omnicom, Interpublic, XLS, Publicis and Havas, Omnicom led with a gain of +2.8%, while XLS was weakest at -3.0%.*

3. *Looking at the US/North America only, results were once again relatively soft, with a +0.7% gain during 3Q17. Among the six, Publicis' 3.0% growth was the strongest during 3Q17, while XLS's -5.9% was the weakest.*

4. *We believe factors causing deceleration include the following:*
   - *Large brands are not growing by much, as they are commonly losing market share to smaller upstart brands or disruptors. While this has been true for some time, what is new is the use of zero-based budgeting processes by some of the impacted marketers. ZBB is having a disproportionate impact on spending by these companies on agency services.*

- *Like-for-like fee compression has been a persistent fact-of-life for agencies for many years. While it's hard to say that the pace at which those like-for-like fees are compressing has increased, in the wake of the K2 media transparency report[1], clients have generally tightened up contract language to have the effect of eliminating some of the ways in which agencies generated some of their media revenues over the past decade. This means that holdco media contracts and media fees will be under downwards pressures.*
- *Holdco creative agencies have generated profits and growth during the past few years largely from downsizings, eliminating the surplus resources that they once enjoyed during the media-commission days, and it now seems that they may have reached the end of this game. Indeed, we believe that the deterioration in creative agency relationships with their clients, as evidenced by shorter relationships and the accelerated pace of agency reviews is evidence that the downsizings have gone very far, affecting creative agency quality. Downsizings have had a negative impact on their ability to generate profit and sales growth rates consistent with healthy client relationships. Downsizings may also be a contributing factor to the lack of advertiser brand growth, since marketing problems associated with millennials, e-commerce and private label competitive products do not appear to be solved.*
- *Digital media has required more labour and more services to manage non-standardized and fragmented activities. It seems likely that slowing growth of digital media spending among larger marketers restrains related growth for agencies. Advertisers are showing skepticism about the results achieved from their digital and social spends, and although this does not suggest a return to TV advertising, it casts doubt on long-term spending levels across all media.*
- *In-housing of creative and media appears to be more common now vs. two or three years ago among the clients that*

agencies service. Advertisers are increasingly developing their own in-house agencies for digital, social and media planning operations. It's too early to know how permanent this might be, but in the short-term it is having an impact on holdco results.

- *Competition from IT services and consulting firms may be responsible for some of the quarter's results. The new competitors are large enough in the marketing services space to hurt the holdcos. Agencies may increasingly look to add many of the same services the consultants offer presently, but whether they have the skills or culture to become more "consultative" with their clients is an open question.*

- *Still, businesses we call "agencies" can be remarkably entrepreneurial, providing us with some confidence that new sources of revenue which are either modest today or not yet established could expand or emerge in some form, supporting incremental growth opportunities. The investment community is now more acutely aware of the challenges facing the industry than before. We think this may bring increased scrutiny of the holdcos to investors, for better or for worse, depending on the success of holdco initiatives.*

5. *VALUATION. We value companies on a DCF basis. Key variables driving valuations across the agencies include long-term costs of capital ranging from 11.5% to 12.0% (XLS on the low end and IPG, OMC and PUB on the high end) and long-term growth rates ranging from 3.5% (for IPG and OMC) to 5.75% (for WPP). We're revising our classification of XLS to "sell" from "hold" in view of our assessment that their long-term growth rate is flat or low.*

6. *RISKS. Agency risks relate to squeezing fees from clients, competition from adjacent industries, reduced competition between marketers and demand for advertising services.*

Pressure on XLS's performance had been building for some time. The 2016 and 2017 budget exercises had been painful for Rogers-Smith. As usual, he and his finance team encouraged (or required) XLS companies to submit aggressive annual budgets, showing strong (above industry) revenue and profit growth as a way of maintaining XLS's share price. Unusually, though, the agency CEOs and CFOs pushed back on the targets in an uncharacteristic way, claiming that the efforts to "get blood out of a stone" (in the words of Nigel Heathcliff, CEO of Icarus Global, one of XLS's major ad agencies) were "misguided." Heathcliff and others asked for a relaxation of some of the targets while the agencies invested in new people and new skills. A common theme was their stated need to "become more analytical" and "more consultative" with their clients, requiring more expensive people to be brought in from the outside.

The media agency heads wanted lower financial targets, referencing the consequences of the June 2016 K2 consulting report in the USA[2], which claimed (unfairly, Rupert thought) that there was fraud in the conduct of media operations by holding companies and their media agencies, including their receipt of non-transparent "rebates" from media owners to media agencies, designed to enhance holding company income from media operations.

Rogers-Smith rebuffed the agency efforts to relax budget targets and continued to ask for "stretched" financial performance from the XLS media and creative ad agencies.

It was becoming clear, though, that the agency executives were no longer "delivering the goods," and this led to weakened XLS performance and the evaluation contained in Foresight's report.

XLS was not the only holding company with performance problems, of course. Foresight's report made it clear that XLS was part of an industry that had industry-wide problems. Each holding company faced somewhat different conditions, depending on client mix, currency issues and the composition of their portfolios.

Rogers-Smith resolved to find alternative solutions during 2018, but he was not sure what direction he should go.

During the sleepless night, he mentally reviewed what he knew about his alternatives, based in part on what other holding companies were doing and in part on a theoretical list of alternatives that he considered. He rapidly filled several pages of his yellow pad of paper.

To be honest, though, he did not think through the consequences of each of the alternatives, and he knew that he would need to be much more thorough in his thinking before he raised his list of strategic alternatives to his management team and the Board of Directors.

Pressure was building, though, for him to begin the dialogue, so he resolved to dig deeper and outline in a more thorough way what alternatives he faced, and what their effects might be.

BACKGROUND AND HISTORY

XLS was created in 1984 by Rupert Rogers-Smith, who bought the controlling interest in a small direct-mail agency in London and named it XLS Results. Direct mail was a competitive business based on the use of mailing lists purchased from a variety of sources to develop and mail credit card solicitations (and similar materials) to potential customers. Rupert discovered that he had a unique ability to purchase, analyse and merge mailing lists that delivered higher than the typical 1% to 2% success rate that other direct mail operators experienced. His success in delivering a higher rate of qualified customers for his clients at lower costs made his direct mail operation successful, and customers of XLS Results encouraged the company to diversify into Customer Relationship Management, which involved the analysis of customer databases and the development of "loyalty programmes." XLS Results expanded into other forms of marketing, like sales promotion, print and even local TV commercials.

Rogers-Smith could see that he was developing the mastery of a number of disciplines that had a positive effect on client results, but the scale of XLS Results' operations was too small, and conflict-of-interest considerations prevented him from expanding his customer base. He decided to create a holding company, named XLS, and begin an acquisition programme of agencies in different disciplines. He and his XLS management team would work with the acquired companies to help them develop marketing campaigns that were more effective than what they were currently developing, and thus improve their capabilities and expand their programmes with existing customers.

During the next few years, from 1986 through 1992, he made a significant number of acquisitions in traditional and direct advertising, using borrowed money and XLS equity. The agencies he bought were not terribly profitable, which kept the acquisition prices low, and Rogers-Smith soon realized that there were massive cost-reduction opportunities that could be achieved, since most of the agencies he acquired were significantly overstaffed.

He shifted XLS's strategy from "helping agencies improve their competence" to "helping agencies become more efficient and profitable," using a small team of finance and budgeting people to work with agencies on their annual budgets and plans.

Rogers-Smith became highly competent at this financial re-engineering, and the growing results of XLS encouraged bankers to lend the company even larger sums to pursue its aggressive acquisition and profit-improvement programmes.

In 1994, XLS went public, ten years after its founding, and by 2016 it had developed an extensive portfolio of marketing communications companies in media, advertising, direct marketing, digital, research, public relations, branding, healthcare, promotions, consulting, and specialist communications. Revenue was more than $8 billion.

THE YELLOW-PAD INSOMNIA LIST OF STRATEGIC ALTERNATIVES – ROGERS-SMITH'S PERSONAL NOTES FOR HIMSELF

1. **Business as usual.** Continue the programme of acquisitions and aggressive budgeting that has generated increases of shareholder value for the past 20+ years. Continue to work with agencies on an arms-length basis, interacting through financial means only. Agencies will remain independent profit centres. If necessary, change the leadership (CEOs and CFOs) of the existing agencies, since the incumbents no longer appear to be able to generate the required results. This strategy only makes sense if we believe that we have "unrealized profit potential" from our existing portfolio of businesses. We need an analysis of this question. Should we hire a consulting firm for this task?

2. **Intervene in our portfolio companies.** Assume that our agencies are being undermanaged, and their operational practices are not up to requirements. We've lost control of pricing with our clients. We've lost control of scopes of work. Our agencies are no longer adding value in the same way, and we've lost the respect of our clients. Let's assume that we've let the quality of our people deteriorate over time. (How would we measure this?) Instead of "arm's length financial relationships," we need to intervene from the centre, and dispatch our people to do various audits of

agency operations and practices in the hope of upgrading them to restore reputations and capabilities. I'm worried, though, that our CEOs will use this as an excuse not to take responsibility, and they will expect XLS to fix their problems. This will put a major hole in performance; they'll stop trying, and they'll beg for reinvestment rather than shoot for better performance. It might kill our performance-oriented culture. Worried about this one.

3. **Imitate WPP's "holding company" initiatives and pursue independent XLS client relationships.** WWP has aggressively pursued holding company client relationships, independent of its agencies, promising clients that they will get fully-integrated teams drawn from the best WPP agencies across all marketing disciplines. Evidently, WWP thinks that its agencies are not doing enough of this, even though many of them are as diversified as WPP. Ogilvy & Mather is itself a holding company, with 10-11 separate brands under the O&M name. (John Seifert, CEO, is now rationalizing these brands under a single O&M name.) We're organized like WPP, but we're not pursuing XLS relationships. Do clients really want one-stop shopping, or do they want "best-in-class?". Can they get best-in-class from a holding company? It sounds like a price-competitive approach, and on top of this I'm not sure that XLS executives can pull together the various pieces to make these relationships work. The WPP agencies, I'm told, hate having their best people pulled out to work on WPP clients. Bad knock-on effects for the branded agencies. I wonder how badly the fees are discounted? Are the holding company relationships managed any better than agency relationships? Fees? Resources? Scopes of work? Or is it just a bigger way of managing things in the same dumb way? How can we find out?

4. **Imitate Publicis Groupe's "Power of One" initiative and pursue independent XLS client relationships.** Arthur Sadoun

took over from Maurice Lévy and seems intent on making one big giant agency out of Publicis Groupe, downgrading his branded agencies in the process[3]. Not at all the same as WPP. Saatchi & Saatchi. Leo Burnett. Publicis agency. All of them being downgraded and marginalized. Shuffling around the top management responsibilities at the agencies[4]. Saatchi oversees Leo's clients in Europe. Fallon takes over Saatchi CEO position in UK[5]. Seems like a screwed-up management mess. Geographical rather than brand-name form of organization. Can Publicis Groupe become one giant global agency? One that's like a consulting firm, built on the Sapient foundation? It's a big stretch. We don't have a Sapient capability, so I don't see how this makes sense for us, but Publicis is growing now, so maybe there's something to be learned about what they're doing.

5. **Sell to Accenture or IBM**. Accenture and Deloitte are very large, and they could buy us with petty cash. Both have been aggressive in buying up advertising agencies and stealing clients from us (and the others)[6]. They are highly analytical consulting firms, and they are fully capable of dealing with their clients' brand stagnation problems, following it up with advertising and media executions. They'd love our portfolio of businesses – they would get a huge package of agencies with one transaction. But they'd have to decide what to keep and what to dump, and that might be a bigger job than they'd like. Maybe it's easier for them to take this one bite at a time, buying smaller independent agencies. I'm unsure about their strategies. It would be hard to approach them without it leaking somehow, and if our investors heard that we were looking for a sale, they might think that we've lost confidence in the future. They might be overjoyed, though, if they had more confidence in the new owners than in us. Surely, though, we can keep this a secret? Would Accenture or Deloitte keep it quiet? Tough to know. Should I ask our investment

bank to make some quiet explorations? Who on the Board could help me with this? Seems complicated at this point. Selling out. It runs against my instincts.

6. **Shareholder value break-up**. We may get to the point where the parts are worth more than the whole, and our agencies should be spun off as separate operations with their own shares. Saatchi & Saatchi plc "demerged" in 1997, splitting into two equal-sized companies, Saatchi & Saatchi Advertising and Bates Worldwide Advertising, with each company holding an interest in Zenith Media, the media entity in the holding company[7]. Everyone got rich in the process, especially the holding company CEO. He stayed on as CEO of Saatchi & Saatchi Advertising and sold it to Publicis Groupe in 2000. Made an additional fortune with this. Bates, renamed Cordiant, went bust in 2003[8]. There's irony for you. Must have been poor leadership and a terrible strategy. Isn't demerger better than letting a slow death continue? Better to demerge early when we're relatively strong and profitable than to do this after WPP, Interpublic or Omnicom do it?

The problem is, I don't know what the knock-on effects of any of these strategies are.

How can I figure this out?

CASE ANALYSIS QUESTIONS

1. Do the in-depth thinking of these alternatives for Rupert Rogers-Smith.
2. Make this an exercise of pure logic. Diagram all the players in XLS's "Game of Advertising": investors, securities analysts, clients, ad agencies, employees, top management and others that you might identify.
3. Determine the various outcomes. What happens to share price? Clients? Investors? Employees? To all the players in XLS's "Game of Advertising?"
4. Can Rogers-Smith improve shareholder value through any of these strategic directions? Are some better than others? Why?
5. What should Rogers-Smith do?

APPENDIX B – ICARUS ADVERTISING AGENCY NEW YORK INC.: A BUSINESS CASE

In 2016, Kathy Morrison, newly hired chief executive officer of the New York office of Icarus Advertising Agency, stared out of her corner office at the growing traffic jam below on Madison Avenue – yellow cabs, blue-and-white buses, black Lincoln Town Cars, delivery vans. *Ok, enough of that, Kathy, get on with it*, she scolded herself.

She snapped around to her desk and looked at the inch-thick pile of typed papers in front of her. They were interview notes from her first three months on the job, written and edited by herself for her personal records. Morrison was an inveterate note taker, and she always typed up her notes in a first-person narrative style, as if the person she was talking to was giving her a coherent, logical story. This narrative device helped Morrison make sense out of what she heard in interviews.

The answer's somewhere in here, she thought. *I'll figure it out.*

HISTORY

Icarus New York was the headquarters office of Icarus Global Network, the number-four advertising agency in the world, with 124 international offices and operations in traditional advertising (TV, radio, print), direct marketing, public relations, events/sponsorship, sales promotion, digital and media. The agency operated under the Icarus brand name: Icarus Advertising was the traditional agency; Icarus DM handled direct marketing; Icarus PR was the public relations agency; Icarus Media handled media planning and buying, and Icarus Digital, a new company where Morrison had been CEO, handled web design, digital and social advertising.

Icarus Advertising was founded in New York in 1936 and had a proud tradition of creating some of the world's best-known advertising in print and radio. When television began to boom after the Second World War, Icarus was quick to exploit its potential. Icarus's fabled creative director, Harrison G. Gold, drove the creative department to: "win awards and then win more and more!" and the growing creative reputation of the agency guaranteed its success with big-spending clients who remained with the agency for decades.

Icarus, like others in the industry, used to collect a 15% commission on its clients' media expenditures, and this revenue, plus a 17.5% markup on production costs, covered all the agency's costs. If a client spent, for example, $100 million on the purchase of TV/radio time and print space in publications, the agency automatically received $15 million. This was a long-standing, profitable arrangement that permitted the agency to do "whatever the client wanted or needed, no questions asked." It also permitted the agency to allocate as many people as it wanted to deal with creative challenges. Under the commission arrangement, Icarus could allocate two, three, four, or even five creative teams to an assignment – assuring that the client received a full range of creative ideas from which to choose. "We wow them with choice," bragged Gold.

Icarus's executive management team had a clear and definitive view about itself, loudly proclaimed in 1985, when Harrison Gold received a "lifetime creative award" at the annual Cannes Festival. "Icarus is pure creativity," declared Gold. "It's as simple as that. Throughout our history, as long as we focused on creativity, and pushed its limits, both we and our clients thrived. What was true in the past will be true in the future. Creativity and success are permanently wedded in the advertising industry."

In the 1970s, Icarus went public and expanded through acquisitions in Europe, Latin America and Asia-Pacific. Subsequently, in the 1990s, it acquired activities in direct marketing and other forms of "nontraditional marketing," culminating in a number of acquisitions that solidified its presence across all media types. Significantly, though, Icarus did not integrate these operations – each marketing discipline was kept in its original organization and office. Thus, the Icarus network of 124 offices was essentially a federation of independent offices, each of them operating as profit centres, responsible for generating 15% profit margins, and the task of integrating their various capabilities for clients fell on the shoulders of the client heads. A global client using Icarus for traditional and direct marketing in, say, ten major markets around the world had to tap into the operations of 20 separate offices involving Icarus Advertising and Icarus DM.

During the post 9/11 recession, Icarus ran into financial difficulties, and its share price declined by 35%. XLS Ltd., the aggressive British holding company, made a public bid for the company in late 2002, and the Icarus board of directors decided to yield to its offer – it would be personally rewarding for each of them to be paid off in XLS shares, and it would get them off the hook, they thought, from continuing the annual heroics to maintain the profit margins that supported Icarus's share price. Furthermore, they knew that they would need to invest in digital capabilities, and ownership by XLS might make this more financially possible.

Indeed, with XLS's help, Icarus made a major digital acquisition in 2009, completing the diversification of its media portfolio. Kathy Morrison, the founder and head of Morrison Digital, an independent agency, joined the Icarus family of companies. Morrison was unusual in the advertising agency world, having earned an MBA at MIT before joining a software company and later founding Morrison Digital. As part of the acquisition, Morrison Digital was renamed Icarus Digital, and Morrison took on the task of running her agency within the Icarus corporate structure and learning how to work with the Icarus offices on an integrated basis.

SHIFT TO FEE-BASED REMUNERATION

The 1990s proved to be difficult for Icarus, despite its excellent creative reputation. Clients throughout the industry began to abandon the 15% media commission as the way of remunerating their agencies, shifting instead to "fee-based remuneration." Under the most usual fee scheme, clients paid their agencies an amount equal to the salaries of the professional people working on the account, plus an additional amount to cover a portion of agency overheads, plus an amount to cover profits.

Each of the three pieces of the remuneration was negotiated separately. First, clients wanted and needed to know the average salaries of the professional people working on the account; they compared these salaries to "benchmarked levels of salaries" in the industry, which they obtained through various means. Second, they expected to know how much overhead they would have to cover. This was calculated as an "overhead rate," based on the agency's *dollars of overhead per dollar of professional cost*. If an agency had, say, $20 million in overhead costs and $20 million in professional salaries, then the overhead rate was 100% (a fairly typical rate). Third, clients paid a negotiated profit margin of anywhere between 10% and 20%. It was generally known that the holding companies expected their agencies to earn a 15-20% profit margin, but not all clients were disposed to pay at this rate.

Once the salary levels, overhead rates and profit margins were negotiated, the fee could be budgeted for the year. Let's assume that the average agency professional person assigned to a given client earned $150,000 in salary and benefits, and that the client agreed to pay for 10 creatives (five teams in total), eight account executives, two strategic planners and eight production people, or $4,200,000 in salaries for 28 full-time equivalents (FTEs). If the overhead rate were 100%, then there would be an additional $4,200,000 for overheads. Total costs would be $8,400,000. To determine a fee for a 15% profit margin, the client would divide these total costs by 85%, and the fee would be $9,882,353. Profit would be the fee less total costs of $8,400,000, or $1,482,353.

This profit figure divided by the $9.882 million of fee calculates to 15%, the agreed profit margin.

One convention that the industry used to simplify these discussions was to divide the fee by the professional costs and calculate the "multiple," sometimes called a billing multiple. The $9.882 million fee divided by the professional costs of $4.200 million yields a "multiple" of 2.35.

These fee-based calculations required an exchange of financial information between ad agencies and their clients. This represented a dramatic change in the way the partners operated with one another. Under the commission arrangement, the only relevant information was "how much is the client going to spend on media and production." This determined the agency fee – 15% of media spend and a markup on production costs. Under the fee arrangement, though, agencies had to provide headcounts, average salary levels, overhead costs and profit margins. Armed with this information, clients began to negotiate in an aggressive manner.

Agencies resented the intrusive nature of this information exchange and felt that it degraded the quality of their relationships with their clients.

The marketing people at their clients were ill-equipped to deal with the financial aspects of the new fee-based remuneration schemes, so they passed them on to their procurement colleagues. As far as agencies were concerned, this added insult to injury; procurement, they believed, might know something about negotiating the cost of pens, pencils and travel arrangements, but they were ignorant about creativity and were sure to make a mess of things.

From 1992 to 2016, procurement departments, believing that agencies were overpaid, uncooperative and inefficient, drove down agency fees in four different ways. First, they used salary "benchmarking data" to drive down the average salary levels that they were prepared to pay for. Second, they negotiated agency headcounts to lower levels. Third, they negotiated lower levels of overhead rates.

Fourth, they reduced profit margins. All of these efforts had the effect of driving down agency headcounts and multiples, and this put agency profits under severe pressure. The profit pressures only intensified with the advent of digital advertising, which caused agency workloads to grow substantially.

One industry consultant documented the effects of growing workloads and declining fees, graphing the industry's "fees per typical ad" in constant dollars from 1992 to 2015, using a "ScopeMetric® Unit" (SMU) as the measure of a "typical ad." Although the data were controversial ("What's an SMU, anyway?") the data showed a clearly declining fee trend.

AGENCY FEES PER SMU 1992-2015

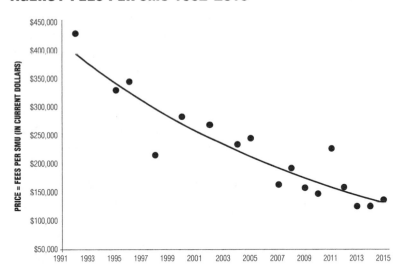

Source: SMU = ScopeMetric® Unit, a uniform measure of scope of work workload developed by Farmer & Company

MANAGEMENT CHANGES BY XLS

Shortly after the acquisition of Morrison Digital by Icarus, the incumbent chief executive officer of Icarus took early retirement in 2009, and Nigel Heathcliff was transferred from another XLS agency to take the helm of Icarus. He brought with him John "Jack" Pratt as his global chief financial officer. Heathcliff, a well-known industry figure, was a rare creature – a creative who rose to become CEO of a major agency. Pratt had been his loyal financial partner in a number of agency assignments. They were seen as a "right brain and left brain" team. Together they pledged to raise the creative profile of Icarus, which had suffered recently, and to shore up its profitability by touting the commercial benefits of Icarus's superior creativity. To this end, winning awards was a major priority.

Between 2009 and 2016, Heathcliff and Pratt changed office heads and executive creative directors around the Icarus network. Inevitably, the axe fell on Andrew Ravenswood, head of the New York office, after the loss of two major clients and weak financial performance for fiscal 2015. Poor creative quality was cited by each lost client as one of the contributing issues leading to Icarus losing the account. The executive creative director of Icarus NY, Tom Riley, was a highly respected, award-winning creative director, but he did not get along with Ravenswood, and he blamed his failure to win awards on Ravenswood's interference in his department, which principally involved downsizing, particularly of senior creative people, in an effort to reduce costs and generate profits for XLS.

Kathy Morrison was brought in to replace Ravenswood in early 2016. Morrison came from Icarus Digital, where she was known to be a tough-minded negotiator with her digital clients and an excellent leader of people. Heathcliff thought that Morrison's digital credibility could make it easier to provide integrated digital solutions for clients. Morrison was an unknown factor in television and print advertising, where the bulk of Icarus's advertising was focused (and was still growing despite the higher growth of digital advertising), but this did not cause him any major concerns.

Heathcliff and Pratt put in a lot of personal time recruiting and orienting Morrison for her new responsibilities.

Soon, Kathy Morrison joined Icarus New York as the new CEO for this headquarters office. Her first order of business was to meet one-on-one with the client heads and the finance director to figure out what was going on and what to do about it. It was clear from her interviews with client heads and other executives that there were mixed attitudes about how to manage the agency for the future.

She also had the recent 2015 report of a management consultant on Icarus' operations, but she was not certain what to make of it. The work had been commissioned by Andrew Ravenswood, her predecessor, during the final six months of 2015, when he was under pressure over the office's profitability. The client heads had participated in the consulting study by providing scopes of work to the consultant, but they had not seen the results of the work.

Morrison thought it might be useful to gather her senior team for an off-site meeting and lay out what she heard and what she thought the client heads and the executive team ought to do about it.

KATHY MORRISON'S INTERVIEW NOTES
(Summarized and Edited)

NIGEL HEATHCLIFF, GLOBAL CEO, ICARUS

Harrison G. Gold created the soul of this agency – we're about creativity, plain and simple, and I've watched our creativity slip through the cracks during recent years. We have to be at the forefront of creativity in everything we do. Creativity is what generates value for our clients. It's been proven that the most creative agencies that win the most awards bring the most value to clients.

One thing I will be expecting is a resurgence of creativity at Icarus NY. I know that this is not your particular expertise, but you're a clever person, and if you let your creative director Tom Riley take the lead on this, then you'll be ok. The problem with Andrew Ravenswood was that he interfered with the creative department and downgraded it with more junior people over time. This is not the way to win awards or deliver value to clients.

If we step up our creativity, I'm sure that it will secure our clients and our profitability. Both of these declined under Ravenswood – it's why he had to leave. Better work, better clients, better profits – and it will keep XLS off our backs.

JOHN "JACK" PRATT, GLOBAL CFO, ICARUS

I'm sure that you've spent enough time with Nigel to know that he lives and breathes creativity. Make sure you support Tom Riley, your creative director.

I'd like to emphasize, though, that you've been part of the XLS family before, and you know the rules of the game. Deliver your profit margin. Nothing else matters if you don't deliver the profits. They pay your bonus and my bonus and Nigel's as well. Missing your numbers is simply not acceptable.

I know that it is not easy in the current financial environment. Client fees have been lousy, and they will probably continue to get lousy. No matter. Do what you have to do to balance your head-counts with the fee structure. We have no flexibility to invest in this business; we have to match our resources to our fees.

My advice to you is to keep an eye on your monthly P&L, and no matter what else, ensure that you make your numbers.

I'll help in any way I can.

ROGER ADAMS, FINANCIAL DIRECTOR, ICARUS NY

Most of our contracts are pure fee contracts – we're paid for the resources we provide, and we have to prove to our clients that we're generating the hours that they expect. I keep abreast of our timesheet hours, even though our people are not very good at keeping timesheets up to date. We're reconciled every quarter – if we don't deliver the promised hours, we have to refund money to the client.

Here's a list of our clients and staffing. It's hard to analyse client profitability, given the poor nature of timesheet reporting, but best I can tell, we're making reasonable margins on our clients this year.

Client Name	Fees	FTEs
Alpha	$5,695,246	28.8
Bravo	$6,562,373	68.3
Charlie	$3,368,207	21.4
Delta	$2,000,017	8.1
Echo	$14,951,362	55.6
Foxtrot	$269,380	1.2
Golf	$7,953,370	45.0
Hotel	$29,858,075	85.1
India	$7,120,038	24.9
Juliet	$14,234,312	37.7
TOTAL	**$92,013,180**	**376.2**

Our biggest problem is that most clients expect to reduce their fees to us by 5% to 10% annually, and that will make it hard to make a 15% margin in the future. We lost two clients last year – Andrew was terminated because of this – and even though we added three new clients, their fees were worse, so we were behind the eight-ball even with new client wins.

We had to reduce our staff by 12% in the fourth quarter to make up for the shortfall, and Tom Riley, the head of creative, was upset by this. He feels that we have not been supporting him. Well, something has to give – it's not as if his department is the only one that has been hurt by client fee issues.

We have things under control for this fiscal year, I think. I'm concerned about a number of our clients – we've been told that we can expect $8 million in fee reductions over the next three years or so, so we know what's coming down the road.

Our client heads are not much help. They should "push back" a bit whenever the client talks about fee reductions, but our client heads are so service-oriented that they simply nod their heads and agree. They'll do whatever the client asks, whether it's more work or less fee. They're afraid of losing their clients, so they simply roll over and play dead. They're more on the clients' side than on ours!

It would be helpful for us if you could put some pressure on them to be more business-like, although I know this is not an easy thing to do. Honestly, I don't have the slightest idea what actually goes on between us and our clients.

We need more new business as a cushion – and better fees and more internal discipline, but I guess I'm hoping for the impossible.

I don't envy you for getting into this situation.

ADAM (CLIENT ALPHA)

We do a huge amount of work on Alpha, but we're coping, and I'm happy to say that we deliver the 15% profit margin to the agency. Our account people are great – they chip in when there's a creative crunch, and the digital work (banners and the like) is not so challenging that they can't make a creative contribution.

We have terrific spirit. Of course, I'd like to get greater fees, but we share this client with another agency, not part of XLS, and I don't dare bring up the subject of fees. Things are stable at present. I think things are going well.

BETH (CLIENT BRAVO)

Bravo was an international client last year, in that we had to develop marketing strategies for their expansion into the Asia-Pacific, where they work with other agencies to develop specific ads. This cost us, because we were not paid enough for this strategic work. Still, we're happy to be the thought leader on the account, because this will help us in the future.

I don't think we have big client issues.

What I really wanted to tell you was how much I appreciate having a woman as CEO, because this office is disgustingly macho, and there aren't enough women anywhere, especially in the creative department. Tom Riley, the creative director, doesn't have a single female copywriter. And I won't bother to tell you about your predecessor, Andrew Ravenswood, who was a little too "hands-on" for my taste. I'm glad he's gone – the office has been very sexist, and it has to stop.

COLIN (CLIENT CHARLIE)

I have a small piece of a big soft-drink company, and it's a great start, so the sky's the limit. I just need some time to develop it. This is a great office, and I'm sure you'll fit in well here.

EDWARD (CLIENT ECHO)

We won a creative award last year at Cannes, and I think we can do it again. Not bad for the number-two client in the office! Tom Riley does what he can with our limited creative resources. My advice for you – hire more creatives and undo the damage Andrew did to the office.

GARY (CLIENT GOLF)

We don't have to do much work on this client every year, but we get a whacking great fee because the client loves our team and will pay for it, even if the work goes up and down. Nothing to worry about at all. We're under control.

HARRY (CLIENT HOTEL)

We're under review, now, but I think that we'll win more of the total business next year. The decision will be made in six weeks, we're told. We've got a very senior team on the client, and we're giving it our all. Nothing you can do at this point; I've got it under control.

IRWIN (CLIENT INDIA)

This is a great client, but we have to service it to death because they can't make up their minds. Lots of rework and rebriefings. If you have any thoughts about how to make things smoother, we're prepared to listen. Fees are high and stable, I think.

JOHN (CLIENT JULIET)

Tom Riley loves this client, because it gives us the best shot at winning awards year after year. We double up on our creative resources to generate extra ideas, and the client loves it. We're in terrific shape. There are other clients in the office that you really need to focus on. It's none of my business, but I've been in this office for ten years, and I've seen things come and go. If I were you, I'd work on developing more entrepreneurialism in the office rather than trying to micromanage things. Andrew became a micromanager, and it nearly killed us. Develop the right climate, and good things will happen. We know how to run our clients if we have the freedom to do it properly.

CONFIDENTIAL REPORT FROM GORDON KINSEY, CONSULTANT

(Private for Andrew Ravenswood of Icarus Advertising Agency)

1. We completed our analysis of each of Icarus NY's clients during the past two months, as agreed, using our proprietary technology.
2. We gathered the scopes of work from each client and ran them through our resource model. From these, we were able to calculate the workload of each client and how many people should have been assigned to each client to assure creative quality.
3. We are concerned, as you know, that Icarus, like others in the industry, does not negotiate the amount of work it does with its clients. This is a holdover from the commission days, when remuneration was so high that workloads did not need to be negotiated. Now, though, under the fee-based arrangement, with fees at historical lows, it no longer makes sense to "do whatever the client wants, whenever the client wants it," which is still the governing MO of the agency. Icarus does too much work for the resources it has if all clients are taken into account.
4. Client heads admit that Icarus is doing more work than it can do on a quality basis, but they arc loathe to confront their clients and negotiate for higher fees – they each think that this will simply encourage clients to go outside and find other agencies. So they suffer in silence.
5. Our analysis suggests that there are many clients that are underpaid and understaffed, and that unless you mobilize your client heads to negotiate for higher fees, this trend will continue.
6. Your creative quality is already at risk. The typical creative should be doing 4.1 SMUs of work per year, according to our methodology, and the office average is already 4.9 – and it varies from this considerably by client, based on varying prices (fees per SMU):

ICARUS TOP TEN CLIENTS – 2015 SOWS

Client Name	Fees	Deliverables	SMUs	Price (Fee per SMU)	FTEs	FTE's per SMU	Creative FTEs	SMUs per Creative	CS&P Ratio
Alpha	$5,695,246	1,776	163.5	$34,837	28.8	0.2	9.2	17.8	1.0
Bravo	$6,562,373	1,700	151.8	$43,219	68.3	0.5	28.7	5.3	0.8
Charlie	$3,368,207	244	49.8	$67,611	21.4	0.4	7.8	6.4	0.8
Delta	$2,000,817	292	16.1	$124,160	8.1	0.5	2.9	5.5	1.2
Echo	$14,951,362	132	80.6	$185,459	55.6	0.7	18.9	4.3	1.3
Foxtrot	$269,380	16	1.4	$194,966	1.2	0.9	0.2	8.2	4.1
Golf	$7,953,370	104	29.5	$269,574	45.0	1.5	9.4	3.1	2.5
Hotel	$29,858,075	632	107.1	$278,808	85.1	0.8	32.8	3.3	1.1
India	$7,120,038	68	23.9	$297,627	24.9	1.0	7.1	3.4	1.7
Juliet	$14,234,312	60	34.9	$407,764	37.7	1.1	16.7	2.1	0.6
TOTAL	$92,013,180	5,024	658.7	$139,693	376.2	0.6	133.6	4.9	1.1

The 2015 average of these ten major clients is relatively healthy, but this average is made up of ten clients with highly varied metrics:

✓ Average *price per SMU* is $139,693, at the industry average price for 2015.

✓ Average **resources per SMU** are 0.6 FTEs per SMU, in the middle of the industry range between 0.5 and 0.7 FTEs. This is an appropriate level of average staffing.

✓ Average **creative output per head** is 4.9 SMUs per creative. It is near the upper limit of the productivity range of 4.1 to 5.0 SMUs per creative. This is not a bad average figure, unless it is part of a trend towards increased creative stretching, which I believe to be the case.

✓ Average **CS&P Ratio** (Client Service + Planning FTEs per Creative FTE) is 1.1x, slightly above the industry average of about 1.0x.

The average health of this portfolio is made up of

- Four "underperforming" clients: Alpha, Bravo, Charlie and Delta;

- Six "overperforming" clients: Echo, Foxtrot, Golf, Hotel, India and Juliet:

Client Groups	Fees	% of Fee	SMUs	% of SMUs	FTEs	% of FTEs
4 Underperformers	$17,626,643	19.2%	95.3	57.9%	126.7	33.7%
6 Overperformers	$74,386,537	80.8%	69.4	42.1%	249.5	66.3%
TOTAL	**$92,013,180**	**100.0%**	**164.7**	**100.0%**	**376.2**	**100.0%**

- The four underperforming clients account for only 19.2% of the fees, but 57.9% of the SOW workload and 33.7% of the FTEs.
- The six overperforming clients account for 80.8% of the fees, but only 42.1% of the SOW workload and 66.3% of the FTEs.
- The overperformance of Hotel and India, relatively large clients, represents a vulnerability, since the high prices relative to the lower workloads are probably unsustainable in the long run.

The four underperforming clients are dragging down the average performance of the agency.

The six overperforming clients are shoring up the underperformers, but the outstanding price performance cannot be guaranteed into the future.

7. Icarus, which has built its reputation on creativity, is at risk of letting its creative capability slip between its fingers.
8. The time has come to refocus the agency, and make it more of an "account management" agency, with improved accountabilities for the account management people. They need to be accountable for fees, workloads and profits – items that the creative department cannot deliver.
9. The long-term financial stability of the agency is determined by its fee structure and the number of people the agency can afford to do the agreed work. These factors are significantly out of balance.

CASE ANALYSIS QUESTIONS:

- What is Icarus's strategic and operational situation?
- What should Kathy Morrison do as CEO at Icarus NY?
- What overall message should she deliver at the off-site meeting?

APPENDIX C –
SCOPE OF WORK
DELIVERABLES:
DEFINITIONS

ORIGINATIONS:
THESE ALWAYS INVOLVE ORIGINAL WORK

HIGH CREATIVE COMPLEXITY ORIGINATIONS
These are the truly original deliverables derived from new strategic briefs, requiring many (three or more) new creative alternatives. The development of a new big idea involves high creative complexity originations. Typically, high creative complexity originations are associated with a new product, a launch, a relaunch, a line extension or as the foundation for an entirely new and original multi-media campaign. They can be characterized as "here's something entirely new and original to serve as the basis for our new positioning and thinking." They often require multiple creative teams and have understandably high levels of associated rework. Example: A TV:30 high creative complexity origination has an SMU value of 1.439.

AVERAGE CREATIVE COMPLEXITY ORIGINATIONS
These are deliverables involving further original work, building on the foundation provided by high creative complexity originations. They are secondary/ongoing deliverables from the existing strategic brief, but usually derived from a new creative brief that calls for at least one or two new creative routes, perhaps for a new media mix or in support of a new campaign. They can be characterized as "something new, but in line with the directions

that have been previously established." They usually require only one creative team and should go through only one full rework (three to four tweaks) in most situations. Example: A TV:30 average creative complexity origination has an SMU value of 0.617, or about 43% of the value of a high creative complexity origination.

LOW CREATIVE COMPLEXITY ORIGINATIONS

These, too, are deliverables involving original work, but the degree of originality is less than average creative complexity deliverables. Instead, these low creative complexity deliverables involve a single creative route from an existing strategic and creative brief, with very little need for new creative thinking. This could be characterized as "more of the same, but different in some minor way." They usually require one creative team, with one half of a full rework (i.e., one to two tweaks). Example: A TV:30 low creative complexity origination has an SMU value of 0.411, or about 67% of the value of an average creative complexity origination and 29% of the value of a high creative complexity origination.

ADAPTATIONS: FROM PREVIOUSLY CREATED ORIGINAL WORK

HIGH CREATIVE COMPLEXITY ADAPTATIONS

What makes an adaptation "high in creative complexity" is the degree to which the original work needs to be changed. High creative complexity adaptations involve changes to about two thirds of script/sound/copy, storyboard/layout, or footage/image. They should involve the efforts of ½ of a creative team, with one to two tweaks (half of a full rework). Example: A TV:30 high creative complexity adaptation has an SMU value of 0.185, or about 45% of the value of a low creative complexity origination, 30% of the value of an average creative complexity origination, and 13% of the value of a high creative complexity origination.

AVERAGE CREATIVE COMPLEXITY ADAPTATIONS

These adaptations involve major changes of one third of the original work or minor changes of to up to two thirds of the original work. They should involve the efforts of half of a creative team, with one to two tweaks (half of a full rework). Example: A TV:30 average creative complexity adaptation has an SMU value of 0.123, or about 67% of the value of a high creative complexity adaptation.

LOW CREATIVE COMPLEXITY ADAPTATIONS

These adaptations involve very low-level changes to the original work – minor changes to one third of the original work. They should involve the efforts of half of a creative team, with virtually no rework. Example: A TV:30 low creative complexity origination has an SMU value of 0.086, or about 70% of the value of an average creative complexity adaptation and 47% of the value of a high creative complexity adaptation.

REFERENCES

Adage Data Center, World's 50 Largest Agency Companies, 13 June 2013.

Auletta, Ken, *Frenemies: The Epic Disruption of the Ad Business (and Everything Else)*, (New York: Penguin Press, 2018)

Barton, R. *Advertising Agency Operations and Management.* (New York: McGraw-Hill Book Company Inc., 1995).

Burton, J. *A Marketer's Guide to Understanding the Economics of Digital Compared to Traditional Advertising and Media Services.* (New York: American Association of Advertising Agencies, 2009).

Christensen, C. M.,*The Innovator's Dilemma.* (Boston: Harvard Business School Press, 1997).

Colvin, G.,"The Great CEO Pay Heist", *Fortune Magazine*, 25 June 2001.

Crystal, G. S, *In Search of Excess: The Overcompensation of American Executives* (New York: WW Norton & Company, 1991).

Dan, A., "Advertising Shoots Itself In The Foot. Again." *Forbes.com,* 21 June 2012.

Denning, S. (2013, June 26). "The Origin of the World's Dumbest Idea," Retrieved from www.forbes.com: http://www.forbes.com/sites/stevedenning/2013/06/26/the-origin-of-the-worlds-dumbest-idea-milton-friedman/

Dentsu Taps Aegis Executive, *Advertising Age,* 28 June 2013.

Dougherty, P. H. (1986, April 28). *www.nytimes.com/1986/04/28/business/3-way-merger-to-create-largest-ad-agency.html.* Retrieved June 11, 2013, from New York Times: www.nytimes.com

Femina, J. D, *From Those Wonderful Folks Who Gave You Pearl Harbor,* (New York: Simon and Schuster, 1970).

Fox, S, *The Mirror Makers,* (New York: Morrow, 1984).

Friedman, M. "The Social Responsibility of Business is to Increase its Profits," *New York Times Magazine,* 13 September 1970.

Gerstner, L. V., *Who Says Elephants Can't Dance?* (New York: HarperCollins Publishers Inc, 2002).

Goldman, K., *Conflicting Accounts – The Creation & Crash of the Saatchi & Saatchi Empire* (New York: Simon & Schuster, 1997).

Haase, A. E., *Advertising Agency Compensation: Theory, Law, Practice* (New York: ANA, 1934).

Hammer, M. & Champy, J., *Reengineering the Corporation: A Manifesto for Business Revolution* (New York: Harper Business Books, 1993).

Hegarty, J., *Hegarty On Advertising: Turning Intelligence into Magic* (New York: Thames & Hudson, 2011).

Kiechel, W., *The Lords of Strategy* (Boston: Harvard Business Press, 2010)

Kleiner, A., "Bare Knuckles on Madison Avenue," *The New York Times Magazine,* November 8 1987.

Kleppner, O., *Advertising Procedure* (New York: Prentice-Hall, 1979).

Kuhn, T. S., *The Structure of Scientific Revolutions* (Chicago: The University of Chicago Press, 2012).

Levitt, T., "The Globalization of Markets," *Harvard Business Review*, 1983.

Livingston, J. S., "Pylmalion in Management," *Harvard Business Review*, January 2003.

Mandese, Joe, "ANA Calls Agency Financial Relations 'Disturbing,' Releases Findings to Back It Up," *Mediapost Agency Daily*, http://www.mediapost.com/publications/article/248295/ana-calls-agency-financial-relations-disturbing.html, 23 April 2015.

"Marketers, Agencies, Google Spar Over Brands' Precious Data," *Advertising Age*, 18 March 2014.

Mayer, M., *Madison Avenue, U.S.A.* (New York: Pocket Books, Inc., 1959).

McNamara, J., *Advertising Agency Management* (Homewood: Dow Jones-Irwin, 1990).

Mierau, C., *Accept No Substitutes! The History of American Advertising.* (Minneapolis: Lerner Publications Company, 2000).

N.W. Ayer & Son, *Forty Years of Advertising* (Philadelphia, 1909).

Ogilvy, D., *Ogilvy on Advertising* (London: Prion, 1983).

Parkinson, C.N. (1958). *Parkinson's Law*. London: John Murray.

Popper, N., "CEO Pay is Rising Despite the Din," *New York Times*, 16 June 2012).

Porter, M. E., *Competitive Strategy* (New York: The Free Press, 1980).

Porter, M. E., *Competitive Advantage* (New York: The Free Press 1985).

Porter, M. E., *The Competitive Advantage of Nations* (New York: The Free Press, 1990).

Reichheld, F. F., *The Loyalty Effect: The Hidden Force Behind Growth, Profits, and Lasting Value* (Boston: Harvard Business School Press, 1996).

Rubel, I., *Financial Management and Accounting* (New York: Funk & Wagnalls Company with Printers' Ink Publishing, 1948).

Singer, N., "In Chief Executives' Pay, A Rich Game of Thrones," *New York Times*, 12 April 2012).

Stern, C. W. & Deimler, M. S., *The Boston Consulting Group On Strategy* (Hoboken: John Wiley & Sons, Inc, 2006).

Stewart III, G. B., *The Quest for Value* (New York: Harpercollins, 1991).

Sullivan, L., *Hey Whipple, Squeeze This!* (Hoboken, NJ: John Wiley & Sons, Inc, 2012).

Sutherland, A. B., "Nice Work if You Can Get It," *Daily Mail*, 27 April 2012.

Tungate, M., *Ad Land,* (London and Philadelphia: Kogan Page, 2007)

WPP, *Annual Report* (London, 2003).

ENDNOTES

INTRODUCTION

1   Ken Auletta, *Frenemies: The Epic Disruption of the Ad Business (and Everything Else)*, Penguin Press, 2018

2   As used in this book, *workloads* refer to the creative and production deliverables that represent an ad agency's output for its clients. Included in the workload is the associated brand strategic work that provides "positioning" for the actual deliverables. Creative workloads exist across all media, including TV, print, radio, out-of-home, direct, promotion, sponsorship, digital, social, and every other possible medium that can contain marketing content.

3   I will frequently use the terms "downsize" and "downsizing." By this I mean *"headcount adjustments that do not keep up with changes in workloads."* This includes staffing reductions in the face of flat workloads; zero staffing growth for growing workloads, or modest staffing growth for substantial growth in workloads. "Downsizing," as used here, always leads to increased stretching of agency resources for a given amount of work.

4   Industry estimates of relationship longevity are at a new low – four years or so, according to The Bedford Group, although *Campaign* magazine (UK) puts the figure at below three years.

CHAPTER 1

1   A typical creative team for TV, print and radio ads consisted of one copywriter and one art director who worked closely with one another on all their projects or 'briefs'. Multiple teams could be assigned by the executive creative director to work competitively on a brief to generate more ideas. Each creative team strove to be the one whose ideas were incorporated in the final ad. Obviously, multiple teams were possible only if there was money to support the extra resources.

2   A "brief" is a creative project assigned to an agency by its client. An agency "is briefed" to carry out strategic and creative work, leading in most cases to the production of an ad. The document used to brief the agency is called "the brief." *Brief* is synonymous with *project*, and both terms are used interchangeably in this book.

CHAPTER 2

[1] *USA Today* described Della Femina as "the most colourful creative guy in an industry full of colourful creative guys." (17 May 1994).

CHAPTER 3

[1] https://www.sec.gov/news/press/2008/2008-71.htm)

[2] https://www.cbsnews.com/news/pay-for-failure-mccann-boss-leaves-agency-in-tatters-but-takes-a-37m-pension/)

[3] https://www.sec.gov/litigation/complaints/2008/comp20547-ipg.pdf)

[4] Ignition One was allowed to buy itself out of Dentsu in a management buyout in July 2013.

CHAPTER 4

[1] Howard Morgens, 1910-2000, was CEO of Procter & Gamble from 1957 to 1974. He is credited with leading P&G through its most significant growth period. During his tenure, he introduced the Pampers, Downy, and Bounce brands, acquired Folgers, expanded internationally, and invested heavily in product development. These efforts resulted in a quadrupling of revenues from $1.1 billion to $4.9 billion and quintupling of earnings from $67 million to $316 million. Source: Harvard Business School, https://www.hbs.edu/leadership/20th-century-leaders/Pages/details.aspx?profile=howard_j_morgens

[2] Theodore Levitt, "The Globalization of Markets," *Harvard Business Review*, May 1983.

[3] The Saatchi & Saatchi plc annual report for 1983 stated "the global corporation operates at low relative cost – as if the entire world (or major regions of it) were a single entity; it sells the same things in the same way everywhere."

[4] Brazil, Russia, India and China

[5] Bangladesh, Egypt, Indonesia, Iran, Mexico, Nigeria, Pakistan, Philippines, South Korea, Turkey and Vietnam.

CHAPTER 6

[1] A "full-service" ad agency offered creative services (development and production of ads) and media services (media planning and buying). Both of these services were paid for by the traditional 15% media commission. When the media services were spun out, what was left was the agency's creative services (creatives, production, client service and strategic planning). The spinoff required a change in the way agencies were remunerated, both for the separate media operations and the remaining creative services operations.

²   https://www.nytimes.com/2018/05/25/business/highest-paid-ceos-2017.html

³   Salary "benchmarks" were provided by specialized benchmarking consulting firms who worked on behalf of advertisers. The benchmarker's business was to examine the salary and overhead costs of advertising agencies and find ways to justify cutting their fees. They did this by comparing the costs of the agencies they were investigating to their own "benchmarked cost data." As a matter of practice, the benchmarking firms retained the agency data they gathered during their inquiries and repackaged the data selectively into their benchmark database to be used with subsequent clients. Benchmarking was a highly successful but ethically questionable business, all the more so because the benchmarkers never revealed the source or accuracy of their benchmarking databases. Procurement departments sought out and supported benchmarking firms. Agencies, for their part, tended to believe that many of the salary and overhead benchmarks were pure inventions designed to justify fee reductions.

CHAPTER 7

¹   See www.bain.com; www.bcg.com; and www.mckinsey.com for examples, looking under industry expertise for consumer marketing, media and entertainment, retail or the equivalent.

²   Bruce Henderson published BCG's *Perspective* on The Experience Curve in 1973 and on The Product Portfolio in 1970.

³   Bill Bain's principles, designed to create successful long-term relationships: *1) We must have a three- to- five hour <u>private</u> meeting with the CEO, during which time we will explain our strategic concepts and why they are successful, and he will share with us his aspirations, concerns and fears about his corporate performance. 2) The CEO must be open to the concept that our mission must be to help him improve results through a top-down CEO/Bain-led programme that begins with his most important businesses and continues throughout his portfolio. 3) He must be open to the idea that the relationship will last as long as Bain & Company continues to generate positive results that are a substantial multiple of its fees – it is <u>not</u> a short-term budget-limited project-based relationship like those that exist between most consulting firms and their clients. 4) The CEO must agree not to work with Bain's competitors, and Bain will agree not to work with the client's competitors.*
Source: the author's memory – the principles were not written down.
It should be pointed out that these principles were in effect from 1973 for about 20 years, but they were abandoned after Bill Bain left Bain & Company in the early 1990s, since it was believed that they were no longer needed to sell new business or retain clients for long-term relationships.

4   *AdWeek*, Richard Morais, September 10, 2018, https://www.adweek.com/digital/how-brian-whipple-turned-accenture-into-worlds-largest-digital-agency/

5   S4 Capital prospectus, September 2018

CHAPTER 8

1   Direct mailing lists have been around a very long time. The analysis and selection of targeted mailing lists from broader databases was an early form of big data – useful for soliciting magazine subscriptions, credit cards, donors for fundraising, etc. These were closely followed by customer relationship management (CRM) databases and the ubiquitous loyalty programmes that subsequently developed. Technology and customer databases have continued to evolve since then, and although big data, as it exists today, dwarfs these early incarnations of customer data analysis, we shouldn't forget about the family resemblance. Big data is a product of evolution, not of recent divine creation.

2   Fortune Magazine, 10 April 2018. http://fortune.com/2018/04/10/facebook-cambridge-analytica-what-happened/

CHAPTER 9

1   *The Washington Post*, 13 September 2018

2   Jack Marshall and Suzanne Vranica, "Agency Transparency Concerns Fueled by Former WPP Executive," *The Wall Street Journal*, 6 March 2015.

3   Jack Neff, "Former Mediacom CEO Alleges Widespread US Agency 'Kickbacks," *Advertising Age*, 6 March 2015.

4   Joe Mandese, "ANA Calls Agency Financial Relations 'Disturbing,' Releases Findings to Back It Up," *Mediapost Agency Daily*, http://www.mediapost.com/publications/article/248295/ana-calls-agency-financial-relations-disturbing.html, April 23, 2015.

5   ANA Press Release, "4As and the ANA Create Cross-Industry Task Force to Establish Best Practices in Transparency, a Task Force Comprised of Agency Heads and Senior Marketers," https://www.ana.net/content/show/id/34748, 24 April 2015.

6   Guidelines, surveys and papers from the 4As website at http://aaaa.org

7   Nathalie Tadena, "Advertising Trade Groups Split Over Transparency Guidelines," *The Wall Street Journal*, 28 January 2016.

8   Noreen O'Leary, "4As Issues Media Transparency Guidelines Without ANA Support," *Adweek*, 28 January 2016.

9   Nathalie Tadena, "Advertising Trade Groups Split Over Transparency Guidelines," *The Wall Street Journal*, 28 January 2016.

[10] Noreen O'Leary, "4As Issues Media Transparency Guidelines Without ANA Support," *Adweek*, 28 January 2016.

[11] "An Independent Study of Media Transparency in the US Advertising Industry for the Association of National Advertisers (ANA)," *K2 Intelligence*, 7 June 2016. From the Executive Summary, pp. 1-3.

[12] "Media Transparency: Prescriptions, Principles, and Processes for Advertisers," a report by ANA, Ebquity and Firm Decision (unauthored), 18 July 2016

[13] Tom Finneran, EVP Agency Management Services, 4As, in an email to the author, 16 November 2016.

[14] Adam Buckman, "Gotlieb Slams ANA Report on Transparency," *Media Daily News*, 28 October 2016.

[15] Kana Inagaki and Leo Lewis, "Dentsu Overcharging Scandal Spreads," *The Financial Times*, 23 September 2016.

[16] Suzanne Vranica and Jack Marshall, "Facebook Overestimated Key Video Metric for Two Years," *The Wall Street Journal*, 22 September 2016.

[17] *MediaPost*, Richard Whitman, 17 September 2018. https://www.mediapost.com/publications/article/325225/agency-client-trust-levels-hit-a-new-low.html

[18] *AdAge*, "McKinsey: Not much has changed three years after media uproar," Jack Neff, 30 April 2018.

[19] MediaPost, Steve McClellan, https://www.mediapost.com/publications/article/326302/fbi-seeks-help-in-identifying-advertisers-that-may.html?edition=111306.

[19] "Production Transparency in the US Advertising Industry," ANA Report, 9 August 2017.

[20] *Adweek*, "Report Finds 36% Increase in New Business This Year, Driven by Agency Reviews," Erik Oster, 6 August 2018

[22] Campaign Staff, "Ad Industry Morale Drops 36% from 2015, says *Campaign* US Survey," Campaign, 24 October 2016.

SECTION II

[1] *The Wall Street Journal*, "WPP's Struggles in North America Send Shares Lower," 14 September 2018.

CHAPTER 10

[1] By size, we mean '*agency manhours to complete a deliverable at an appropriate productivity level*', where '*appropriate productivity level*' considers '*appropriate staffing*' (like the appropriate use of multiple creative teams, for example) and '*appropriate levels of rework*'. The subject of deliverable size is explained in detail in Appendix C.

2   Originations and adaptation deliverables can be classified as 'creative development only', 'production only' or 'full-up.' *Creative development only* means that production is done in a different fiscal year or by another agency. *Production only* means the creative development was done earlier or by another agency. *Full-up* means that the creative development and production for the deliverable were done by the same agency in the same fiscal year.
As a consequence, there are six possible origination/adaptation classifications for each deliverable.

CHAPTER 11

1   Bruce Henderson, founder of The Boston Consulting Group, showed in 1968 that prices and costs decline by 20-30% each time accumulated production is doubled. This decline (in constant dollars) goes on in time *without limit*. The concept of price and cost decline is more fully developed in the book *Perspectives on Experience*, published by The Boston Consulting Group, Boston, 1970.

2   Peter Drucker, *Management* (Revised Edition), HarperCollins Publishers, 2009.

3   *Profitability* is used loosely here, since we are ignoring overhead costs. If the cost dimension is limited to FTE costs for the client-facing FTEs, then *profitability* means *"contribution margin"* – income less direct costs, which "contributes" to cover overhead costs and operating profits.

4   According to a vote of more than 1,000 DDB employees around the world in 2011, this particular quote (*"Nobody counts the number of ads you run..."*) is Bill Bernbach's "number one quote of the century." http://www.ddb.com/BillBernbachSaid/why_bernbach_matters/deep-influence.

CHAPTER 12

1   Organizational research shows that collaborative decision-making yields improved results over individual decision-making. See, for example, research from the "survivor training series" offered by Human Synergistics International and other training organizations. http://www.humansynergistics.com/ResourceCenter/ResearchandPublications.

CHAPTER 13

1   Bruce Henderson, founder of The Boston Consulting Group, was a creative thinker and prolific writer. During the early years of BCG, he penned a number of provocative articles and mailed them to potential clients, calling them "Perspectives" – an early version of what we now identify as a blog. The Perspectives were reprinted in 2006 as *The Boston Consulting Group On Strategy*, edited by Carl W. Stern & Michael S. Deimler (Stern CW & Deimler MS, 2006).

[2] If we had included *all rework* as part of our SMU value, rather than "gold standard" levels of rework, then the amount of work in 1992's SOWs would have been higher, and the calculated creative productivity would have been much closer to three ads per year.

CHAPTER 14
[1] Parkinson's Law: The Pursuit of Progress (London, John Murray, 1958)

CHAPTER 15
[1] I've seen many agency offices where each client head kept some form of rudimentary SOW record on the basis of his/her client's fiscal year, and every client head had a different system, but if you tried to add them up in some way to see the office's workload for *its* fiscal year, you could not do so. Most office heads are unaware of the client-by-client workload and of the workload of the total office. In many ways, SOW documentation is no better today than it was when we first encountered it in 1992. The industry has not shown very much progress on this important dimension.

CHAPTER 16
[1] *Salt from My Attic* (1928), The Mosher Press, Portland, Maine; cited in The Yale Book of Quotations (2006) ed. Fred R. Shapiro, p. 705. There are numerous variants of this expression.

[2] I've observed this many times. In one example, the CEO of the European Region of a global ad agency promulgated a written policy that required all European office heads to document all local client briefs in an agreed SOW template. The German office head called me by phone and asked me to pass on a message to the Regional CEO. "*Tell _____ to go f**k himself*," he said. I reluctantly passed on the message. The office head got away with it – he never filled out the template, and he certainly continued in his job.

APPENDIX A
[1] See *Madison Avenue Manslaughter*, Third Edition, by Michael Farmer (2019), Chapter 9, for a discussion of the "media rebate" problem outlined by the K2 report.

[2] http://online.wsj.com/public/resources/documents/Transparency.pdf

[3] See http://www.media-marketing.com/en/theme-of-the-day/publicis-challenge-busting-silos-while-creating-silos/

[4] See https://www.prweek.com/article/1382378/arthur-sadoun-publicis-agency-changes-if-i-didnt-sharing-expertise-id-fool

5   See https://www.campaignlive.co.uk/article/robert-senior-steps-down-saatchi-saatchi/1420445

6   See https://www.campaignlive.com/article/meet-brain-behind-accenture-interactives-acquisition-spree/1444382

7   See http://www.nytimes.com/1997/04/21/business/advertising-giant-likely-to-break-up.html

8   See http://www.economist.com/node/1868008

AN INTRODUCTION TO
MICHAEL FARMER

Michael Farmer is Chairman of Farmer & Company LLC and Executive Chairman of TrinityP3 USA, strategy consulting firms for advertising agencies and advertisers, respectively.

He graduated from Princeton University and Harvard Business School before working for The Boston Consulting Group and Bain & Company around the world.

He has lived and worked in Rio de Janeiro, Lausanne, Munich, Paris, Istanbul and London. He serves as Adjunct Assistant Professor of Branding and Integrated Communications at The City College of New York (CCNY).

He currently resides in Madison, Connecticut and works out of New York City.